NEW X MEN

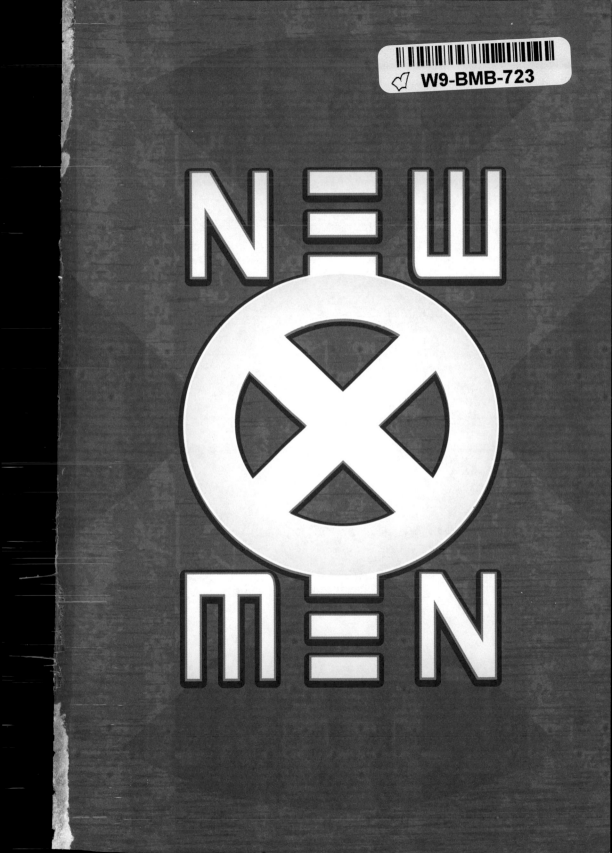

NEW ⊗ MEN

WRITER: *Grant Morrison*

PENCILERS: *Ethan Van Sciver (Issue #118), Igor Kordey (Issues #119-120) and Frank Quitely (Issue #121)*

INKERS: *Prentis Rollins with Scott Hanna & Sandu Florea (Issue #118), Igor Kordey (Issue #119-120) & Frank Quitely (Issue #121)*

COLORIST: *Hi-Fi Design*

LETTERERS: *RS & Comicraft's Saida T!*

COVER ARTISTS: *Frank Quitely, Tim Townsend & HiFi Design*

ASSISTANT EDITOR: *Pete Franco*

EDITOR: *Mark Powers*

COLLECTION EDITOR: *Jennifer Grünwald*

EDITORIAL ASSISTANTS: *James Emmett & Joe Hochstein*

ASSISTANT EDITORS: *Alex Starbuck & Nelson Ribeiro*

EDITOR, SPECIAL PROJECTS: *Mark D. Beazley*

SENIOR EDITOR, SPECIAL PROJECTS: *Jeff Youngquist*

SENIOR VICE PRESIDENT OF SALES: *David Gabriel*

SVP OF BRAND PLANNING & COMMUNICATIONS: *Michael Pasciullo*

EDITOR IN CHIEF: *Axel Alonso*

CHIEF CREATIVE OFFICER: *Joe Quesada*

PUBLISHER: *Dan Buckley*

EXECUTIVE PRODUCER: *Alan Fine*

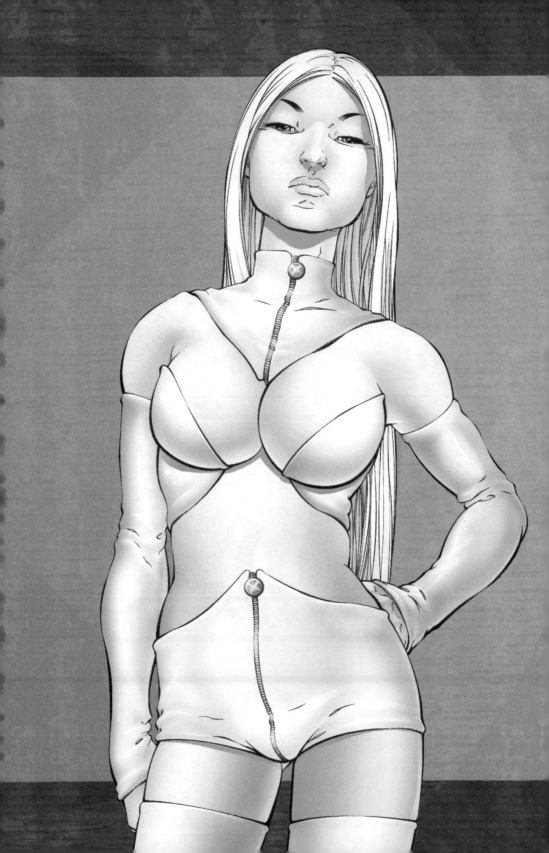

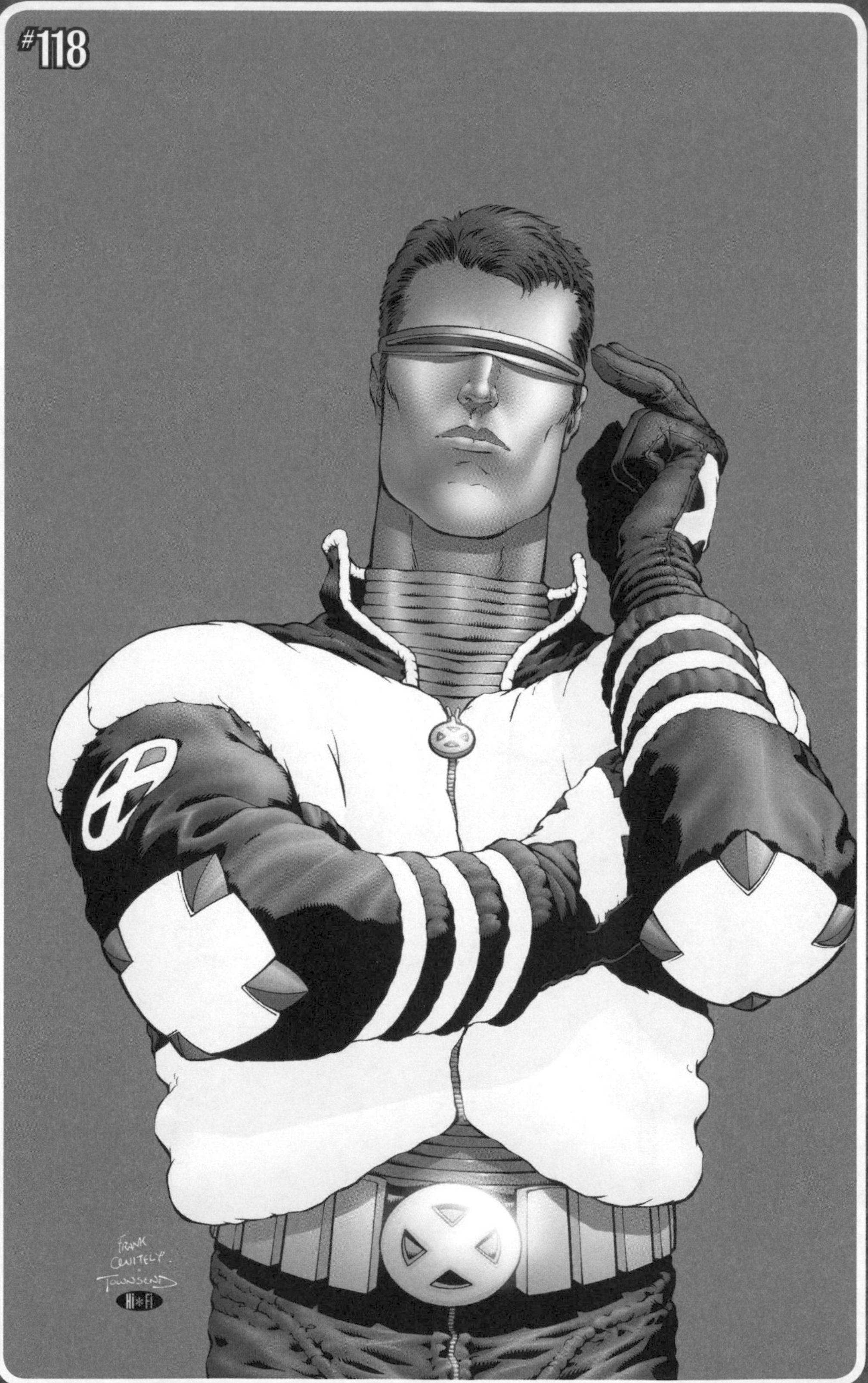
#118
FRANK QUITELY
TOWNSEND
Hi-Fi

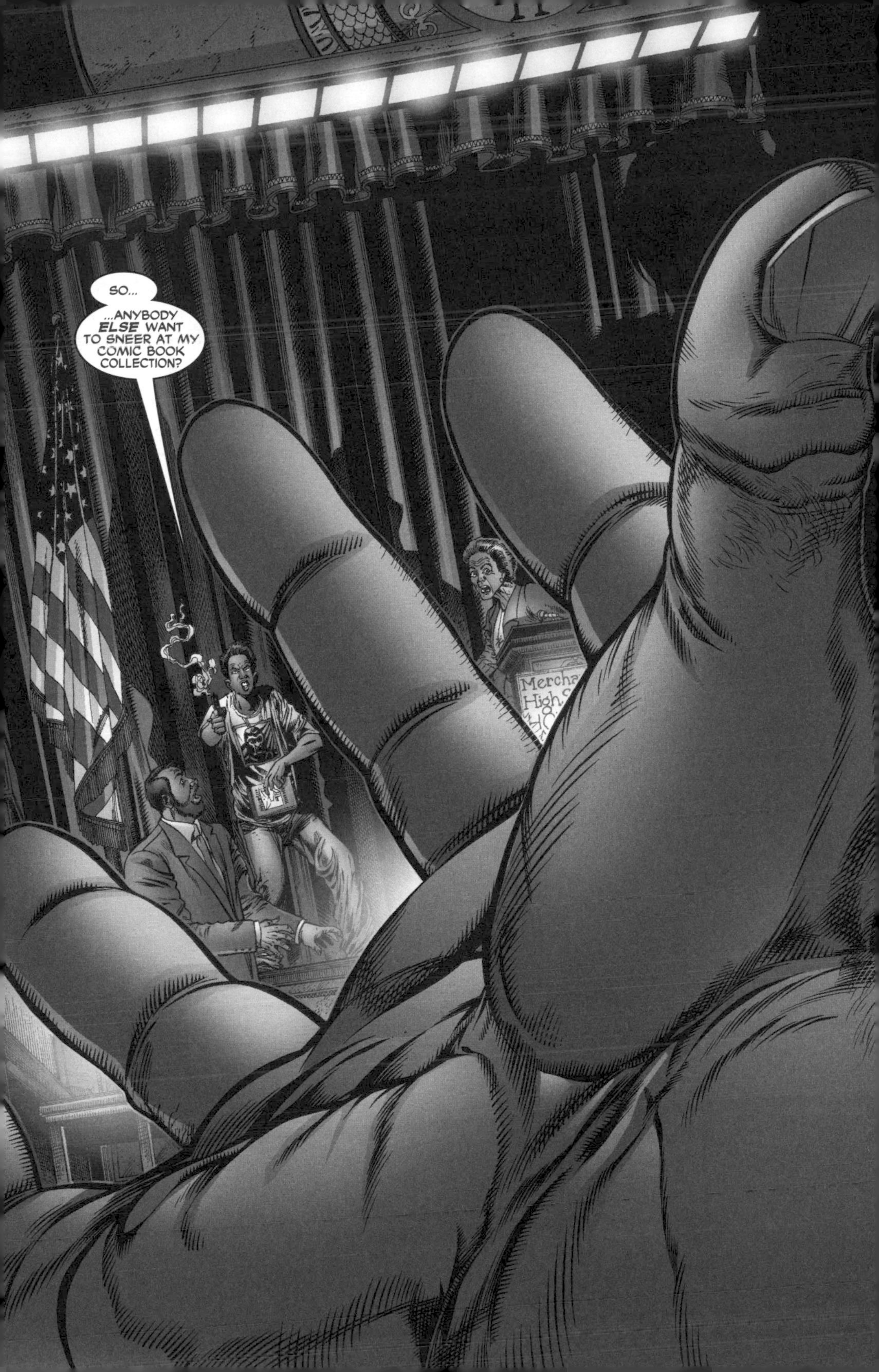
SO...
...ANYBODY ELSE WANT TO SNEER AT MY COMIC BOOK COLLECTION?

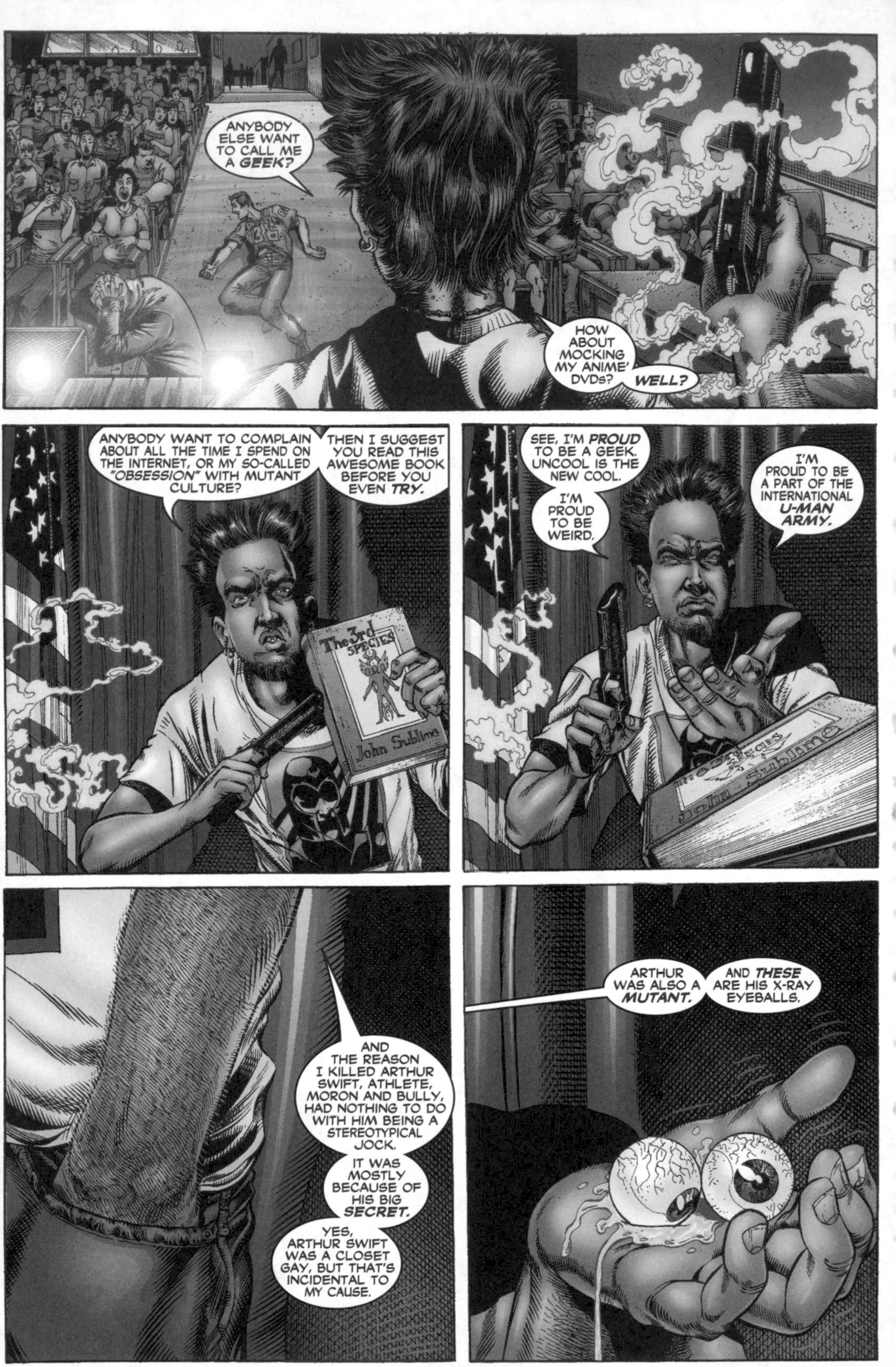
ANYBODY ELSE WANT TO CALL ME A GEEK?
HOW ABOUT MOCKING MY ANIME' DVDs? WELL?
ANYBODY WANT TO COMPLAIN ABOUT ALL THE TIME I SPEND ON THE INTERNET, OR MY SO-CALLED "OBSESSION" WITH MUTANT CULTURE?
THEN I SUGGEST YOU READ THIS AWESOME BOOK BEFORE YOU EVEN TRY.
The 3rd SPECIES
John Sublime
SEE, I'M PROUD TO BE A GEEK. UNCOOL IS THE NEW COOL.
I'M PROUD TO BE WEIRD.
I'M PROUD TO BE A PART OF THE INTERNATIONAL U-MAN ARMY.
AND THE REASON I KILLED ARTHUR SWIFT, ATHLETE, MORON AND BULLY, HAD NOTHING TO DO WITH HIM BEING A STEREOTYPICAL JOCK.
IT WAS MOSTLY BECAUSE OF HIS BIG SECRET.
YES, ARTHUR SWIFT WAS A CLOSET GAY, BUT THAT'S INCIDENTAL TO MY CAUSE.
ARTHUR WAS ALSO A MUTANT.
AND THESE ARE HIS X-RAY EYEBALLS.

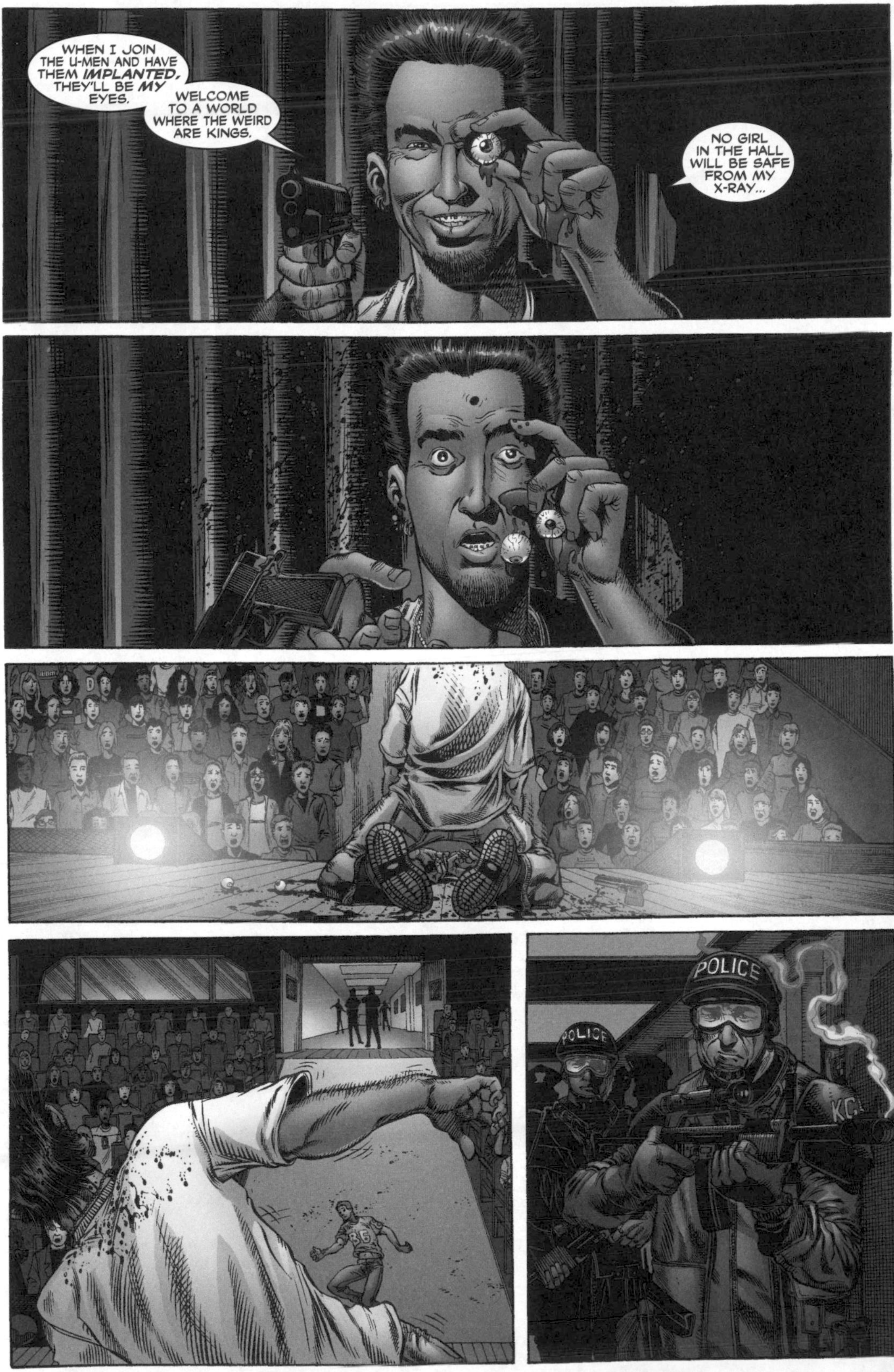
WHEN I JOIN THE U-MEN AND HAVE THEM IMPLANTED, THEY'LL BE MY EYES.
WELCOME TO A WORLD WHERE THE WEIRD ARE KINGS.
NO GIRL IN THE HALL WILL BE SAFE FROM MY X-RAY...
POLICE
POLICE

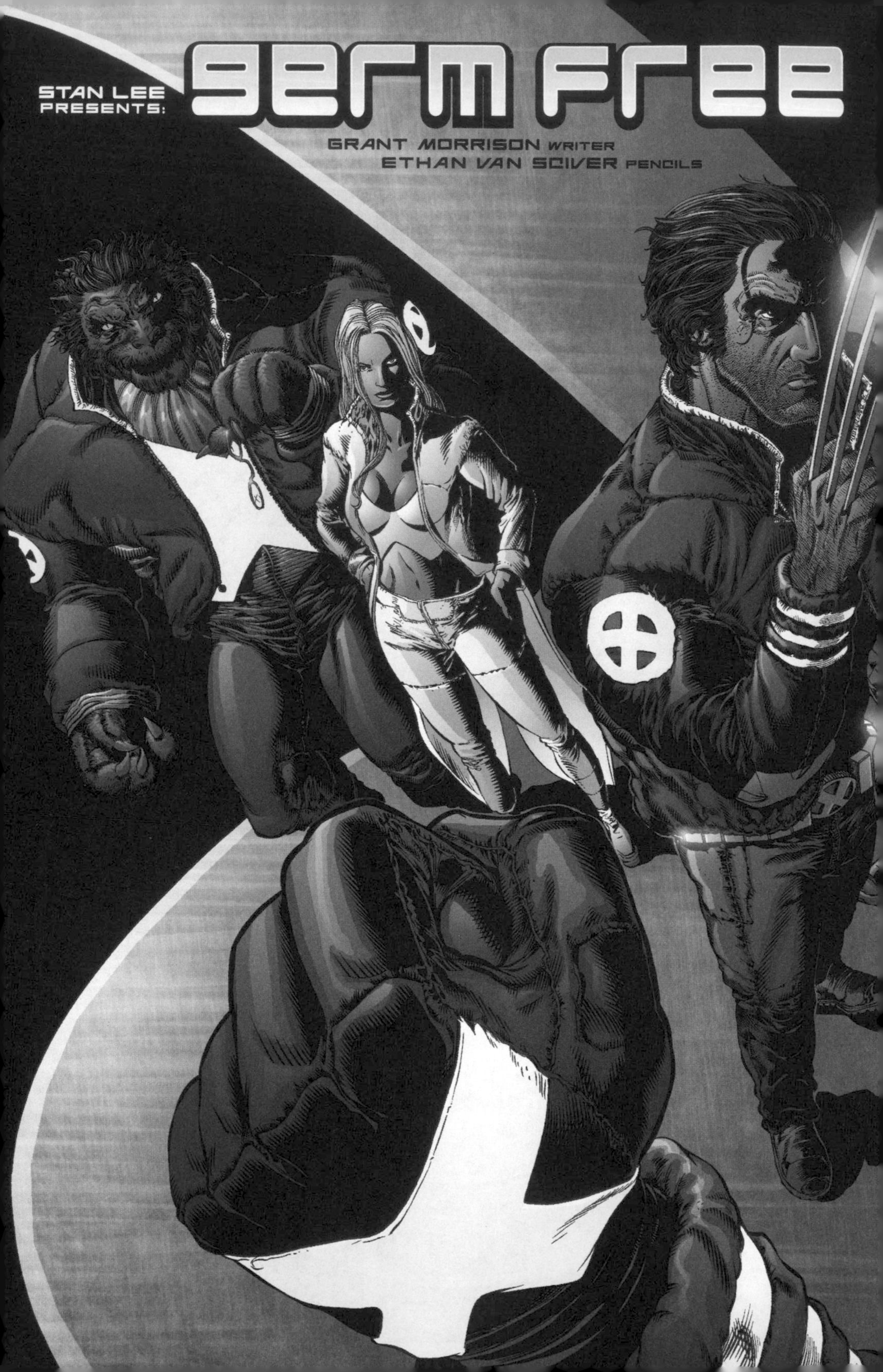
STAN LEE PRESENTS:
GERM FREE
GRANT MORRISON WRITER
ETHAN VAN SCIVER PENCILS

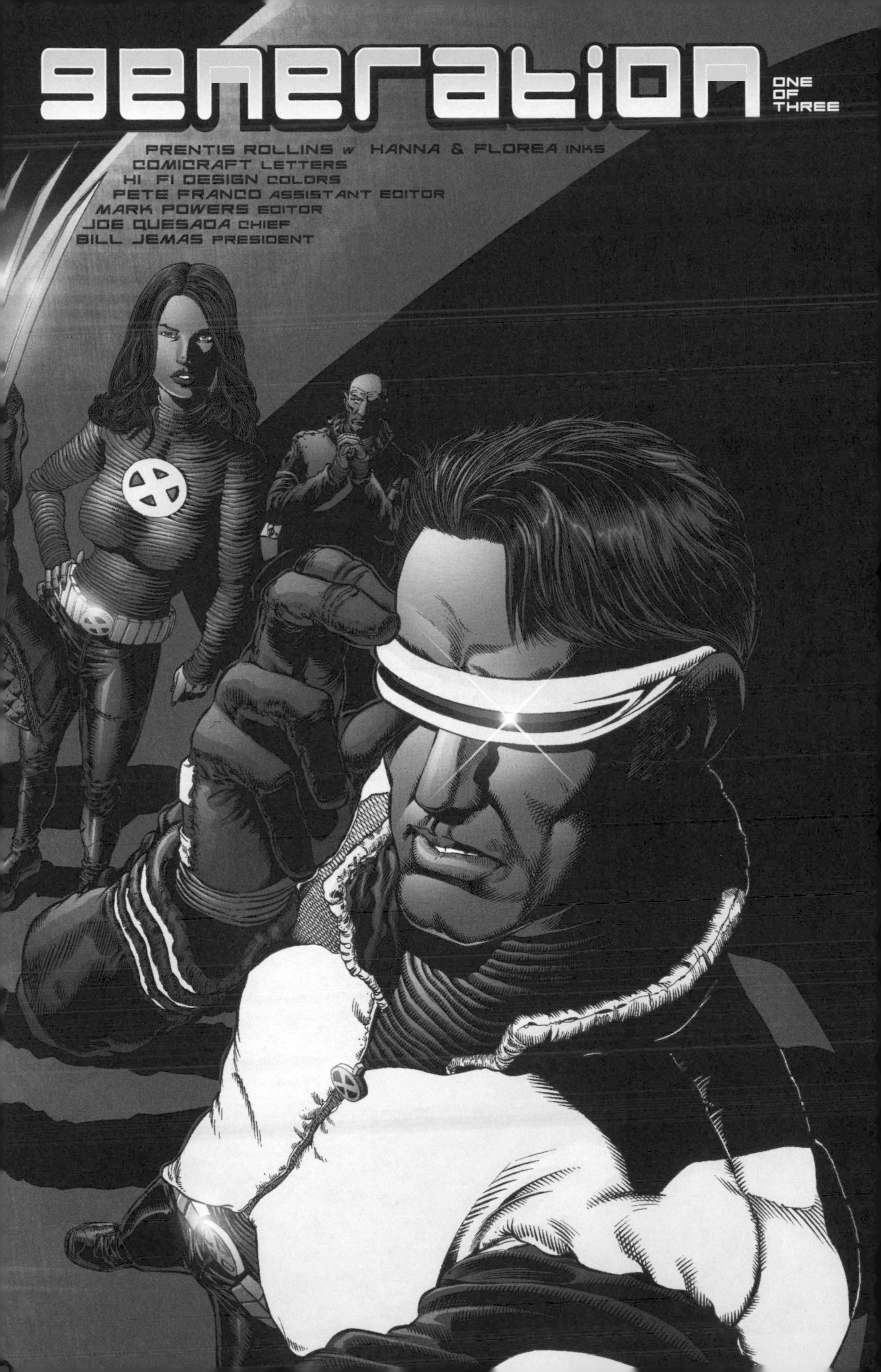
GENERATION
ONE OF THREE
PRENTIS ROLLINS w HANNA & FLOREA INKS
COMICRAFT LETTERS
HI FI DESIGN COLORS
PETE FRANCO ASSISTANT EDITOR
MARK POWERS EDITOR
JOE QUESADA CHIEF
BILL JEMAS PRESIDENT

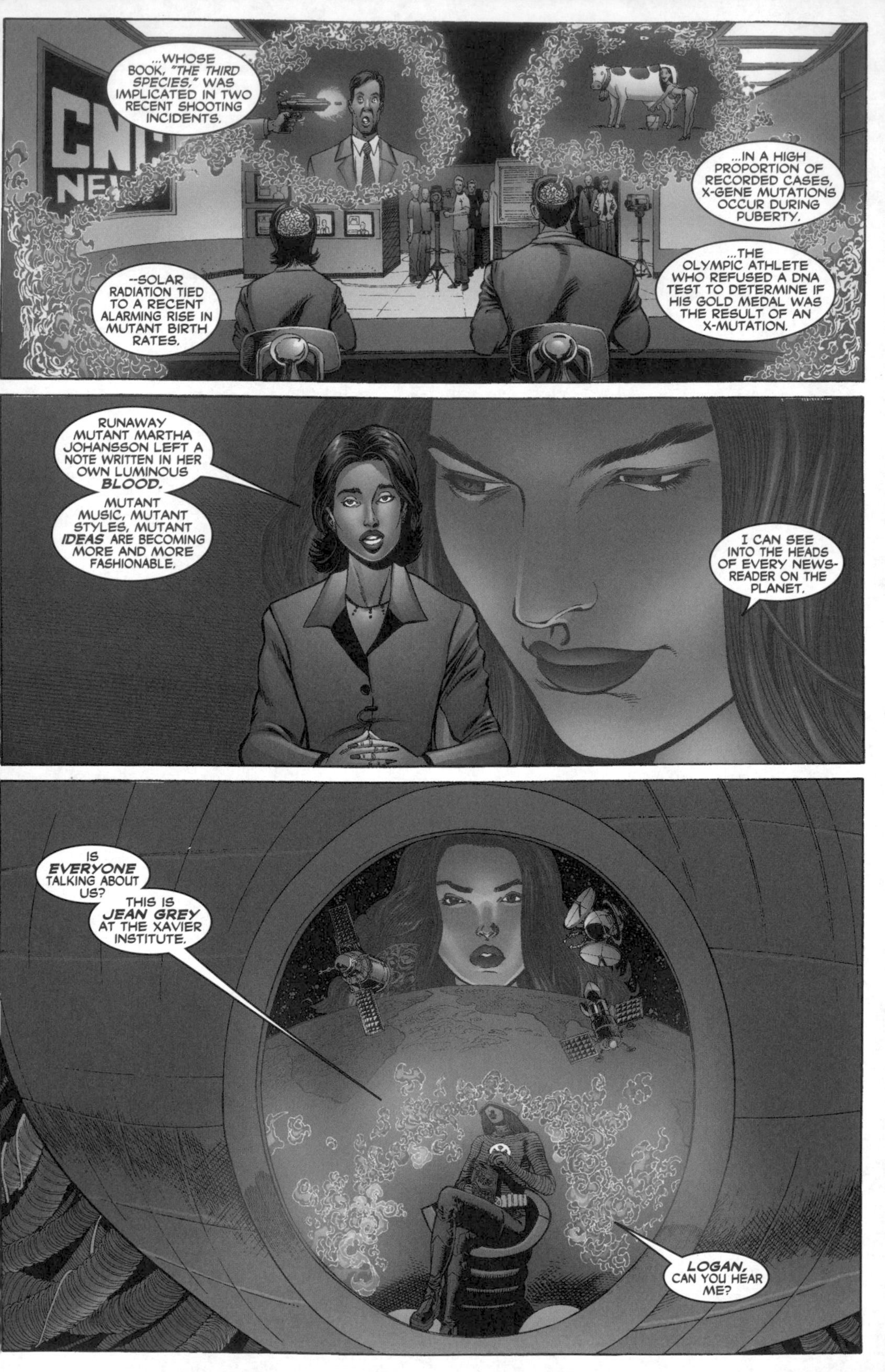
...WHOSE BOOK, "THE THIRD SPECIES," WAS IMPLICATED IN TWO RECENT SHOOTING INCIDENTS.
...IN A HIGH PROPORTION OF RECORDED CASES, X-GENE MUTATIONS OCCUR DURING PUBERTY.
--SOLAR RADIATION TIED TO A RECENT ALARMING RISE IN MUTANT BIRTH RATES.
...THE OLYMPIC ATHLETE WHO REFUSED A DNA TEST TO DETERMINE IF HIS GOLD MEDAL WAS THE RESULT OF AN X-MUTATION.
RUNAWAY MUTANT MARTHA JOHANSSON LEFT A NOTE WRITTEN IN HER OWN LUMINOUS BLOOD.
MUTANT MUSIC, MUTANT STYLES, MUTANT IDEAS ARE BECOMING MORE AND MORE FASHIONABLE.
I CAN SEE INTO THE HEADS OF EVERY NEWS-READER ON THE PLANET.
IS EVERYONE TALKING ABOUT US?
THIS IS JEAN GREY AT THE XAVIER INSTITUTE.
LOGAN, CAN YOU HEAR ME?

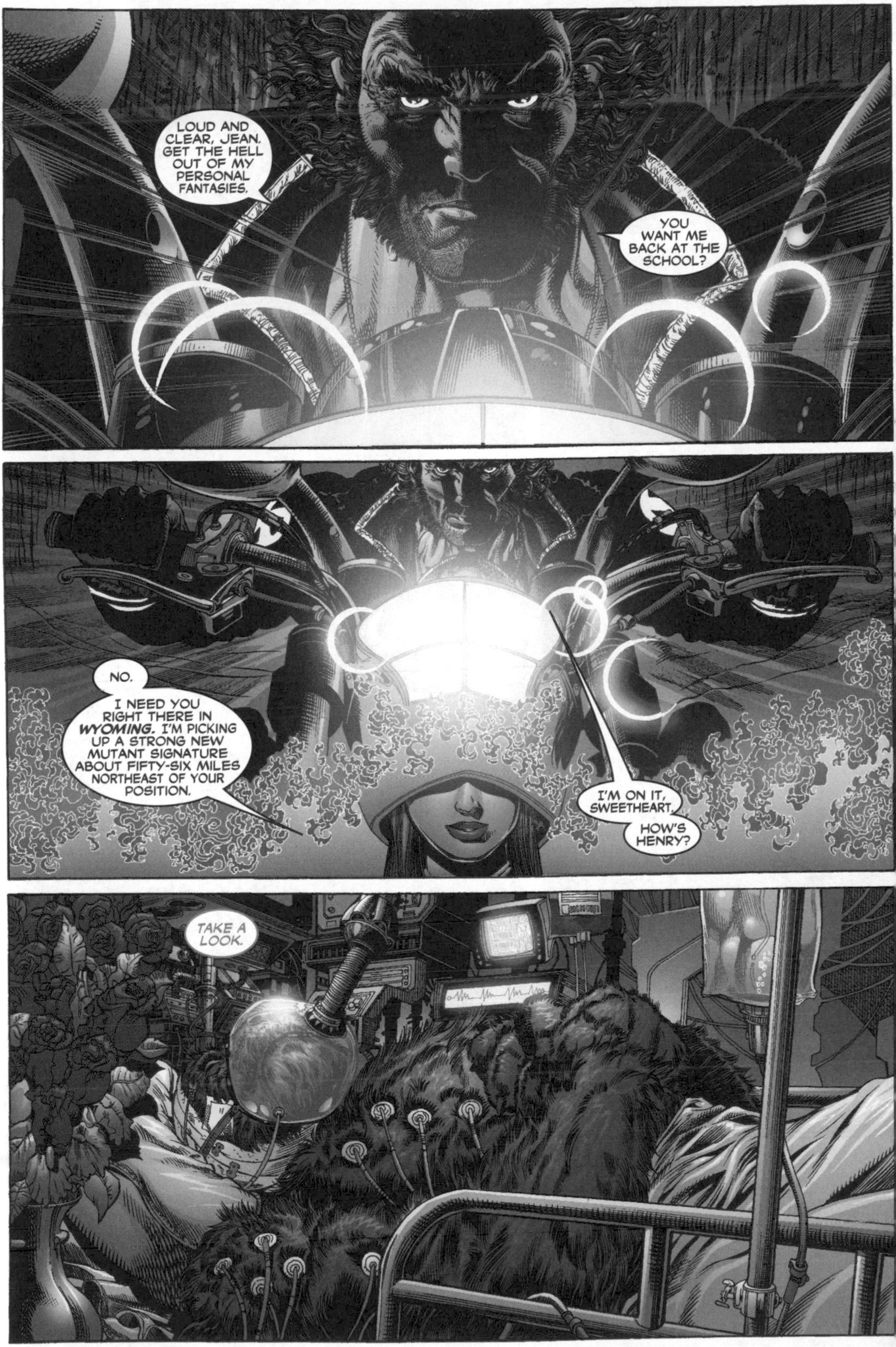
LOUD AND CLEAR, JEAN. GET THE HELL OUT OF MY PERSONAL FANTASIES.
YOU WANT ME BACK AT THE SCHOOL?
NO.
I NEED YOU RIGHT THERE IN WYOMING. I'M PICKING UP A STRONG NEW MUTANT SIGNATURE ABOUT FIFTY-SIX MILES NORTHEAST OF YOUR POSITION.
I'M ON IT, SWEETHEART.
HOW'S HENRY?
TAKE A LOOK.

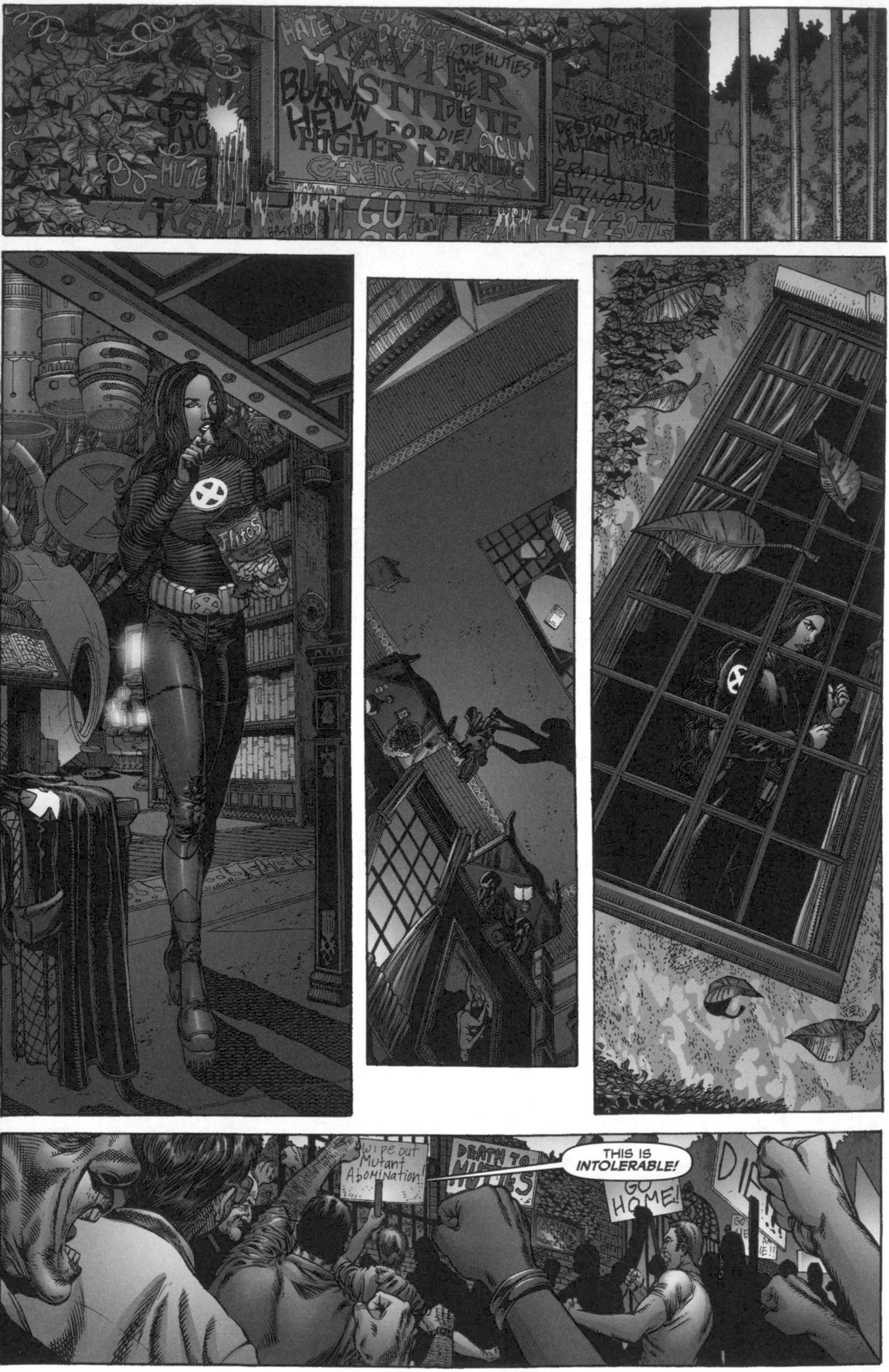
XAVIER INSTITUTE FOR HIGHER LEARNING
BURN IN HELL
DIE MUTIES
SCUM
GENETIC FREAKS
DESTROY THE MUTANT PLAGUE
Flitos
Wipe out Mutant Abomination!
DEATH TO MUTIES
GO HOME!
THIS IS INTOLERABLE!

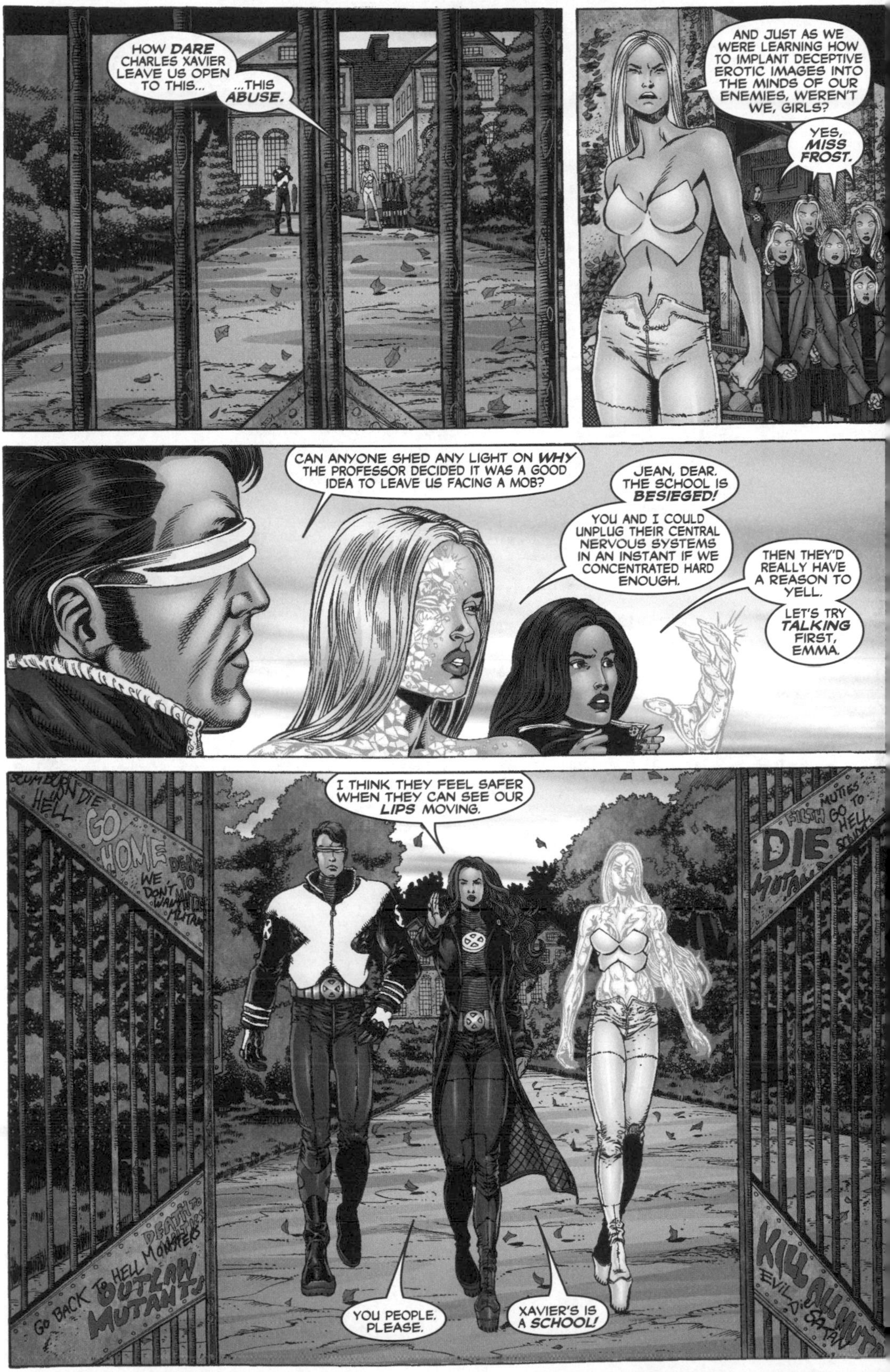
HOW DARE CHARLES XAVIER LEAVE US OPEN TO THIS...
...THIS ABUSE.
AND JUST AS WE WERE LEARNING HOW TO IMPLANT DECEPTIVE EROTIC IMAGES INTO THE MINDS OF OUR ENEMIES, WEREN'T WE, GIRLS?
YES, MISS FROST.
CAN ANYONE SHED ANY LIGHT ON WHY THE PROFESSOR DECIDED IT WAS A GOOD IDEA TO LEAVE US FACING A MOB?
JEAN, DEAR. THE SCHOOL IS BESIEGED!
YOU AND I COULD UNPLUG THEIR CENTRAL NERVOUS SYSTEMS IN AN INSTANT IF WE CONCENTRATED HARD ENOUGH.
THEN THEY'D REALLY HAVE A REASON TO YELL.
LET'S TRY TALKING FIRST, EMMA.
I THINK THEY FEEL SAFER WHEN THEY CAN SEE OUR LIPS MOVING.
GO HOME
DIE
OUTLAW MUTANTS
KILL
YOU PEOPLE, PLEASE.
XAVIER'S IS A SCHOOL!

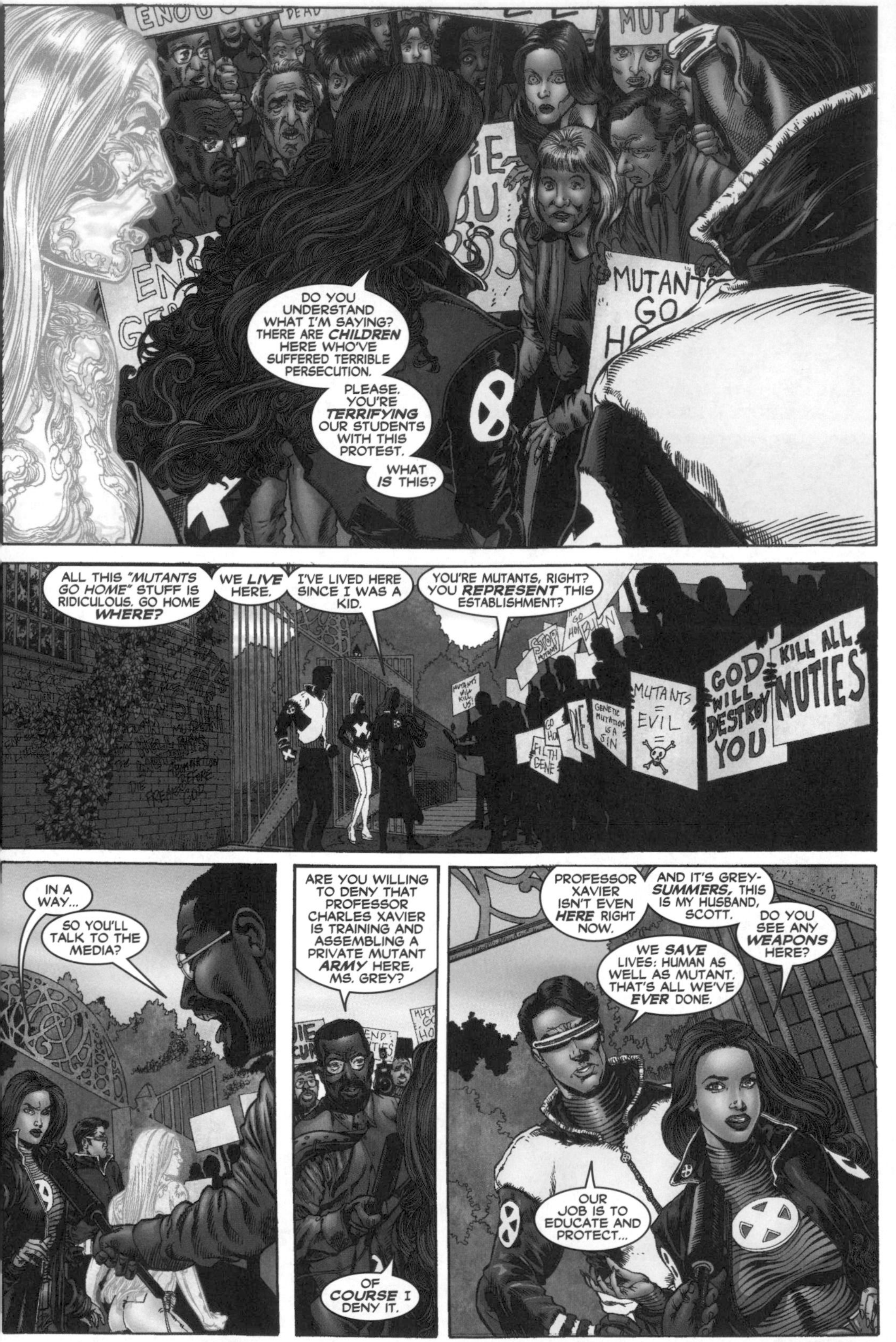
MUTANTS GO HO
DO YOU UNDERSTAND WHAT I'M SAYING? THERE ARE *CHILDREN* HERE WHO'VE SUFFERED TERRIBLE PERSECUTION.
PLEASE. YOU'RE *TERRIFYING* OUR STUDENTS WITH THIS PROTEST.
WHAT *IS* THIS?
ALL THIS *"MUTANTS GO HOME"* STUFF IS RIDICULOUS. GO HOME *WHERE?*
WE *LIVE* HERE.
I'VE LIVED HERE SINCE I WAS A KID.
YOU'RE MUTANTS, RIGHT? YOU *REPRESENT* THIS ESTABLISHMENT?
GENETIC MUTATION IS A SIN
FILTH GENE
MUTANTS = EVIL =
GOD WILL DESTROY YOU
KILL ALL MUTIES
IN A WAY...
SO YOU'LL TALK TO THE MEDIA?
ARE YOU WILLING TO DENY THAT PROFESSOR CHARLES XAVIER IS TRAINING AND ASSEMBLING A PRIVATE MUTANT *ARMY* HERE, MS. GREY?
OF *COURSE* I DENY IT.
PROFESSOR XAVIER ISN'T EVEN *HERE* RIGHT NOW.
AND IT'S GREY-*SUMMERS,* THIS IS MY HUSBAND, SCOTT.
DO YOU SEE ANY *WEAPONS* HERE?
WE *SAVE* LIVES: HUMAN AS WELL AS MUTANT. THAT'S ALL WE'VE *EVER* DONE.
OUR JOB IS TO EDUCATE AND PROTECT...

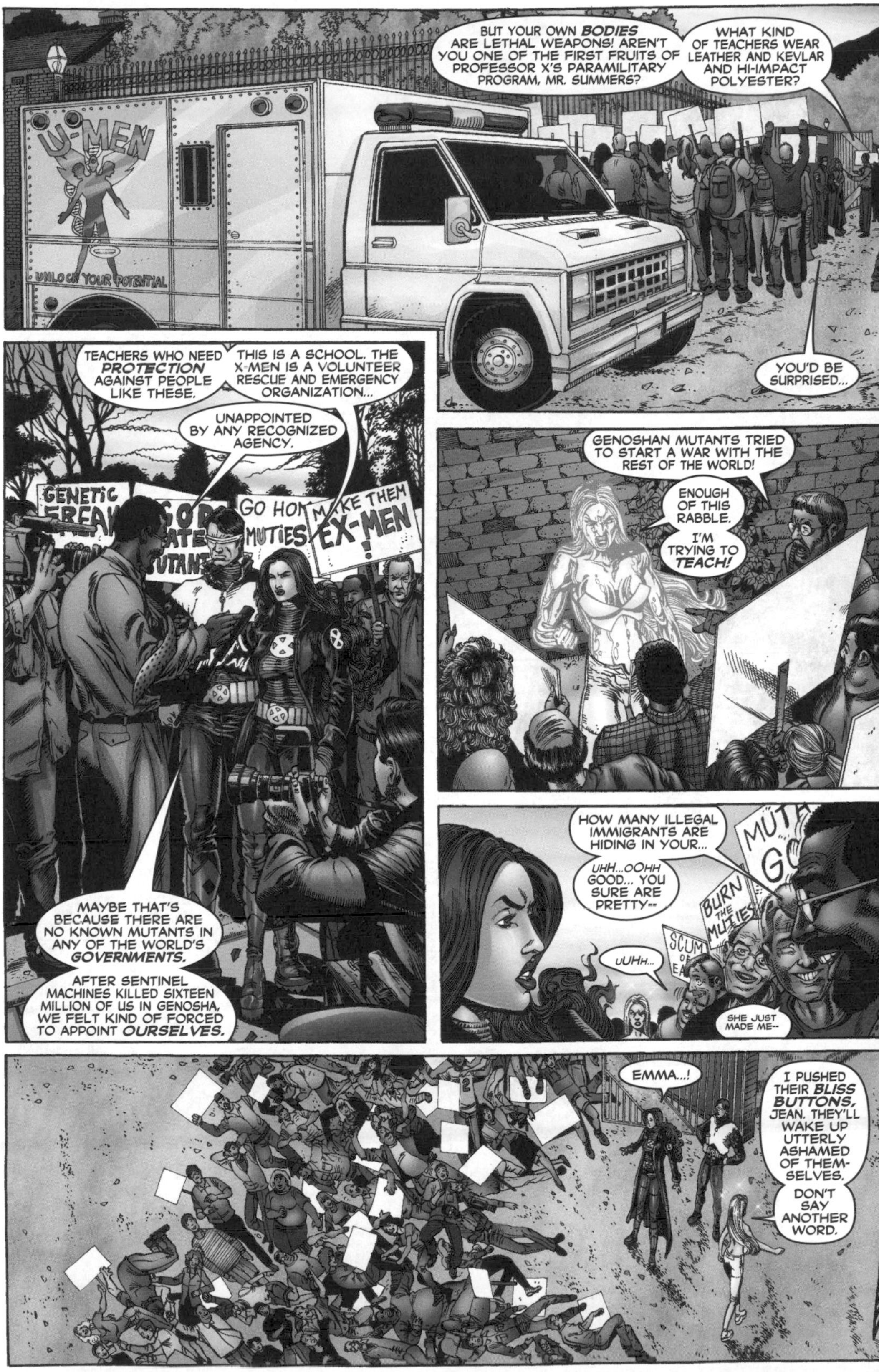
BUT YOUR OWN BODIES ARE LETHAL WEAPONS! AREN'T YOU ONE OF THE FIRST FRUITS OF PROFESSOR X'S PARAMILITARY PROGRAM, MR. SUMMERS?
WHAT KIND OF TEACHERS WEAR LEATHER AND KEVLAR AND HI-IMPACT POLYESTER?
YOU'D BE SURPRISED...
U-MEN
UNLOCK YOUR POTENTIAL
TEACHERS WHO NEED PROTECTION AGAINST PEOPLE LIKE THESE.
THIS IS A SCHOOL. THE X-MEN IS A VOLUNTEER RESCUE AND EMERGENCY ORGANIZATION...
UNAPPOINTED BY ANY RECOGNIZED AGENCY.
GENETIC FREAK
GO HOM MUTIES
MAKE THEM EX-MEN!
MAYBE THAT'S BECAUSE THERE ARE NO KNOWN MUTANTS IN ANY OF THE WORLD'S GOVERNMENTS.
AFTER SENTINEL MACHINES KILLED SIXTEEN MILLION OF US IN GENOSHA, WE FELT KIND OF FORCED TO APPOINT OURSELVES.
GENOSHAN MUTANTS TRIED TO START A WAR WITH THE REST OF THE WORLD!
ENOUGH OF THIS RABBLE.
I'M TRYING TO TEACH!
HOW MANY ILLEGAL IMMIGRANTS ARE HIDING IN YOUR...
UHH...OOHH GOOD... YOU SURE ARE PRETTY--
UUHH...
SHE JUST MADE ME--
BURN THE MUTIES
EMMA...!
I PUSHED THEIR BLISS BUTTONS, JEAN. THEY'LL WAKE UP UTTERLY ASHAMED OF THEM-SELVES.
DON'T SAY ANOTHER WORD.

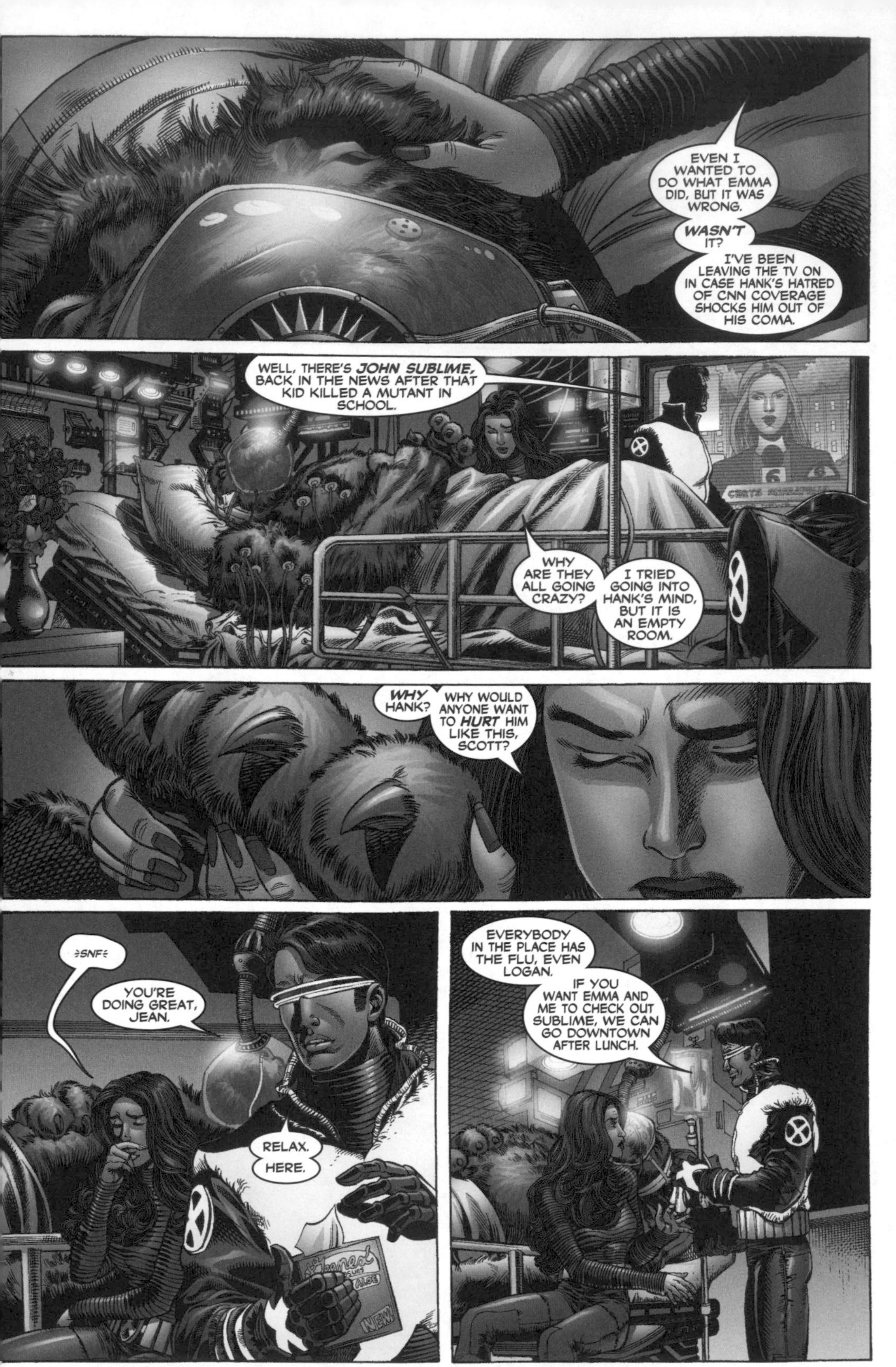
EVEN I WANTED TO DO WHAT EMMA DID, BUT IT WAS WRONG.
WASN'T IT?
I'VE BEEN LEAVING THE TV ON IN CASE HANK'S HATRED OF CNN COVERAGE SHOCKS HIM OUT OF HIS COMA.
WELL, THERE'S JOHN SUBLIME, BACK IN THE NEWS AFTER THAT KID KILLED A MUTANT IN SCHOOL.
WHY ARE THEY ALL GOING CRAZY?
I TRIED GOING INTO HANK'S MIND, BUT IT IS AN EMPTY ROOM.
WHY HANK?
WHY WOULD ANYONE WANT TO HURT HIM LIKE THIS, SCOTT?
SNF
YOU'RE DOING GREAT, JEAN.
RELAX.
HERE.
EVERYBODY IN THE PLACE HAS THE FLU, EVEN LOGAN.
IF YOU WANT EMMA AND ME TO CHECK OUT SUBLIME, WE CAN GO DOWNTOWN AFTER LUNCH.

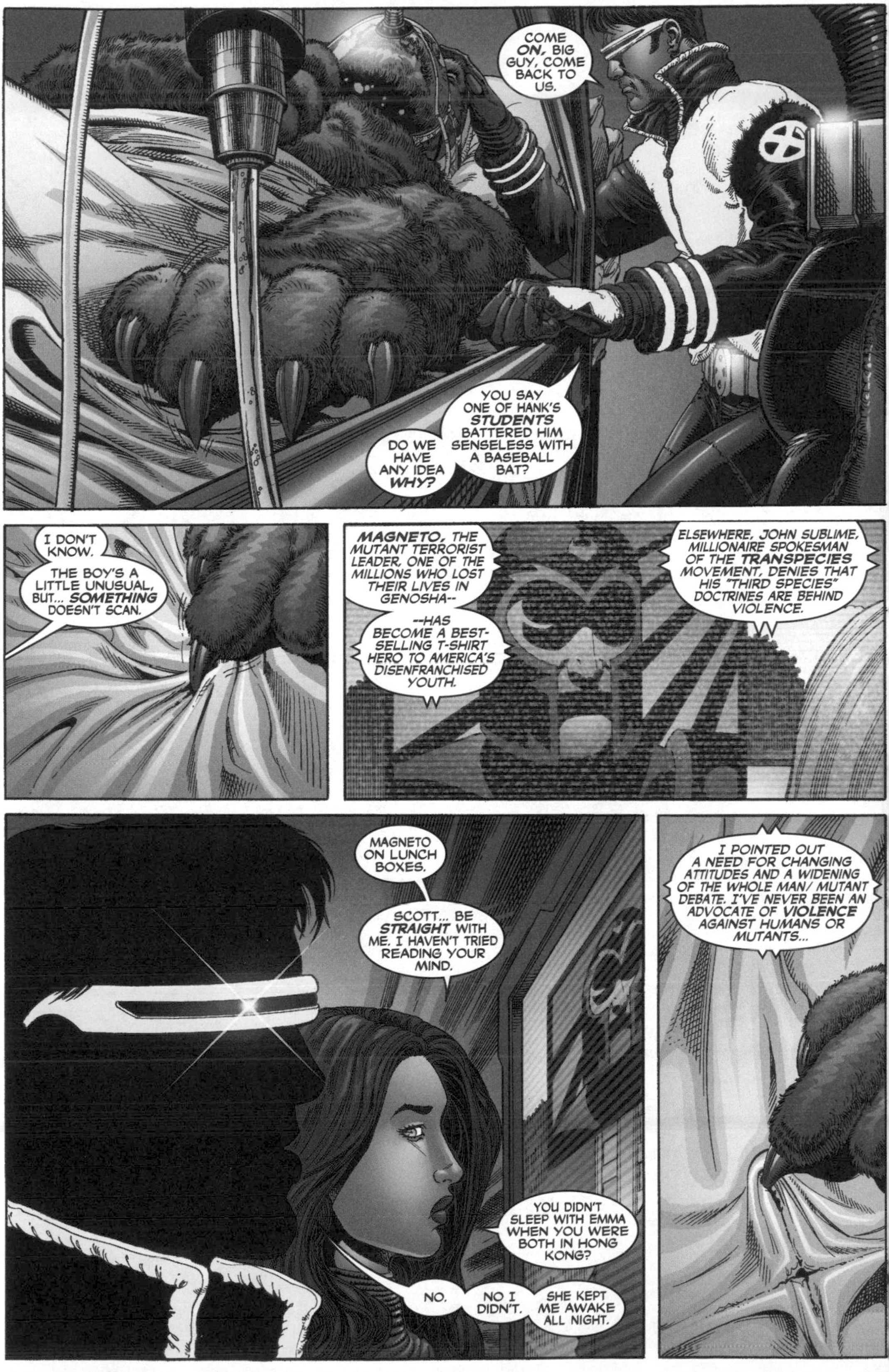
COME ON, BIG GUY, COME BACK TO US.
YOU SAY ONE OF HANK'S STUDENTS BATTERED HIM SENSELESS WITH A BASEBALL BAT?
DO WE HAVE ANY IDEA WHY?
I DON'T KNOW.
THE BOY'S A LITTLE UNUSUAL, BUT... SOMETHING DOESN'T SCAN.
MAGNETO, THE MUTANT TERRORIST LEADER, ONE OF THE MILLIONS WHO LOST THEIR LIVES IN GENOSHA--
--HAS BECOME A BEST-SELLING T-SHIRT HERO TO AMERICA'S DISENFRANCHISED YOUTH.
ELSEWHERE, JOHN SUBLIME, MILLIONAIRE SPOKESMAN OF THE TRANSPECIES MOVEMENT, DENIES THAT HIS "THIRD SPECIES" DOCTRINES ARE BEHIND VIOLENCE.
MAGNETO ON LUNCH BOXES.
SCOTT... BE STRAIGHT WITH ME. I HAVEN'T TRIED READING YOUR MIND.
YOU DIDN'T SLEEP WITH EMMA WHEN YOU WERE BOTH IN HONG KONG?
NO.
NO I DIDN'T.
SHE KEPT ME AWAKE ALL NIGHT.
I POINTED OUT A NEED FOR CHANGING ATTITUDES AND A WIDENING OF THE WHOLE MAN/ MUTANT DEBATE. I'VE NEVER BEEN AN ADVOCATE OF VIOLENCE AGAINST HUMANS OR MUTANTS...

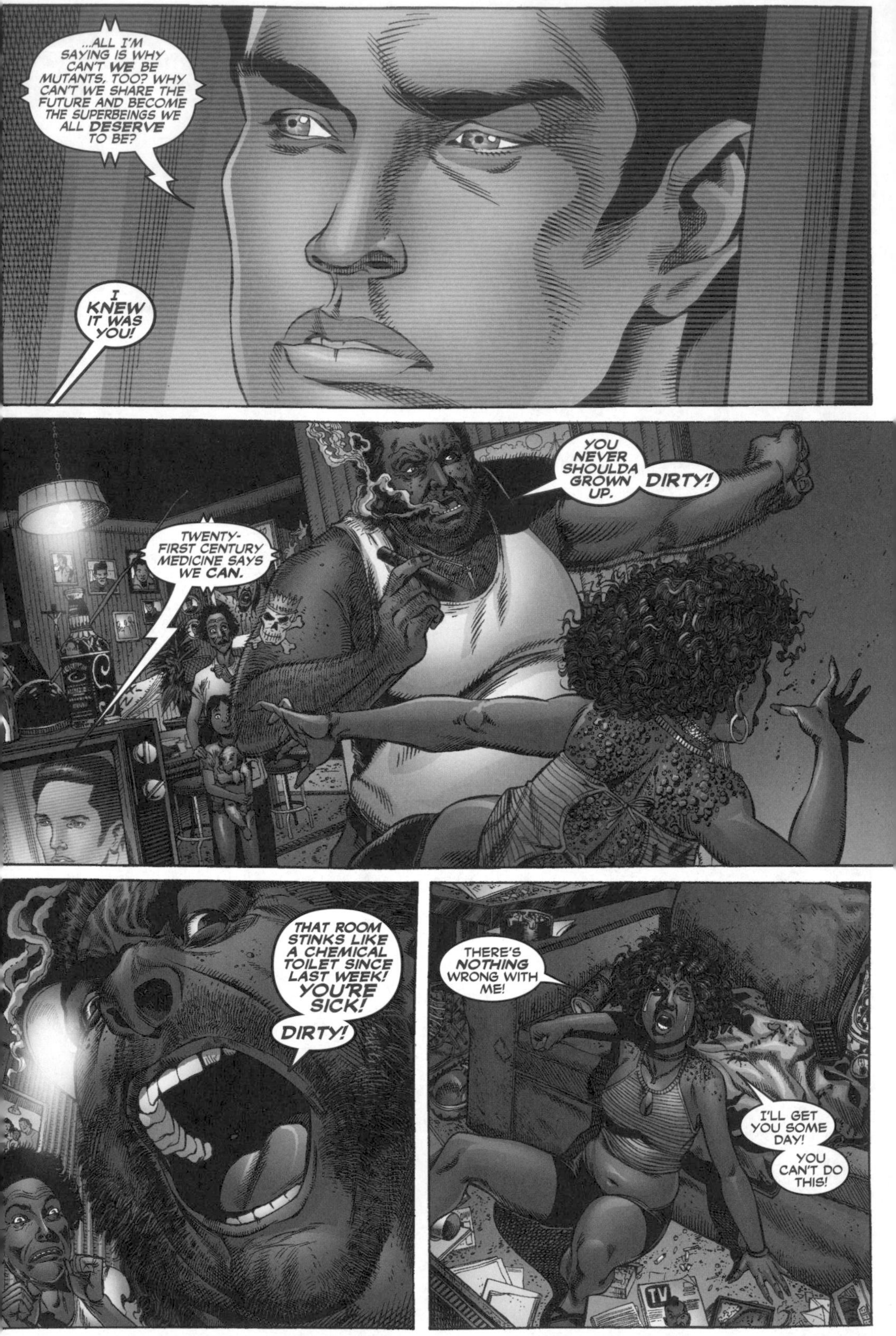
...ALL I'M SAYING IS WHY CAN'T WE BE MUTANTS, TOO? WHY CAN'T WE SHARE THE FUTURE AND BECOME THE SUPERBEINGS WE ALL DESERVE TO BE?
I KNEW IT WAS YOU!
YOU NEVER SHOULDA GROWN UP.
DIRTY!
TWENTY-FIRST CENTURY MEDICINE SAYS WE CAN.
THAT ROOM STINKS LIKE A CHEMICAL TOILET SINCE LAST WEEK! YOU'RE SICK!
DIRTY!
THERE'S NOTHING WRONG WITH ME!
I'LL GET YOU SOME DAY!
YOU CAN'T DO THIS!

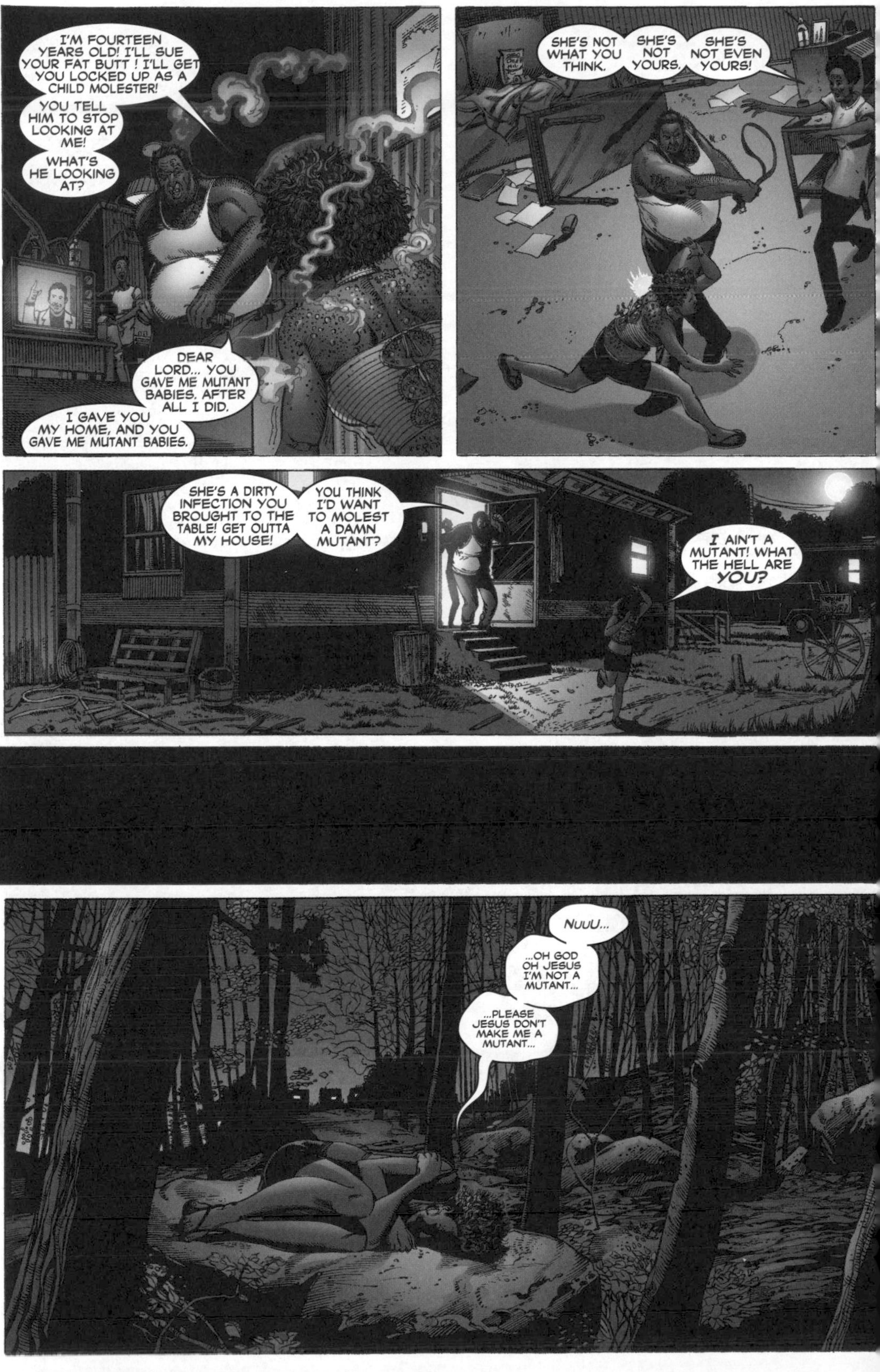
I'M FOURTEEN YEARS OLD! I'LL SUE YOUR FAT BUTT ! I'LL GET YOU LOCKED UP AS A CHILD MOLESTER!
YOU TELL HIM TO STOP LOOKING AT ME!
WHAT'S HE LOOKING AT?
DEAR LORD... YOU GAVE ME MUTANT BABIES. AFTER ALL I DID.
I GAVE YOU MY HOME, AND YOU GAVE ME MUTANT BABIES.
SHE'S NOT WHAT YOU THINK.
SHE'S NOT YOURS.
SHE'S NOT EVEN YOURS!
SHE'S A DIRTY INFECTION YOU BROUGHT TO THE TABLE! GET OUTTA MY HOUSE!
YOU THINK I'D WANT TO MOLEST A DAMN MUTANT?
I AIN'T A MUTANT! WHAT THE HELL ARE YOU?
NUUU...
...OH GOD OH JESUS I'M NOT A MUTANT...
...PLEASE JESUS DON'T MAKE ME A MUTANT...

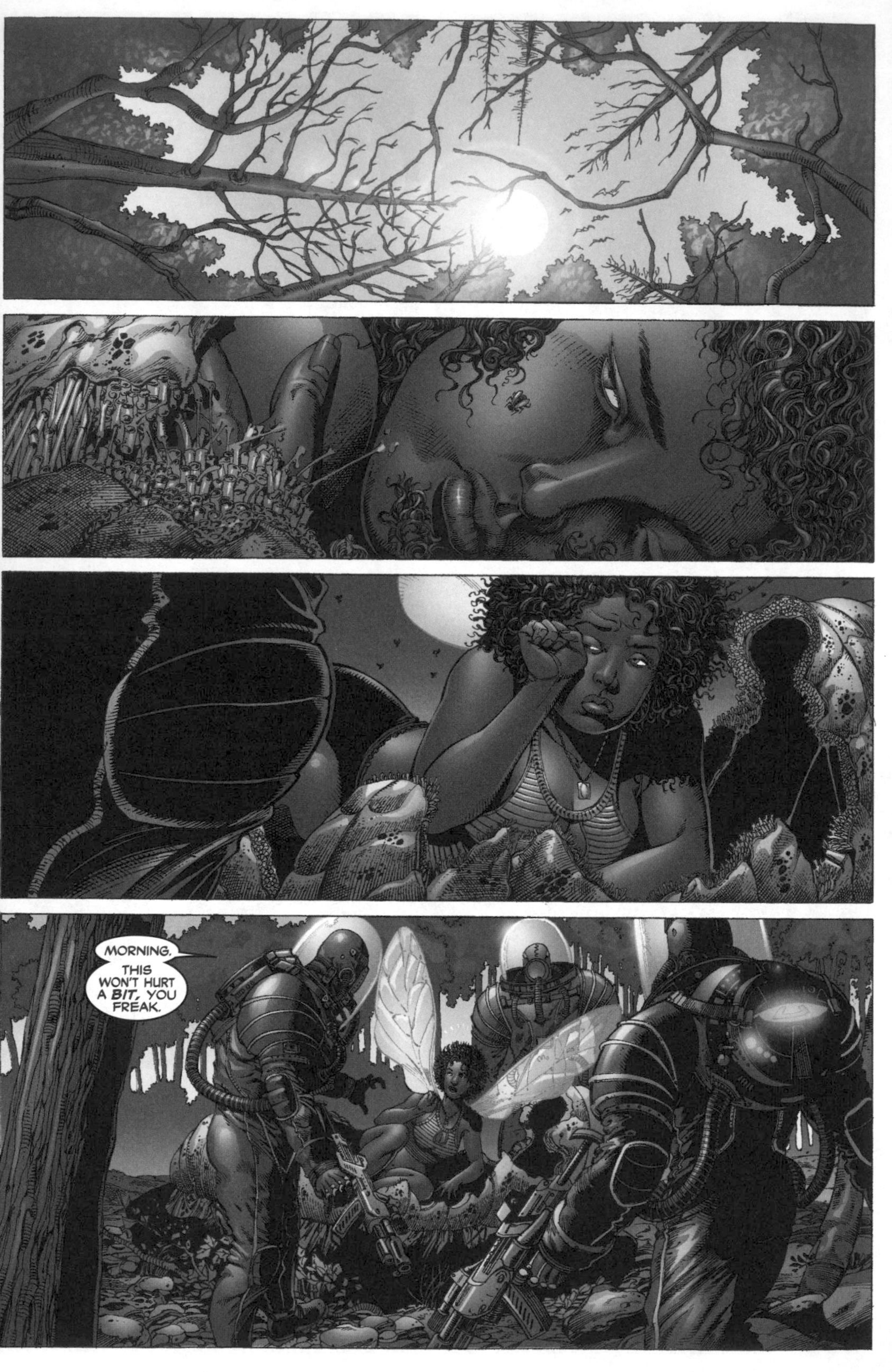
MORNING.
THIS WON'T HURT A BIT, YOU FREAK.

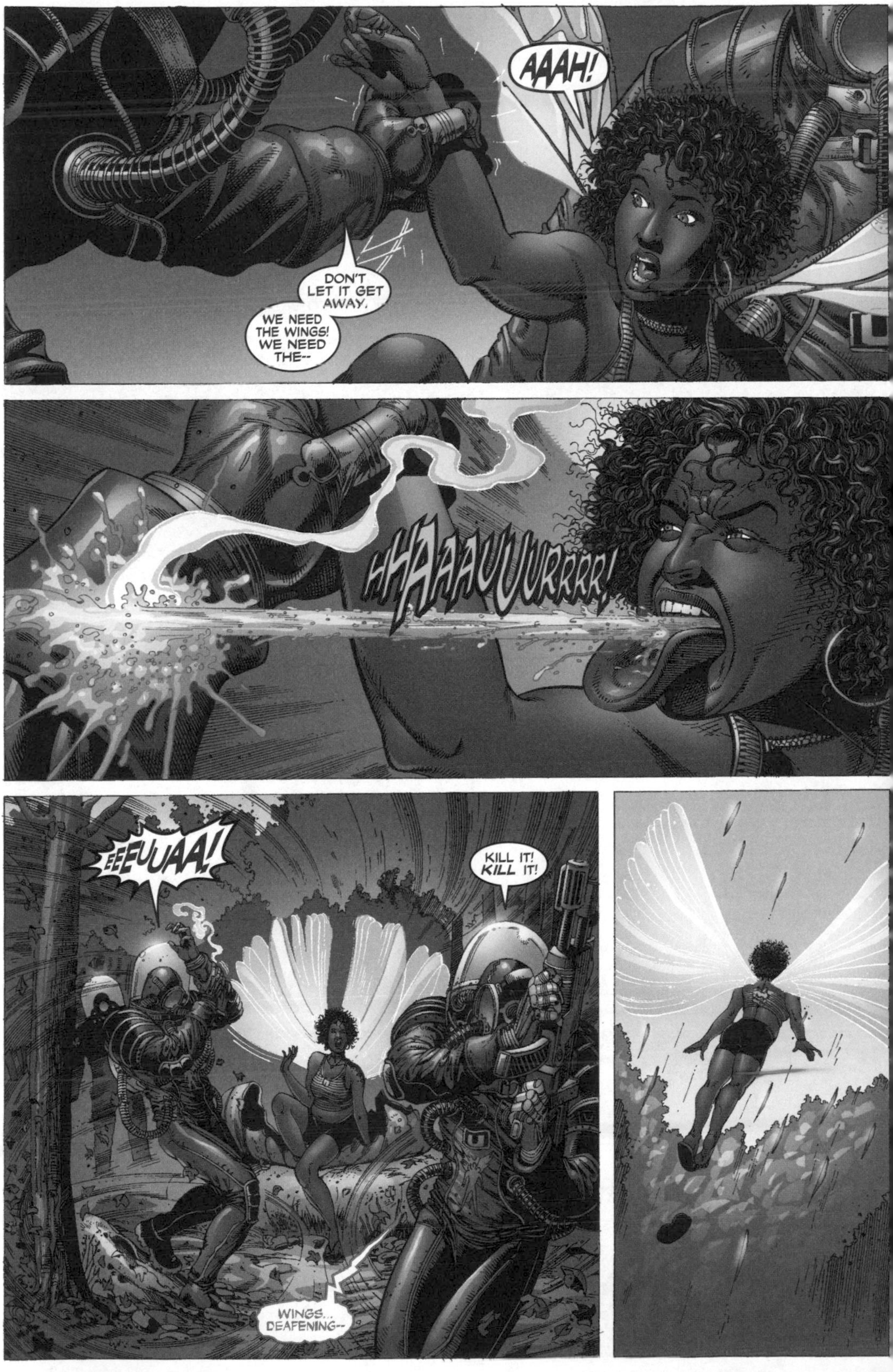
AAAH!
DON'T LET IT GET AWAY.
WE NEED THE WINGS! WE NEED THE--
HHAAAUUURRRR!
EEEUUAA!
KILL IT! KILL IT!
WINGS... DEAFENING--

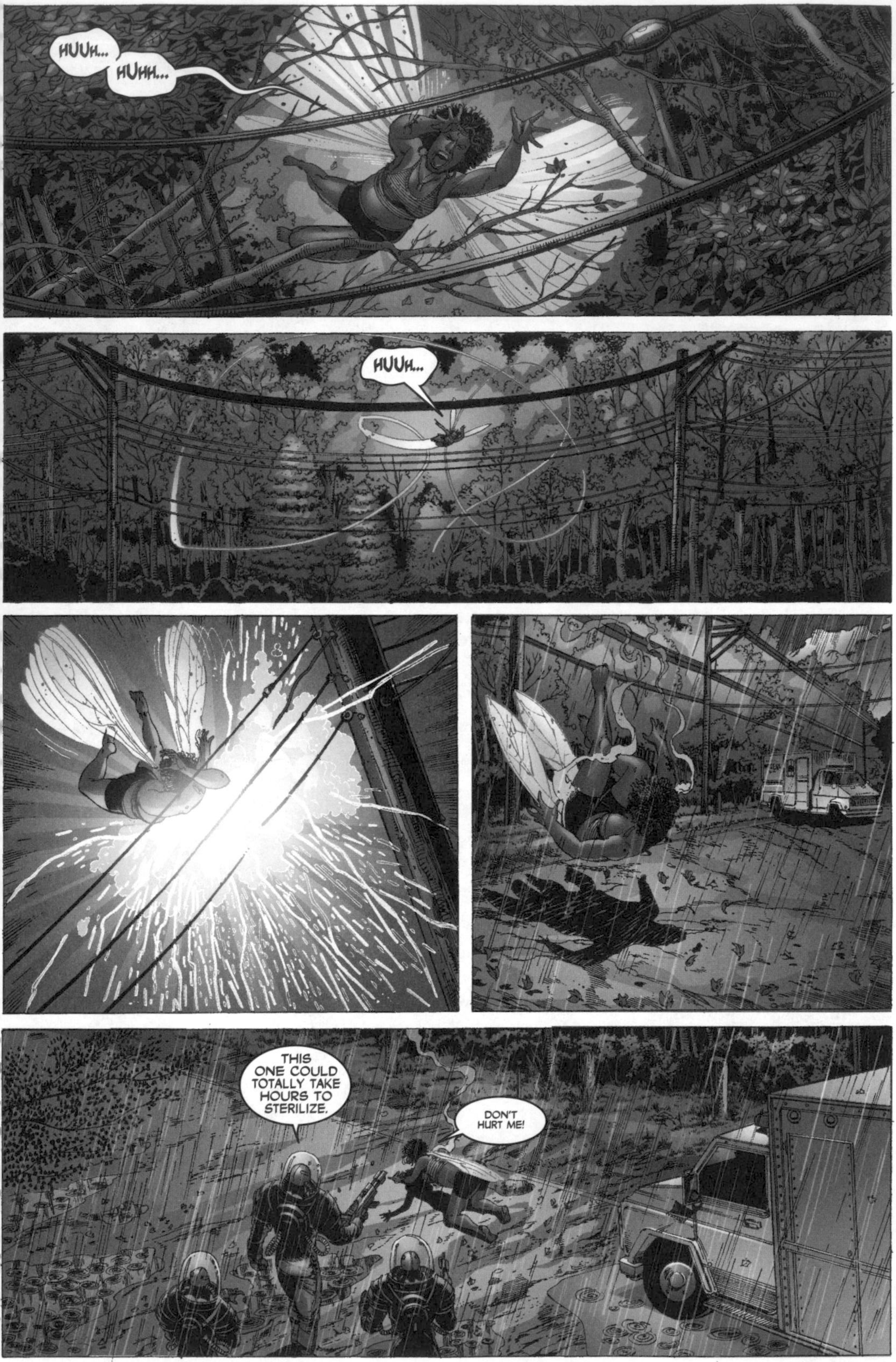
HUUH...
HUHH...
HUUH...
THIS ONE COULD TOTALLY TAKE HOURS TO STERILIZE.
DON'T HURT ME!

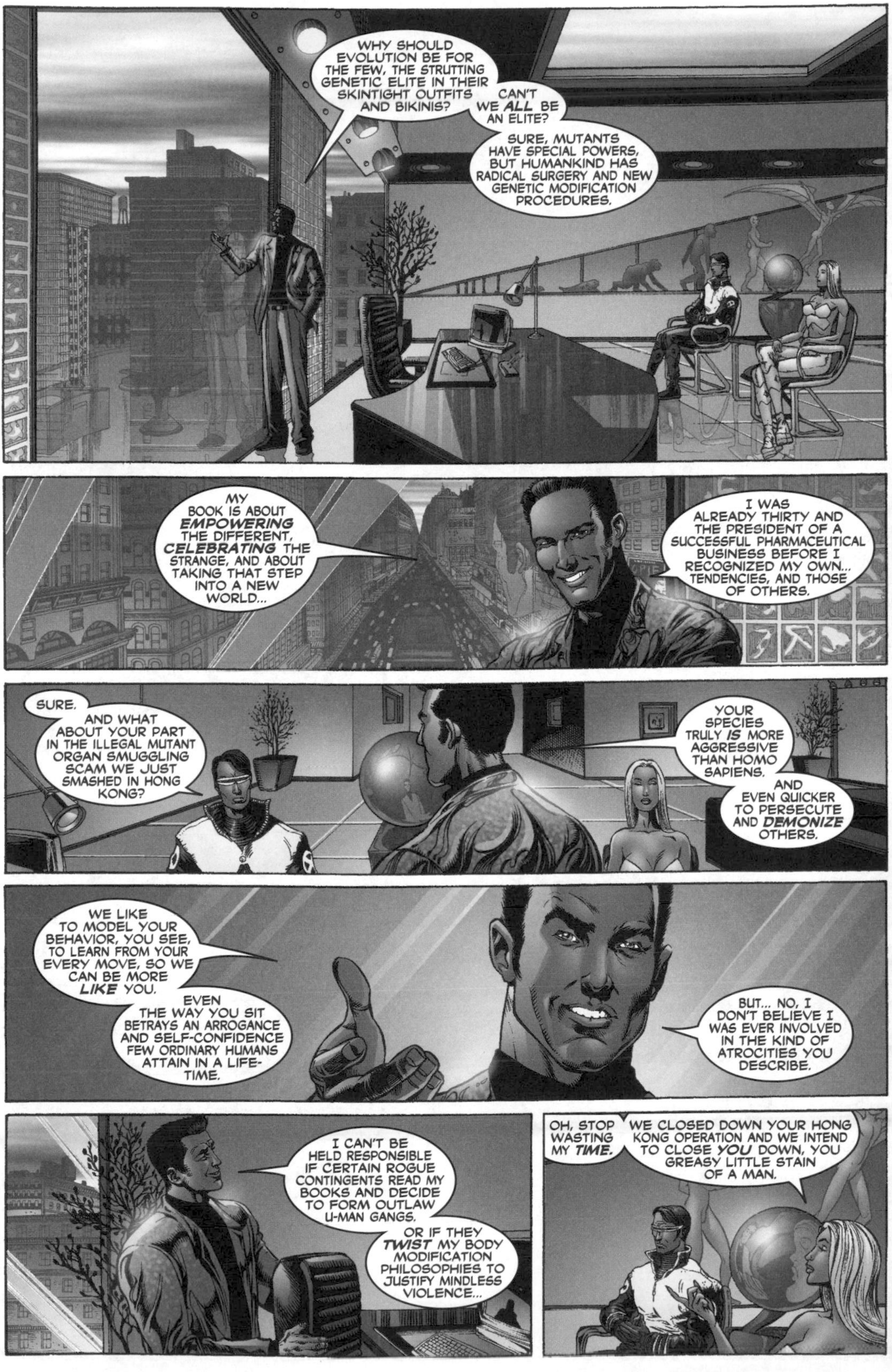
WHY SHOULD EVOLUTION BE FOR THE FEW, THE STRUTTING GENETIC ELITE IN THEIR SKINTIGHT OUTFITS AND BIKINIS?
CAN'T WE ALL BE AN ELITE?
SURE, MUTANTS HAVE SPECIAL POWERS, BUT HUMANKIND HAS RADICAL SURGERY AND NEW GENETIC MODIFICATION PROCEDURES.
MY BOOK IS ABOUT EMPOWERING THE DIFFERENT, CELEBRATING THE STRANGE, AND ABOUT TAKING THAT STEP INTO A NEW WORLD...
I WAS ALREADY THIRTY AND THE PRESIDENT OF A SUCCESSFUL PHARMACEUTICAL BUSINESS BEFORE I RECOGNIZED MY OWN... TENDENCIES, AND THOSE OF OTHERS.
SURE.
AND WHAT ABOUT YOUR PART IN THE ILLEGAL MUTANT ORGAN SMUGGLING SCAM WE JUST SMASHED IN HONG KONG?
YOUR SPECIES TRULY IS MORE AGGRESSIVE THAN HOMO SAPIENS.
AND EVEN QUICKER TO PERSECUTE AND DEMONIZE OTHERS.
WE LIKE TO MODEL YOUR BEHAVIOR, YOU SEE, TO LEARN FROM YOUR EVERY MOVE, SO WE CAN BE MORE LIKE YOU.
EVEN THE WAY YOU SIT BETRAYS AN ARROGANCE AND SELF-CONFIDENCE FEW ORDINARY HUMANS ATTAIN IN A LIFE-TIME.
BUT... NO, I DON'T BELIEVE I WAS EVER INVOLVED IN THE KIND OF ATROCITIES YOU DESCRIBE.
I CAN'T BE HELD RESPONSIBLE IF CERTAIN ROGUE CONTINGENTS READ MY BOOKS AND DECIDE TO FORM OUTLAW U-MAN GANGS.
OR IF THEY TWIST MY BODY MODIFICATION PHILOSOPHIES TO JUSTIFY MINDLESS VIOLENCE...
OH, STOP WASTING MY TIME.
WE CLOSED DOWN YOUR HONG KONG OPERATION AND WE INTEND TO CLOSE YOU DOWN, YOU GREASY LITTLE STAIN OF A MAN.

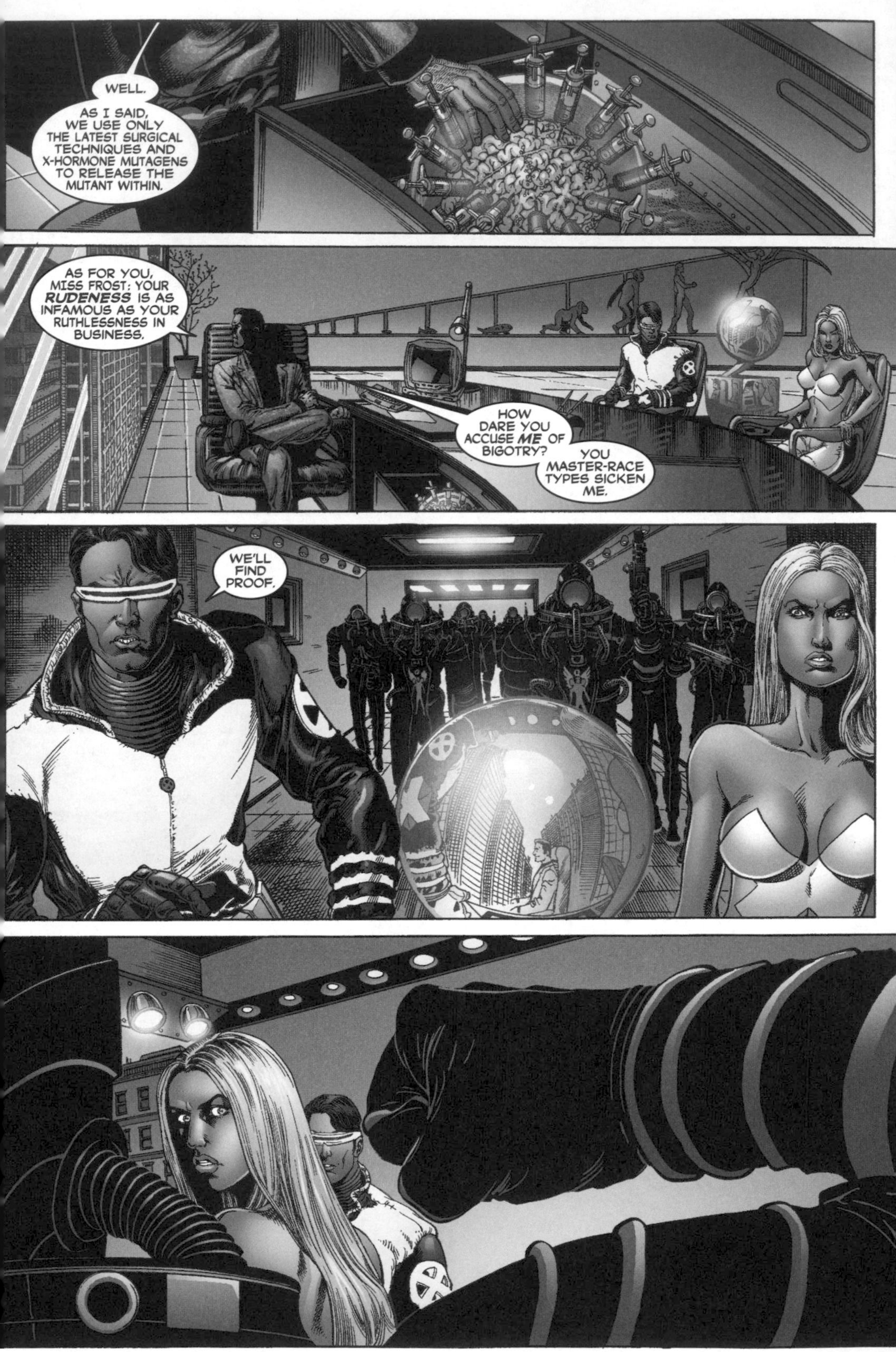
WELL.
AS I SAID, WE USE ONLY THE LATEST SURGICAL TECHNIQUES AND X-HORMONE MUTAGENS TO RELEASE THE MUTANT WITHIN.
AS FOR YOU, MISS FROST: YOUR RUDENESS IS AS INFAMOUS AS YOUR RUTHLESSNESS IN BUSINESS.
HOW DARE YOU ACCUSE ME OF BIGOTRY?
YOU MASTER-RACE TYPES SICKEN ME.
WE'LL FIND PROOF.

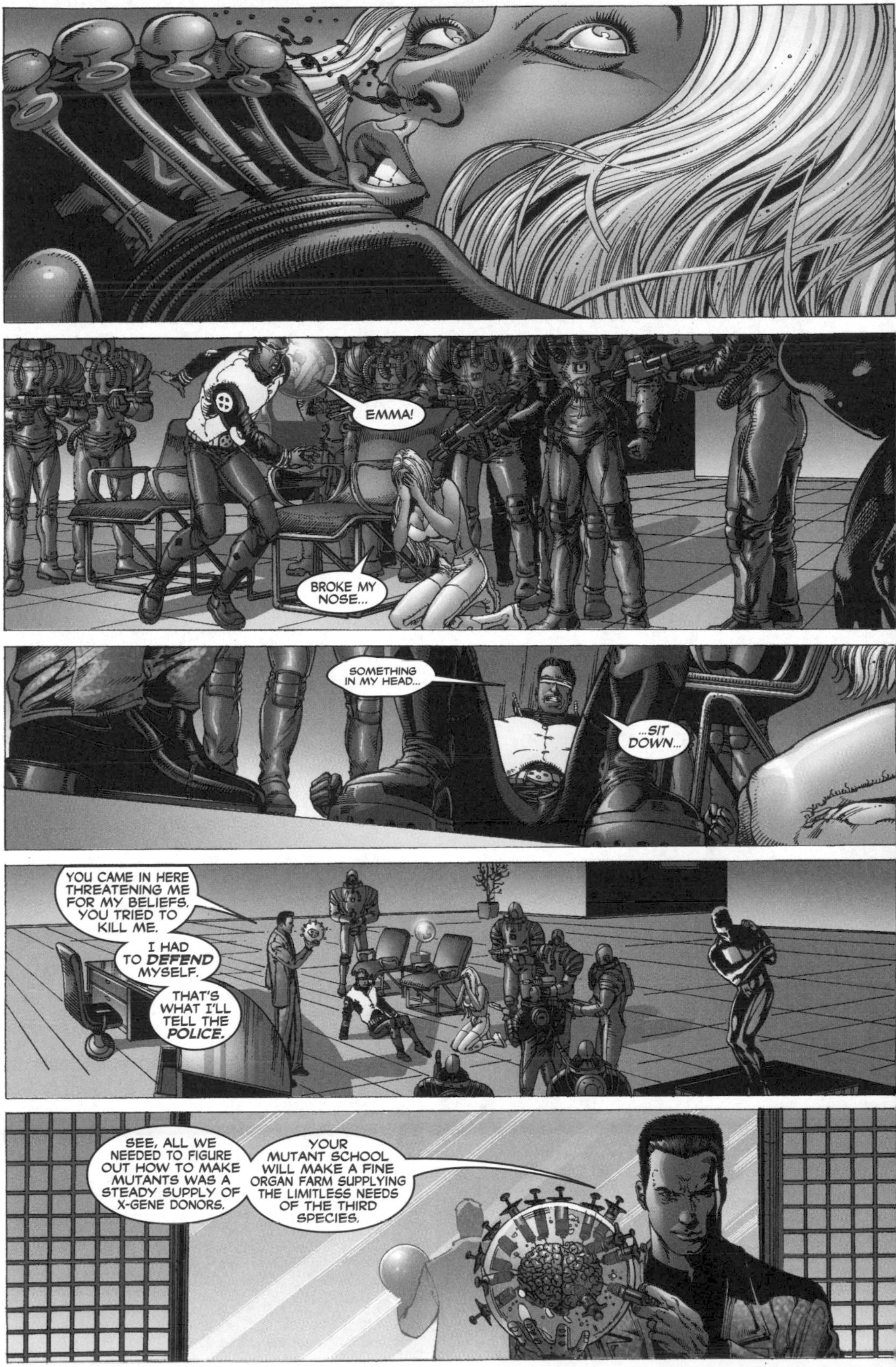
EMMA!
BROKE MY NOSE...
SOMETHING IN MY HEAD...
...SIT DOWN...
YOU CAME IN HERE THREATENING ME FOR MY BELIEFS, YOU TRIED TO KILL ME.
I HAD TO DEFEND MYSELF.
THAT'S WHAT I'LL TELL THE POLICE.
SEE, ALL WE NEEDED TO FIGURE OUT HOW TO MAKE MUTANTS WAS A STEADY SUPPLY OF X-GENE DONORS.
YOUR MUTANT SCHOOL WILL MAKE A FINE ORGAN FARM SUPPLYING THE LIMITLESS NEEDS OF THE THIRD SPECIES.

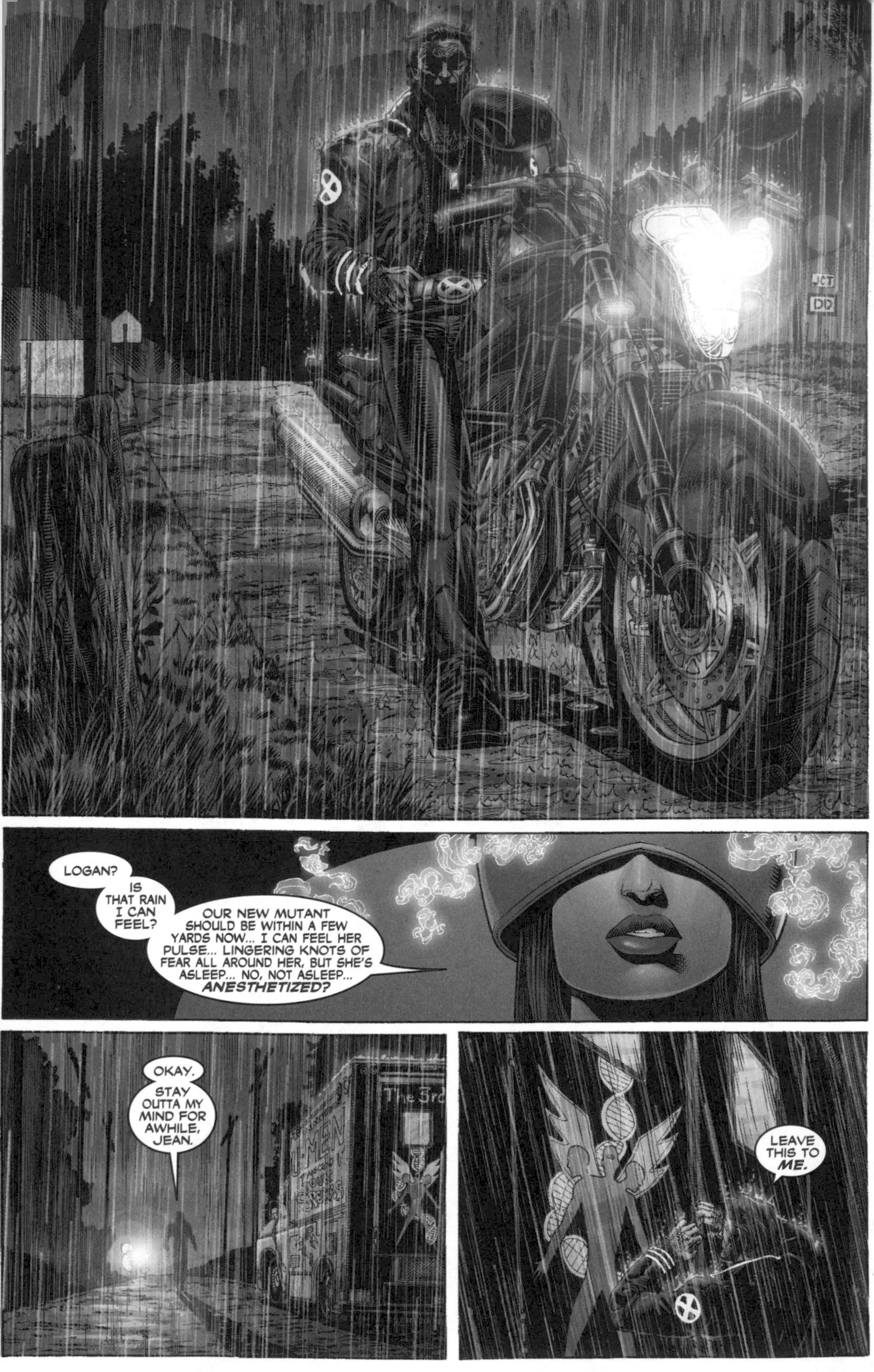
JCT
DD
LOGAN?
IS THAT RAIN I CAN FEEL?
OUR NEW MUTANT SHOULD BE WITHIN A FEW YARDS NOW... I CAN FEEL HER PULSE... LINGERING KNOTS OF FEAR ALL AROUND HER, BUT SHE'S ASLEEP... NO, NOT ASLEEP... *ANESTHETIZED?*
OKAY. STAY OUTTA MY MIND FOR AWHILE, JEAN.
U-MEN
The 3rd
LEAVE THIS TO *ME.*

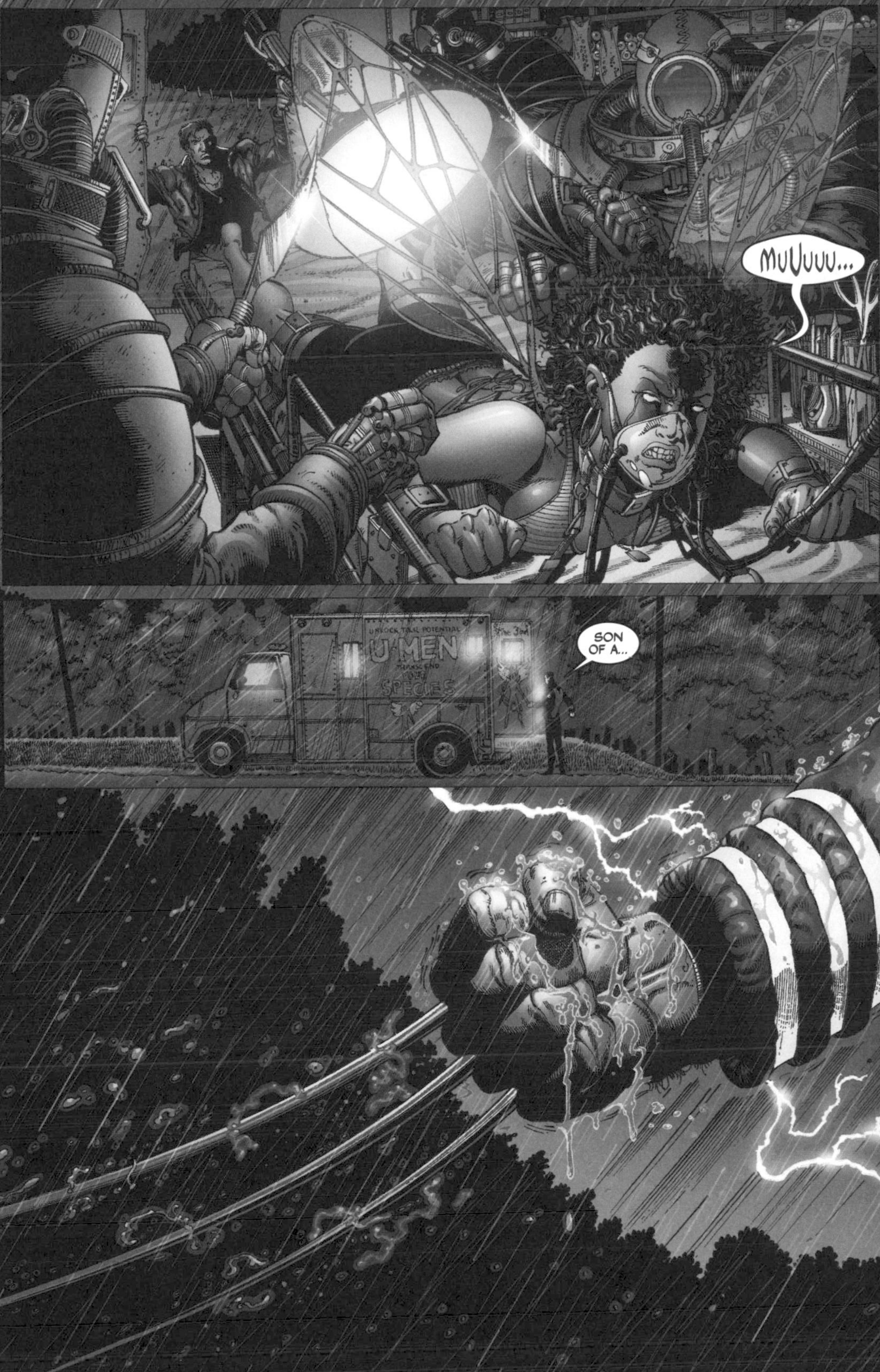
MUUUUU...
U-MEN
SPECIES
SON OF A...

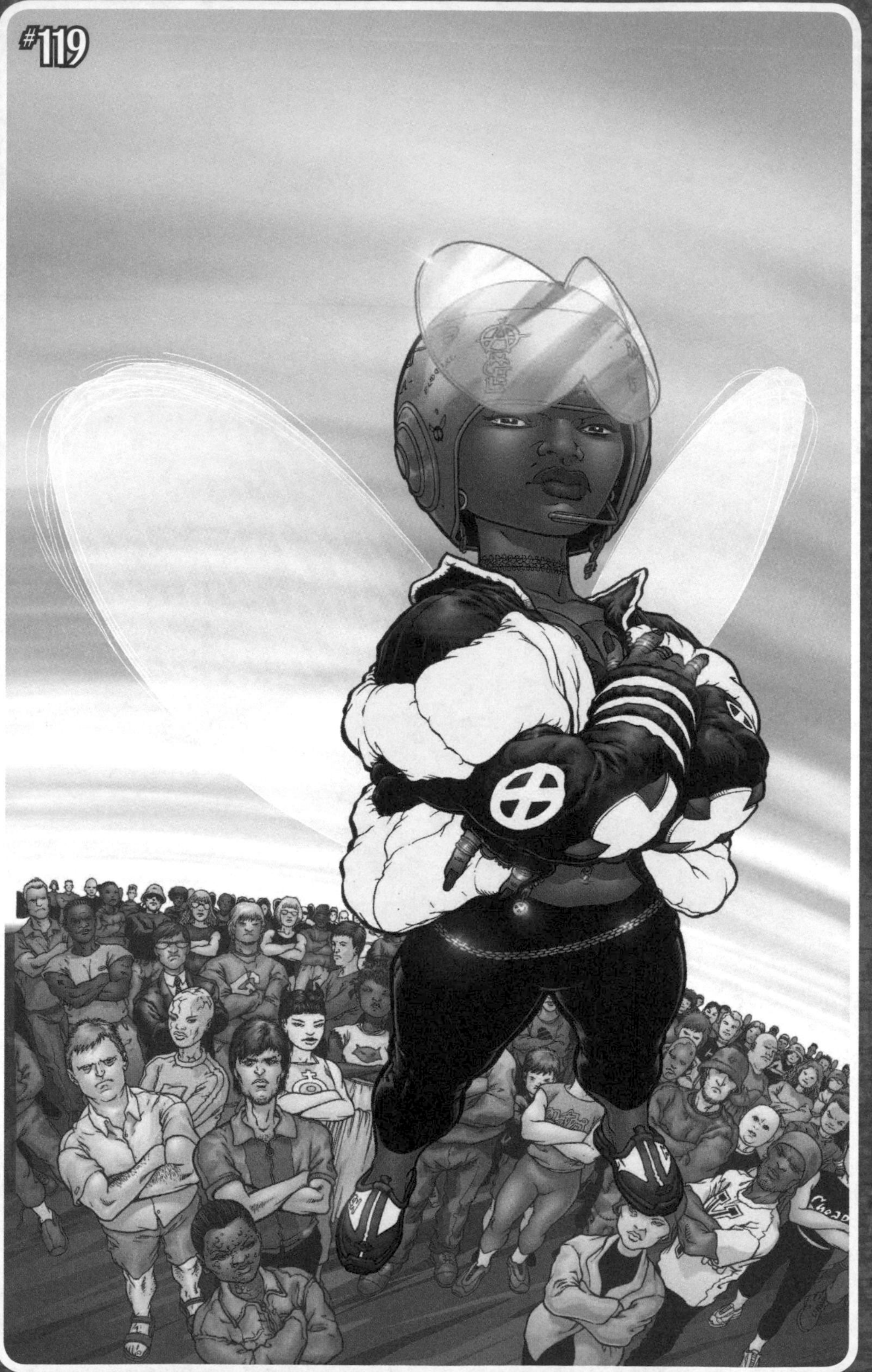
#119

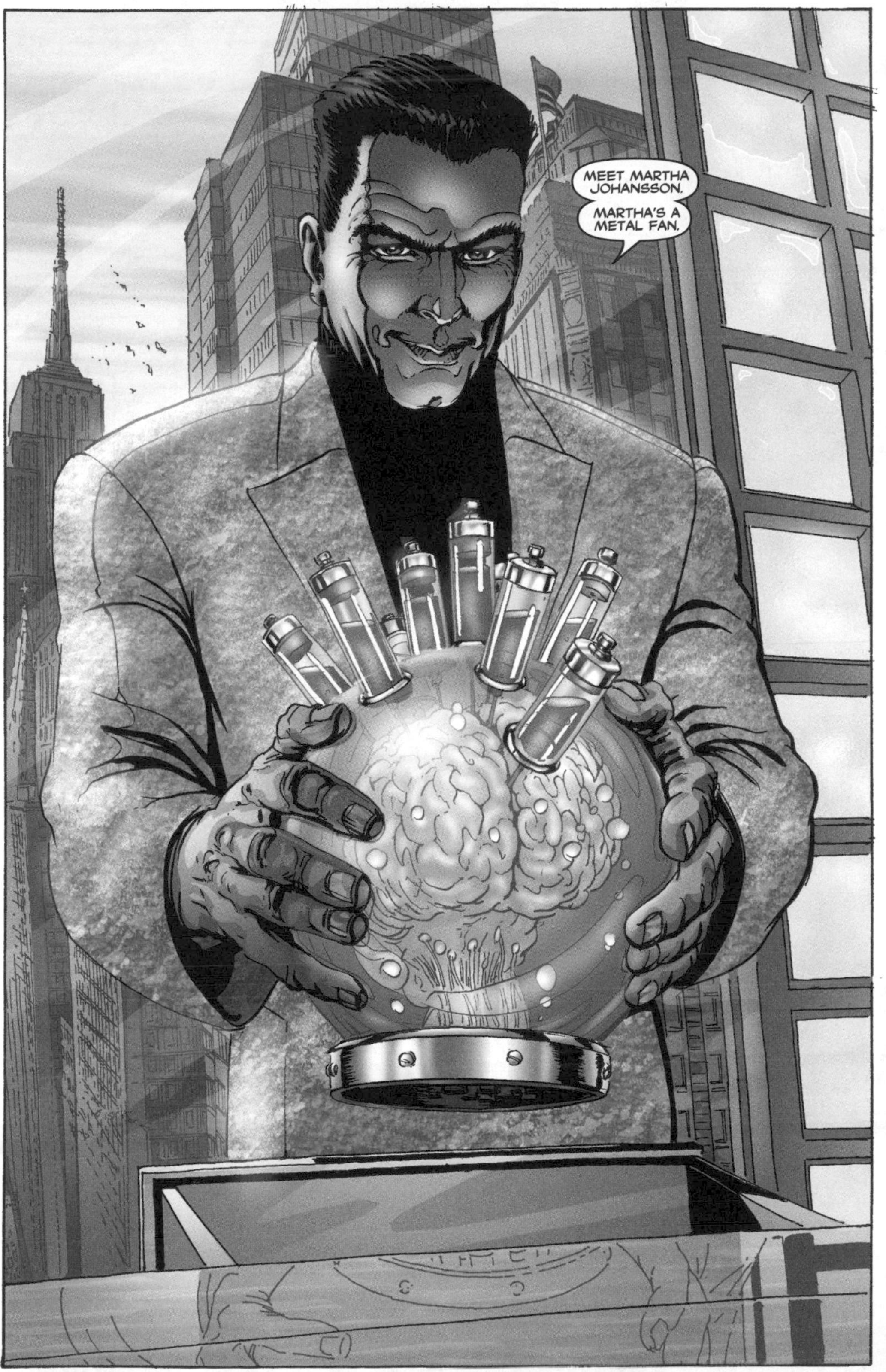
MEET MARTHA JOHANSSON.
MARTHA'S A METAL FAN.

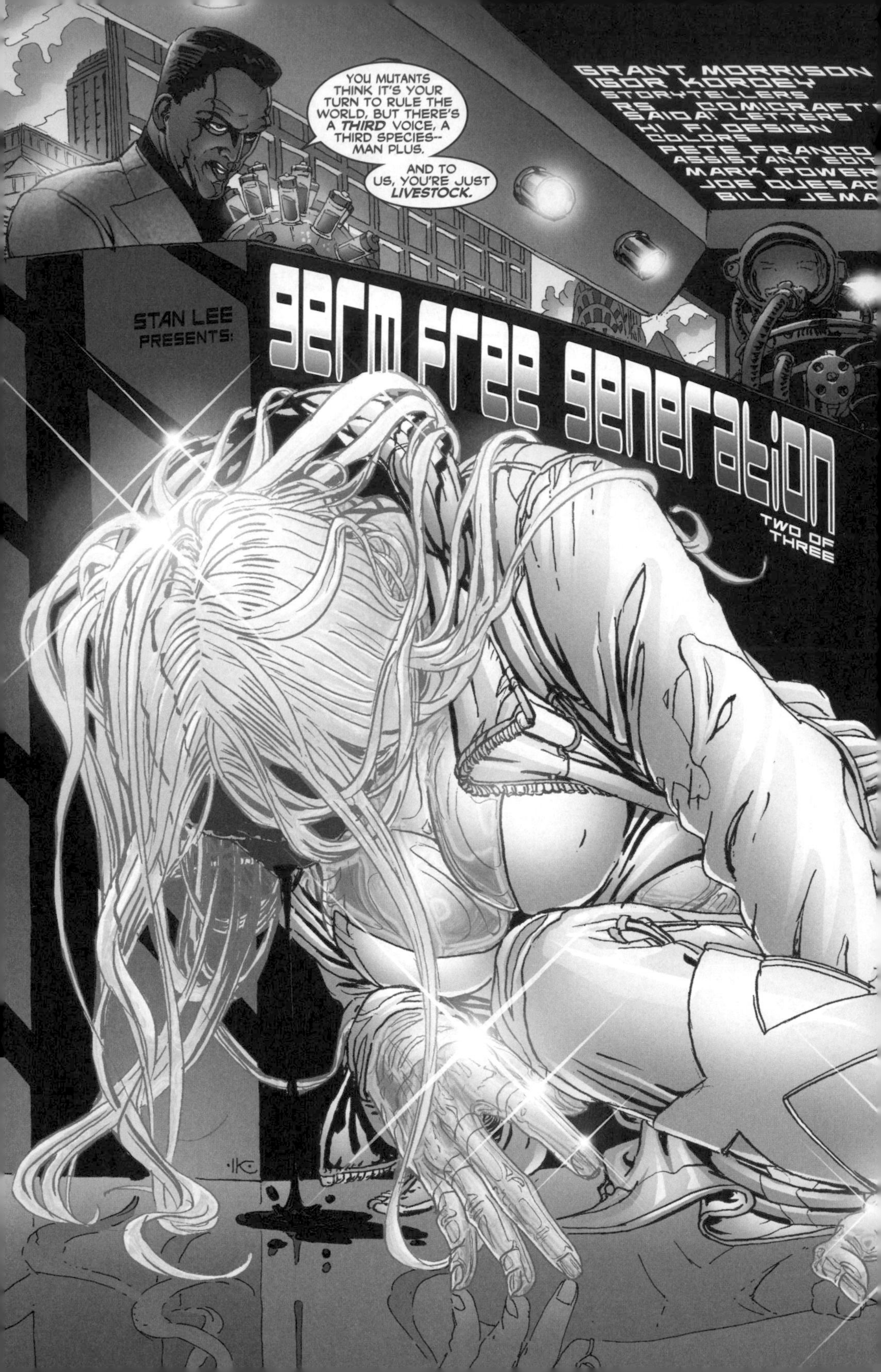

YOU MUTANTS THINK IT'S YOUR TURN TO RULE THE WORLD, BUT THERE'S A *THIRD* VOICE, A THIRD SPECIES-- MAN PLUS.
AND TO US, YOU'RE JUST ***LIVESTOCK.***
GRANT MORRISON
IGOR KORDEY
STORYTELLERS
RS COMICRAFT'
SAIDA! LETTERS
HI FI DESIGN
COLORS
PETE FRANCO
ASSISTANT EDIT
MARK POWER
JOE QUESAD
BILL JEMA
STAN LEE PRESENTS:
GERM FREE GENERATION
TWO OF THREE

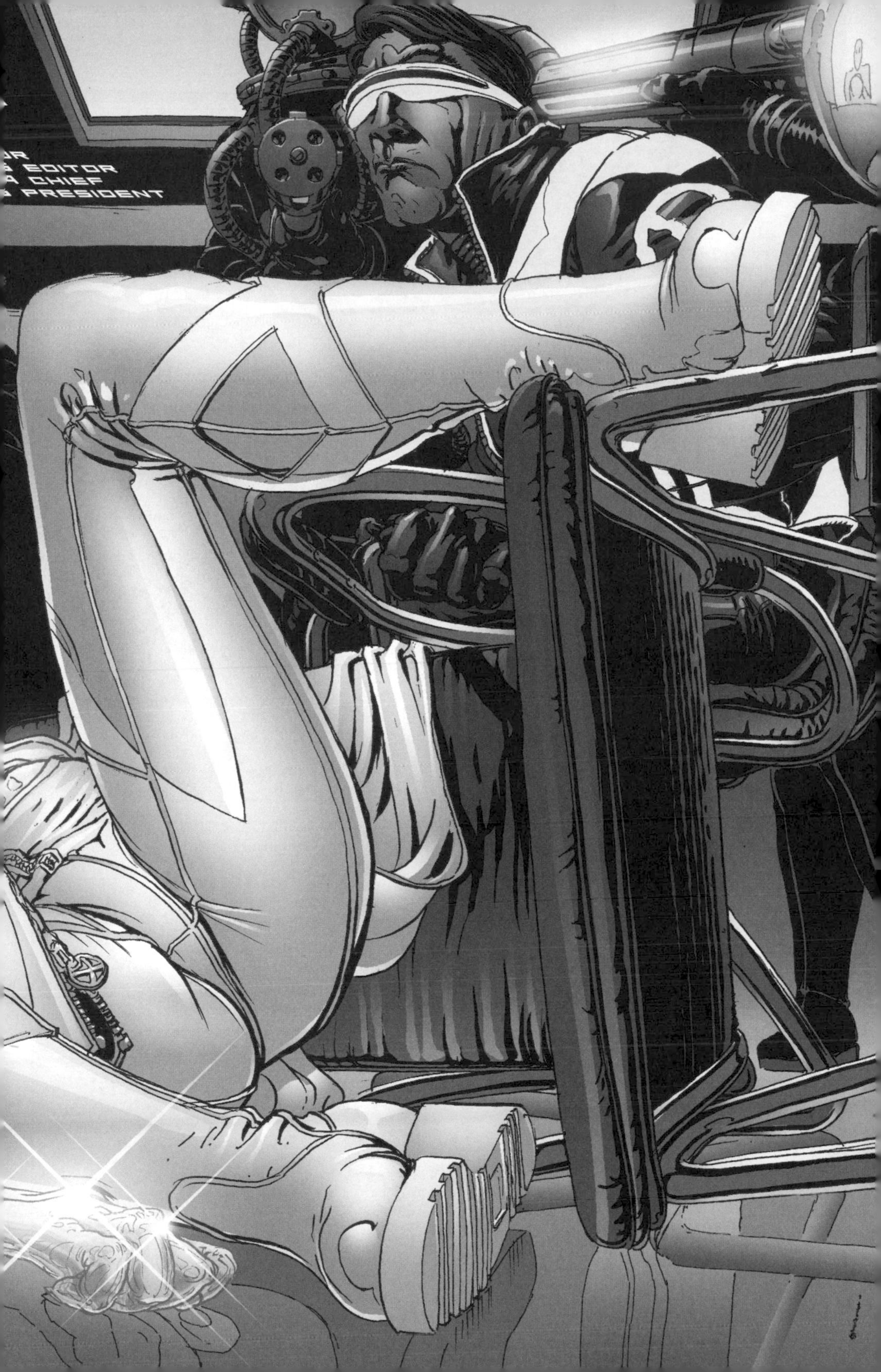
EDITOR
CHIEF
PRESIDENT

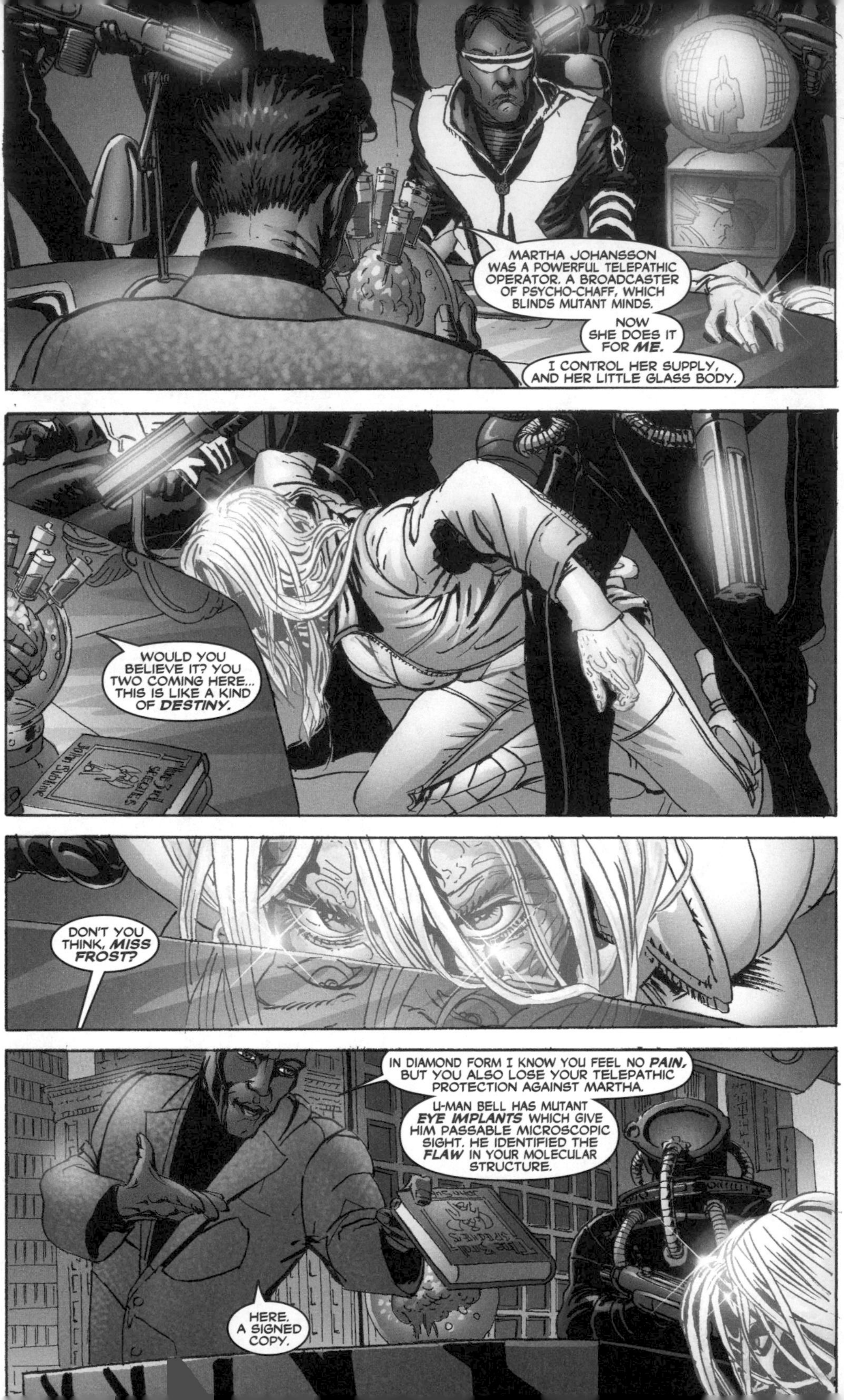
MARTHA JOHANSSON WAS A POWERFUL TELEPATHIC OPERATOR. A BROADCASTER OF PSYCHO-CHAFF, WHICH BLINDS MUTANT MINDS.
NOW SHE DOES IT FOR ME.
I CONTROL HER SUPPLY, AND HER LITTLE GLASS BODY.
WOULD YOU BELIEVE IT? YOU TWO COMING HERE... THIS IS LIKE A KIND OF DESTINY.
DON'T YOU THINK, MISS FROST?
IN DIAMOND FORM I KNOW YOU FEEL NO PAIN, BUT YOU ALSO LOSE YOUR TELEPATHIC PROTECTION AGAINST MARTHA.
U-MAN BELL HAS MUTANT EYE IMPLANTS WHICH GIVE HIM PASSABLE MICROSCOPIC SIGHT. HE IDENTIFIED THE FLAW IN YOUR MOLECULAR STRUCTURE.
HERE. A SIGNED COPY.

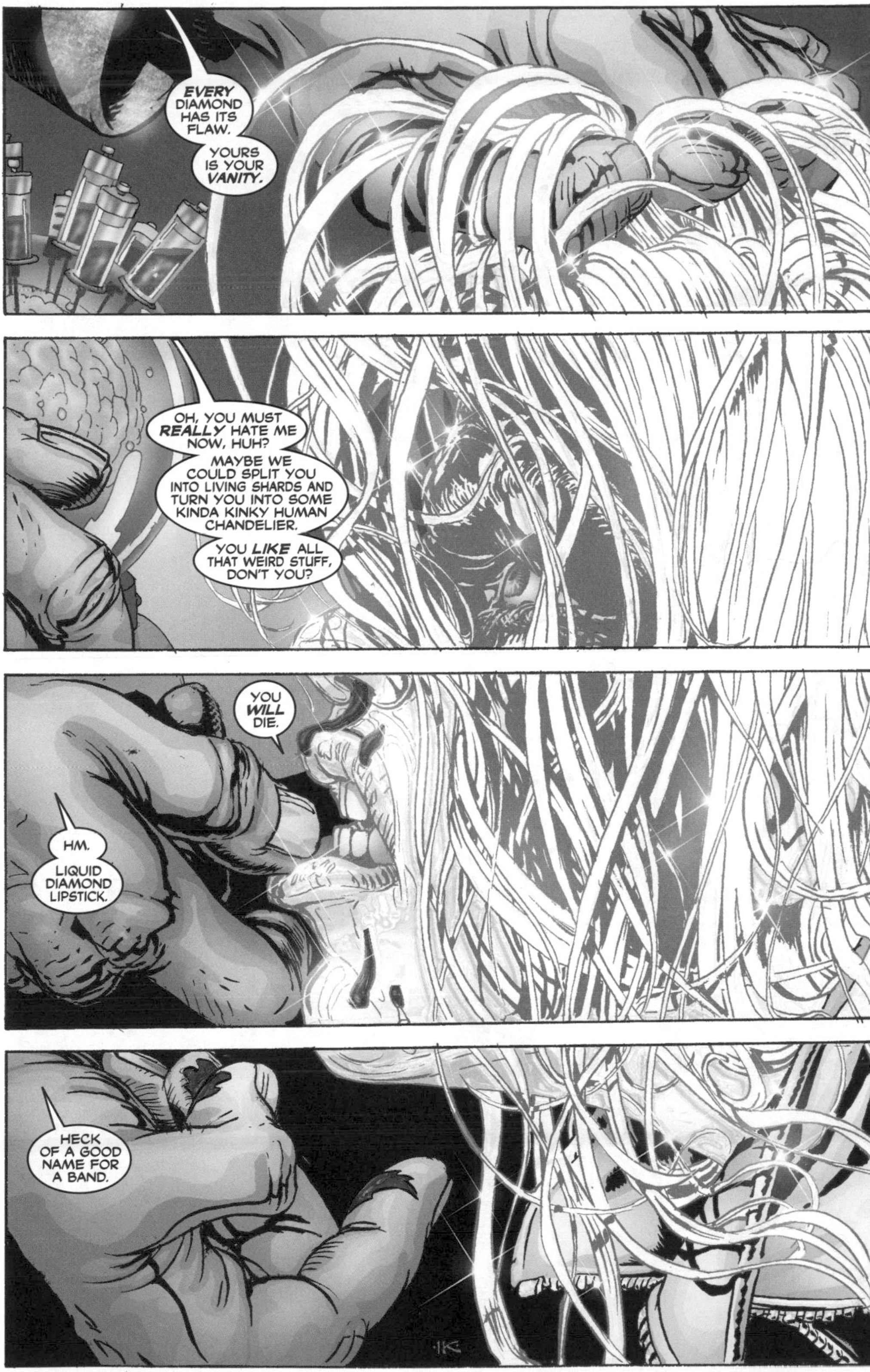
EVERY DIAMOND HAS ITS FLAW.
YOURS IS YOUR VANITY.
OH, YOU MUST REALLY HATE ME NOW, HUH?
MAYBE WE COULD SPLIT YOU INTO LIVING SHARDS AND TURN YOU INTO SOME KINDA KINKY HUMAN CHANDELIER.
YOU LIKE ALL THAT WEIRD STUFF, DON'T YOU?
YOU WILL DIE.
HM.
LIQUID DIAMOND LIPSTICK.
HECK OF A GOOD NAME FOR A BAND.

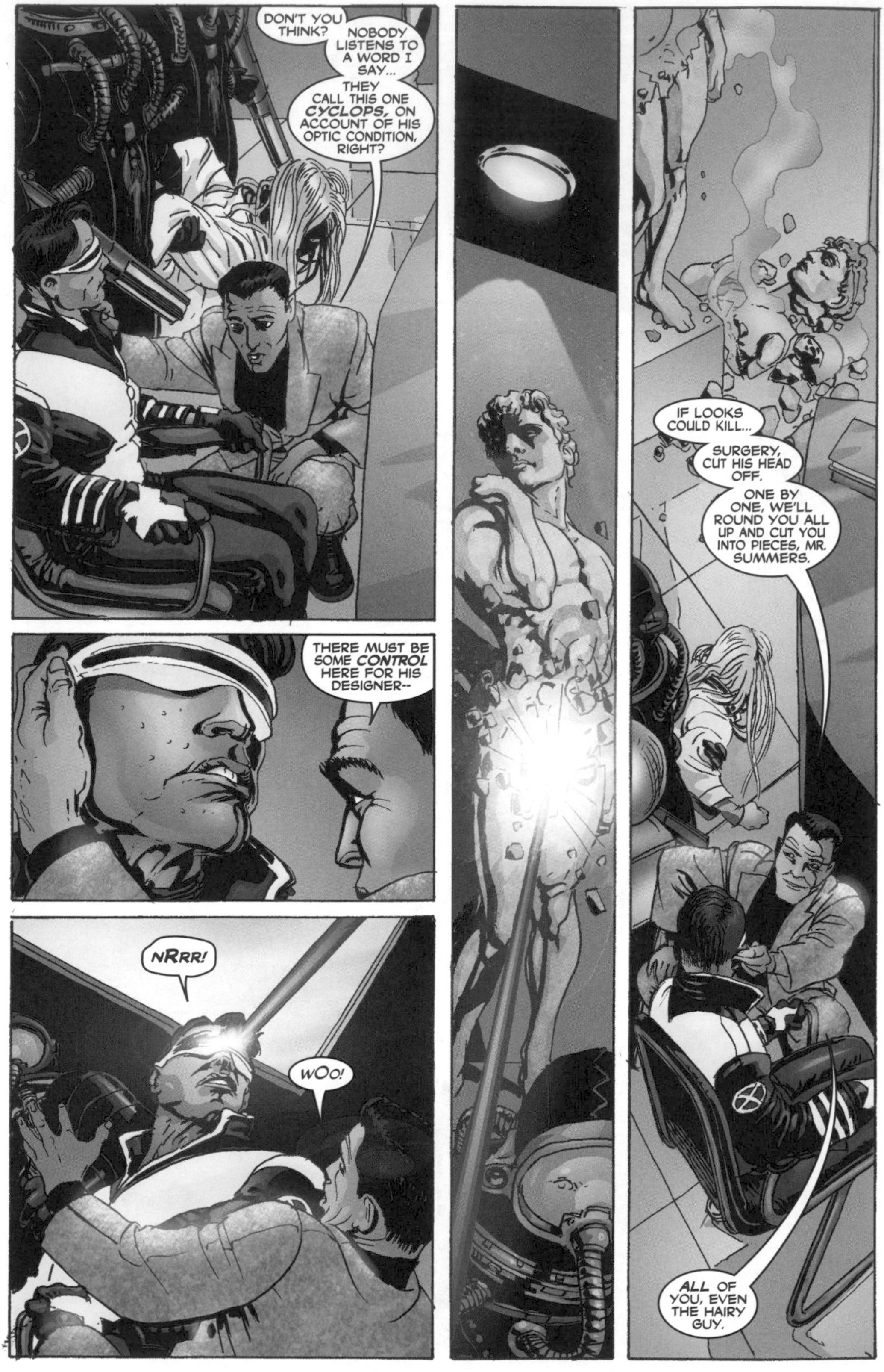
DON'T YOU THINK?
NOBODY LISTENS TO A WORD I SAY...
THEY CALL THIS ONE *CYCLOPS,* ON ACCOUNT OF HIS OPTIC CONDITION, RIGHT?
THERE MUST BE SOME *CONTROL* HERE FOR HIS DESIGNER--
NRRR!
WOO!
IF LOOKS COULD KILL...
SURGERY, CUT HIS HEAD OFF.
ONE BY ONE, WE'LL ROUND YOU ALL UP AND CUT YOU INTO PIECES, MR. SUMMERS.
ALL OF YOU, EVEN THE HAIRY GUY.

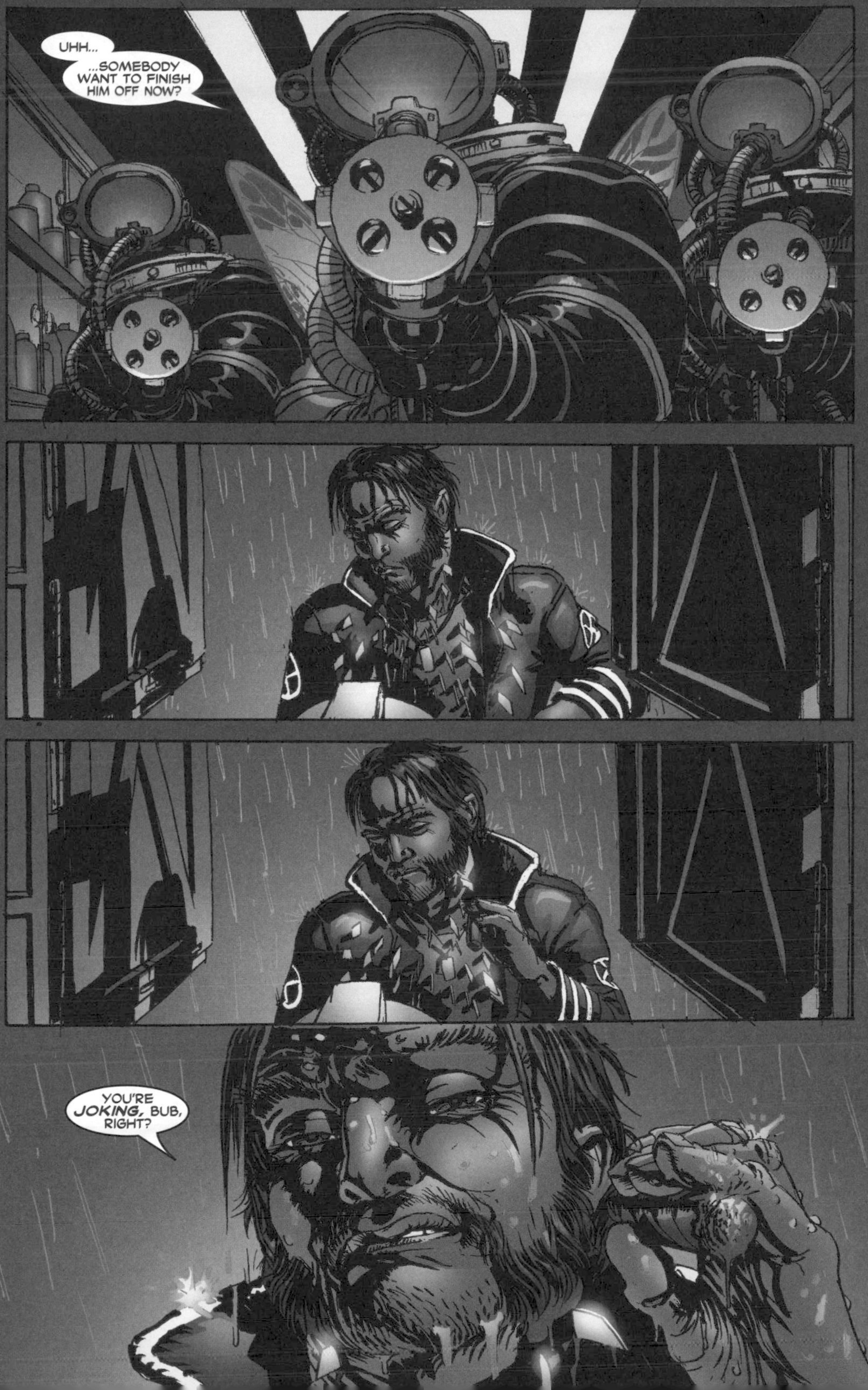
UHH...
...SOMEBODY WANT TO FINISH HIM OFF NOW?
YOU'RE *JOKING,* BUB, RIGHT?

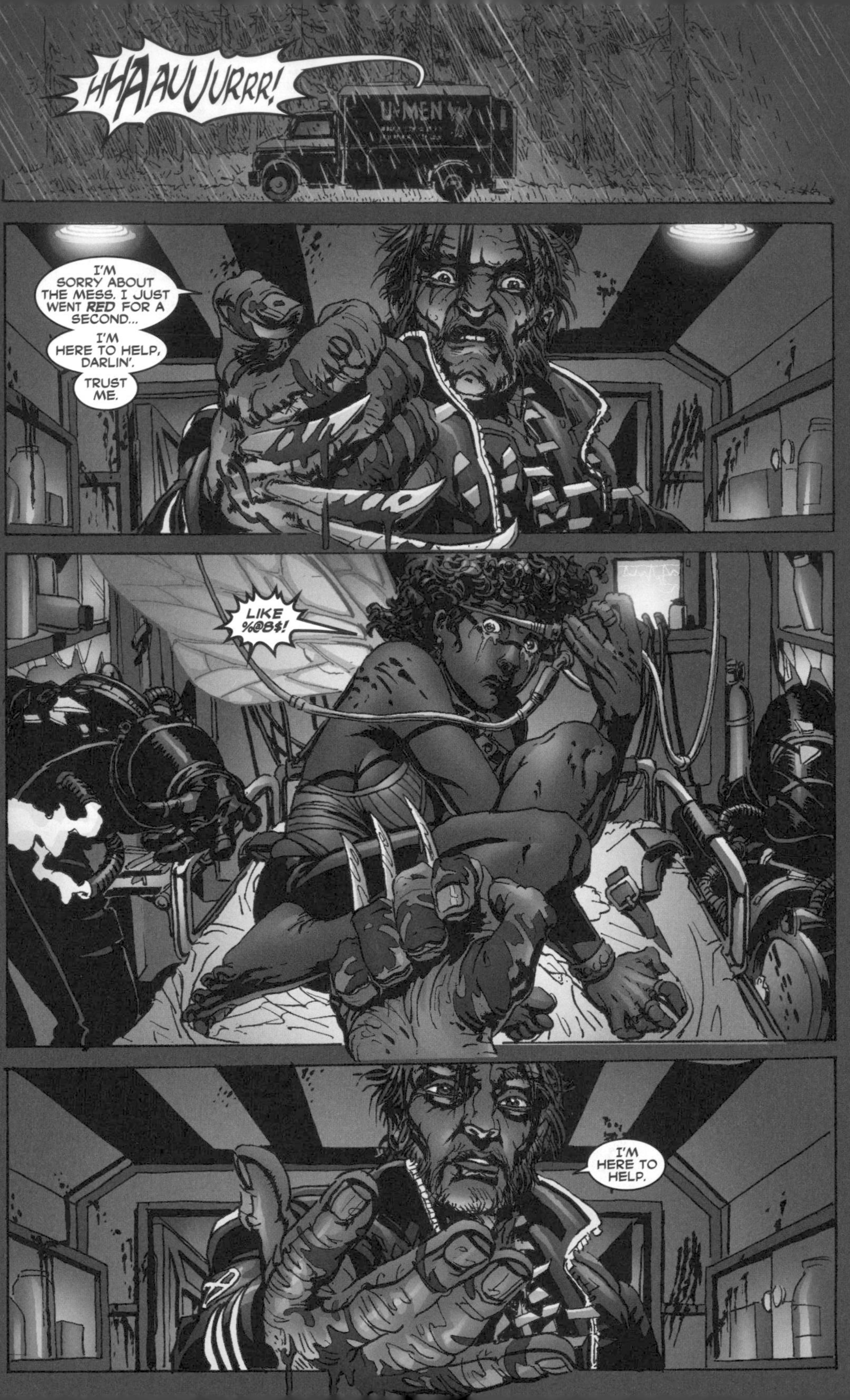
HHAAUUURRR!
U-MEN
I'M SORRY ABOUT THE MESS. I JUST WENT RED FOR A SECOND...
I'M HERE TO HELP, DARLIN'.
TRUST ME.
LIKE %@B$!
I'M HERE TO HELP.

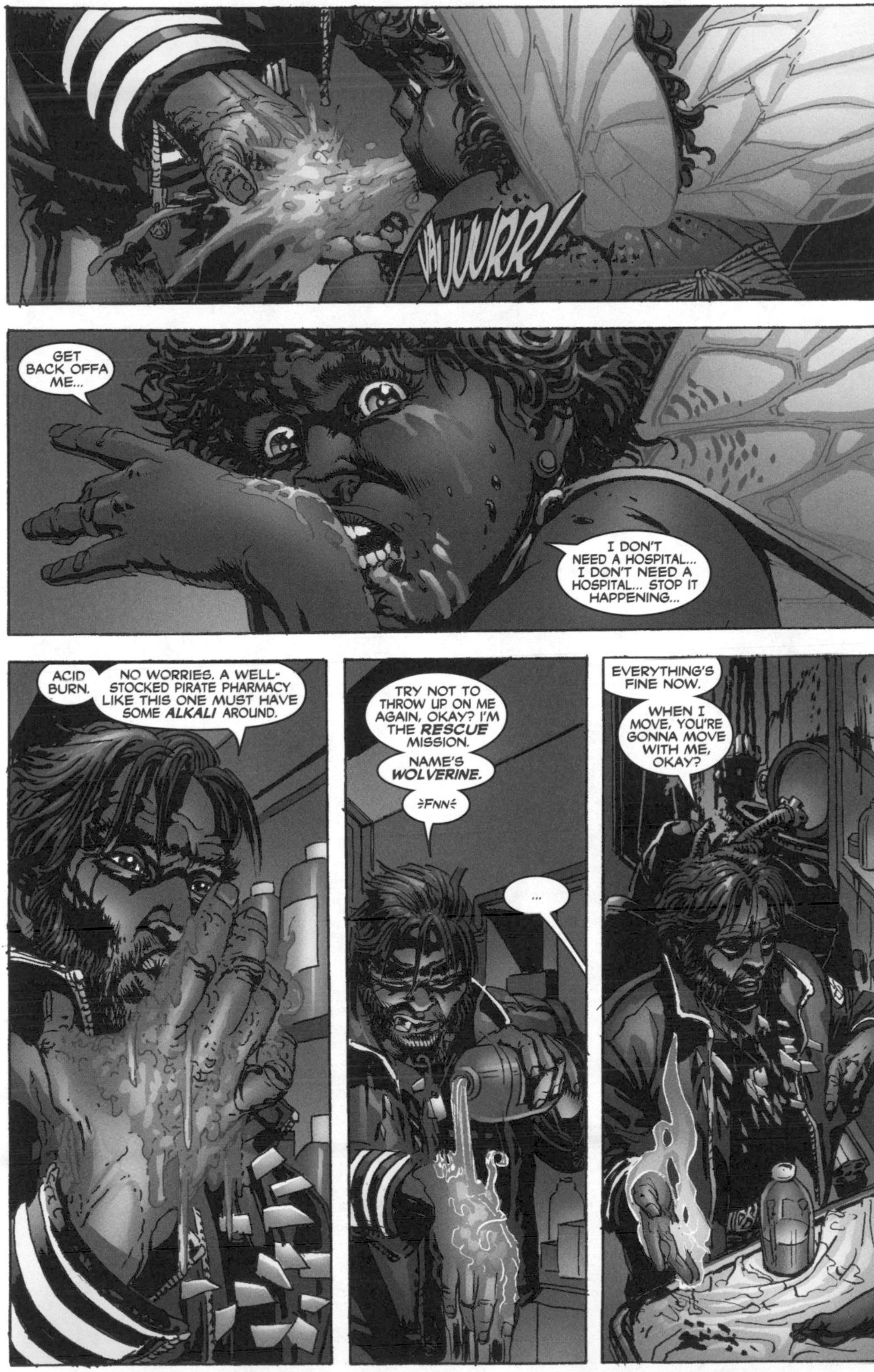
VAUUURR!
GET BACK OFFA ME...
I DON'T NEED A HOSPITAL... I DON'T NEED A HOSPITAL... STOP IT HAPPENING...
ACID BURN.
NO WORRIES. A WELL-STOCKED PIRATE PHARMACY LIKE THIS ONE MUST HAVE SOME ALKALI AROUND.
TRY NOT TO THROW UP ON ME AGAIN, OKAY? I'M THE RESCUE MISSION.
NAME'S WOLVERINE.
FNN
...
EVERYTHING'S FINE NOW.
WHEN I MOVE, YOU'RE GONNA MOVE WITH ME, OKAY?

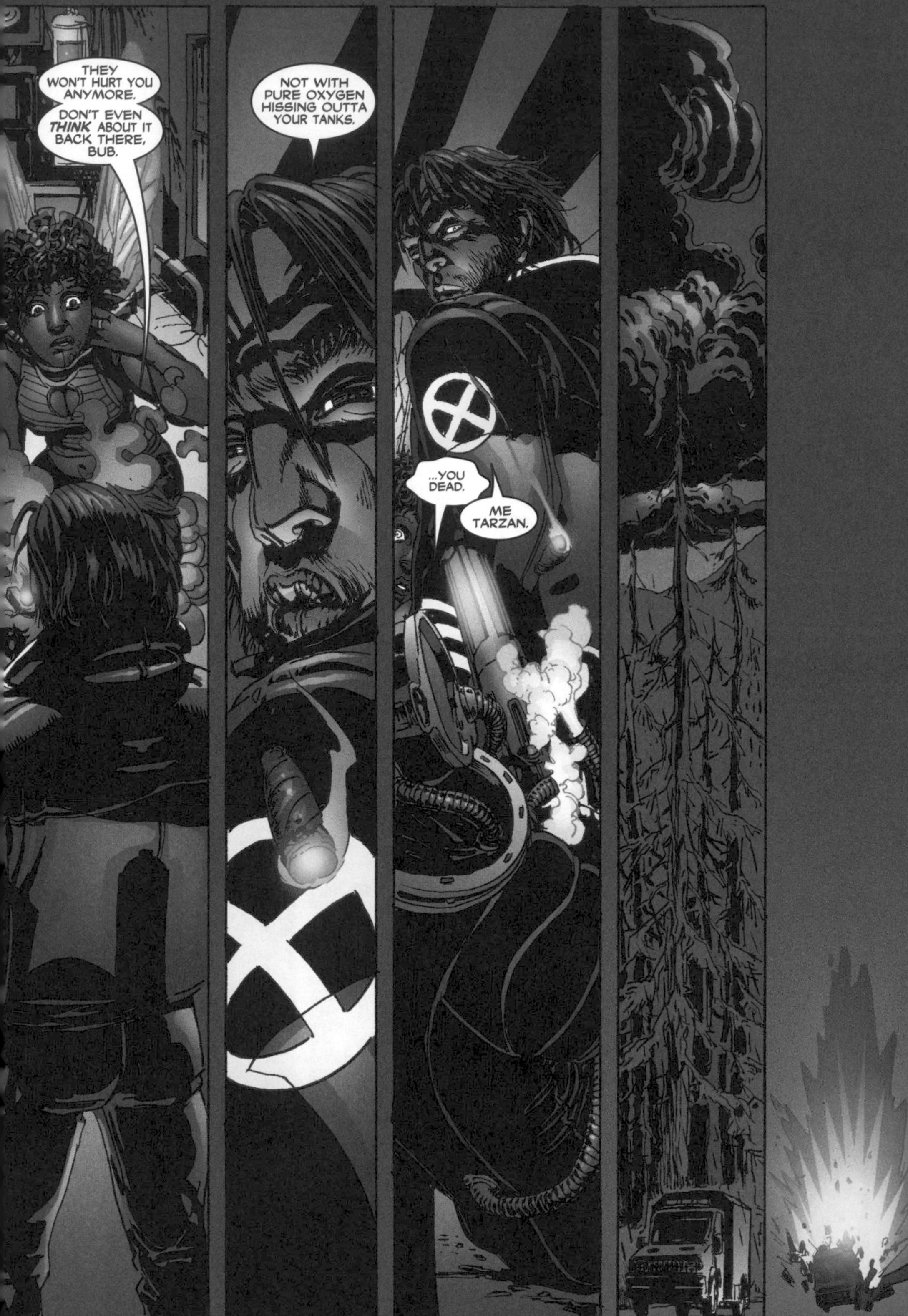
THEY WON'T HURT YOU ANYMORE.
DON'T EVEN *THINK* ABOUT IT BACK THERE, BUB.
NOT WITH PURE OXYGEN HISSING OUTTA YOUR TANKS.
...YOU DEAD.
ME TARZAN.

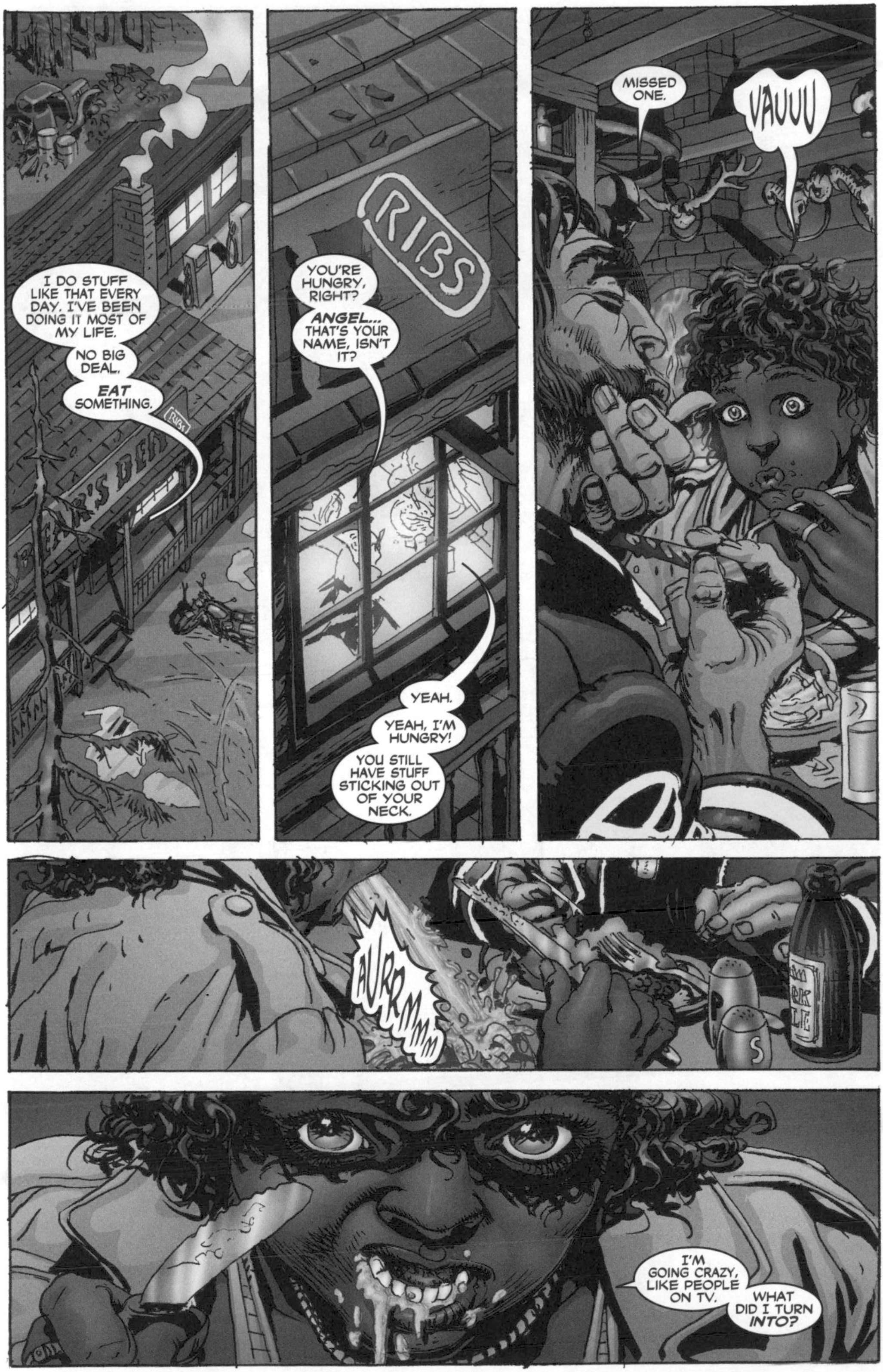
I DO STUFF LIKE THAT EVERY DAY. I'VE BEEN DOING IT MOST OF MY LIFE.
NO BIG DEAL.
EAT SOMETHING.
RIBS
YOU'RE HUNGRY, RIGHT?
ANGEL... THAT'S YOUR NAME, ISN'T IT?
RIBS
YEAH.
YEAH, I'M HUNGRY!
YOU STILL HAVE STUFF STICKING OUT OF YOUR NECK.
MISSED ONE.
VAUUU
AURRMMM
I'M GOING CRAZY, LIKE PEOPLE ON TV.
WHAT DID I TURN INTO?

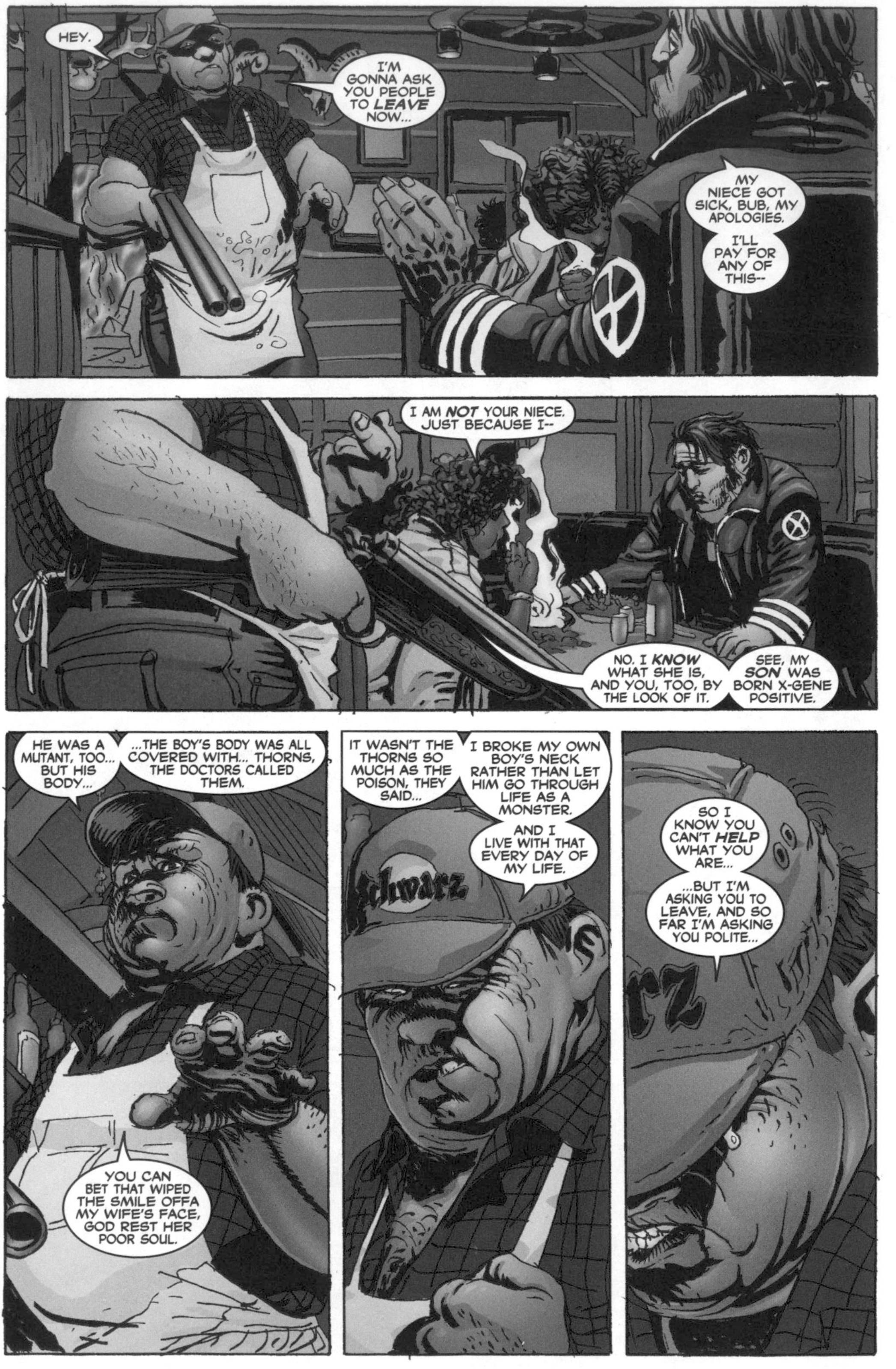
HEY.
I'M GONNA ASK YOU PEOPLE TO LEAVE NOW...
MY NIECE GOT SICK, BUB, MY APOLOGIES.
I'LL PAY FOR ANY OF THIS--
I AM NOT YOUR NIECE. JUST BECAUSE I--
NO. I KNOW WHAT SHE IS, AND YOU, TOO, BY THE LOOK OF IT.
SEE, MY SON WAS BORN X-GENE POSITIVE.
HE WAS A MUTANT, TOO... BUT HIS BODY...
...THE BOY'S BODY WAS ALL COVERED WITH... THORNS, THE DOCTORS CALLED THEM.
YOU CAN BET THAT WIPED THE SMILE OFFA MY WIFE'S FACE, GOD REST HER POOR SOUL.
IT WASN'T THE THORNS SO MUCH AS THE POISON, THEY SAID...
I BROKE MY OWN BOY'S NECK RATHER THAN LET HIM GO THROUGH LIFE AS A MONSTER.
AND I LIVE WITH THAT EVERY DAY OF MY LIFE.
SO I KNOW YOU CAN'T HELP WHAT YOU ARE...
...BUT I'M ASKING YOU TO LEAVE, AND SO FAR I'M ASKING YOU POLITE...

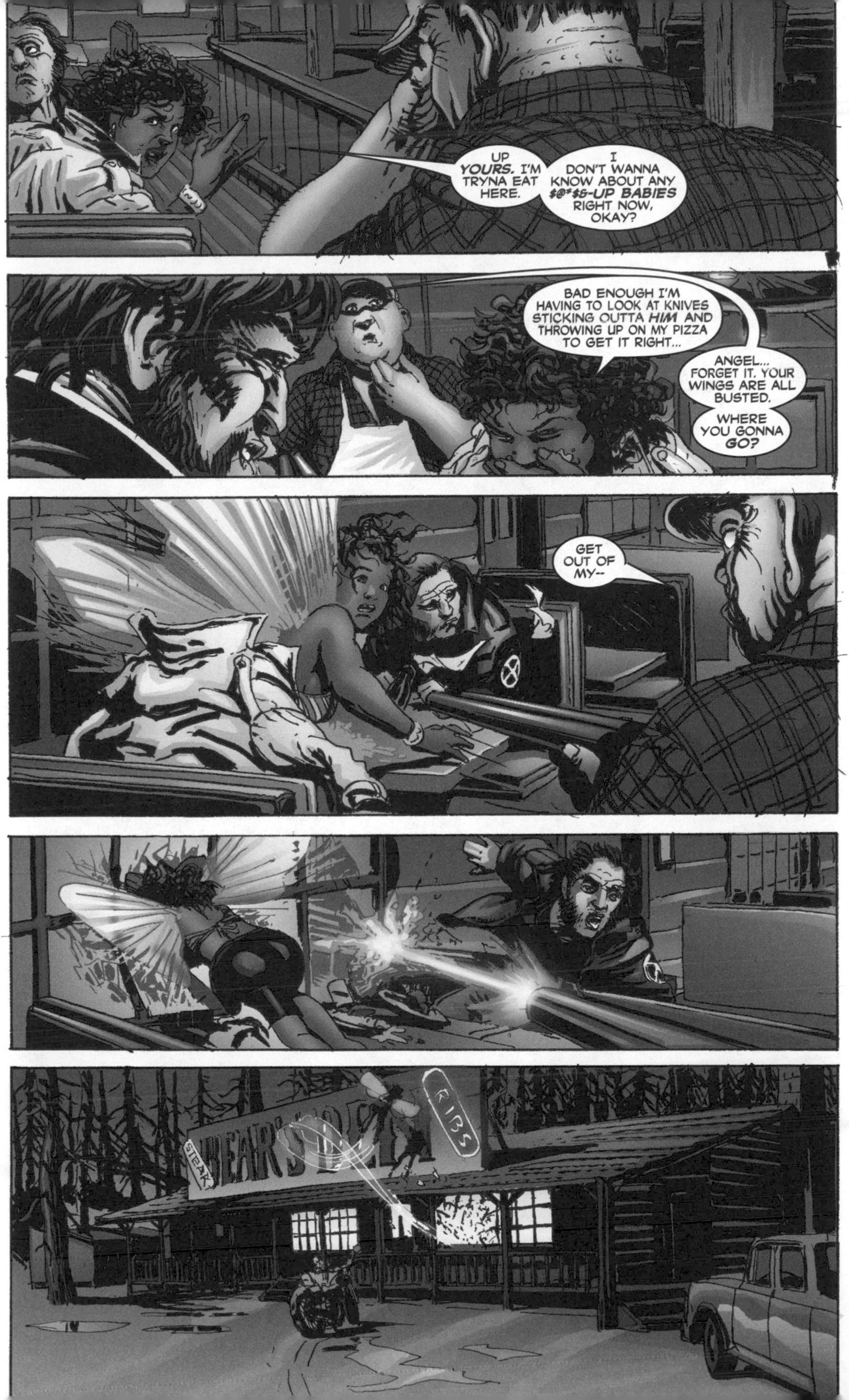
UP *YOURS.* I'M TRYNA EAT HERE.
I DON'T WANNA KNOW ABOUT ANY *$@*$&-UP BABIES* RIGHT NOW, OKAY?
BAD ENOUGH I'M HAVING TO LOOK AT KNIVES STICKING OUTTA *HIM* AND THROWING UP ON MY PIZZA TO GET IT RIGHT...
ANGEL... FORGET IT. YOUR WINGS ARE ALL BUSTED.
WHERE YOU GONNA *GO?*
GET OUT OF MY--
RIBS
STEAK

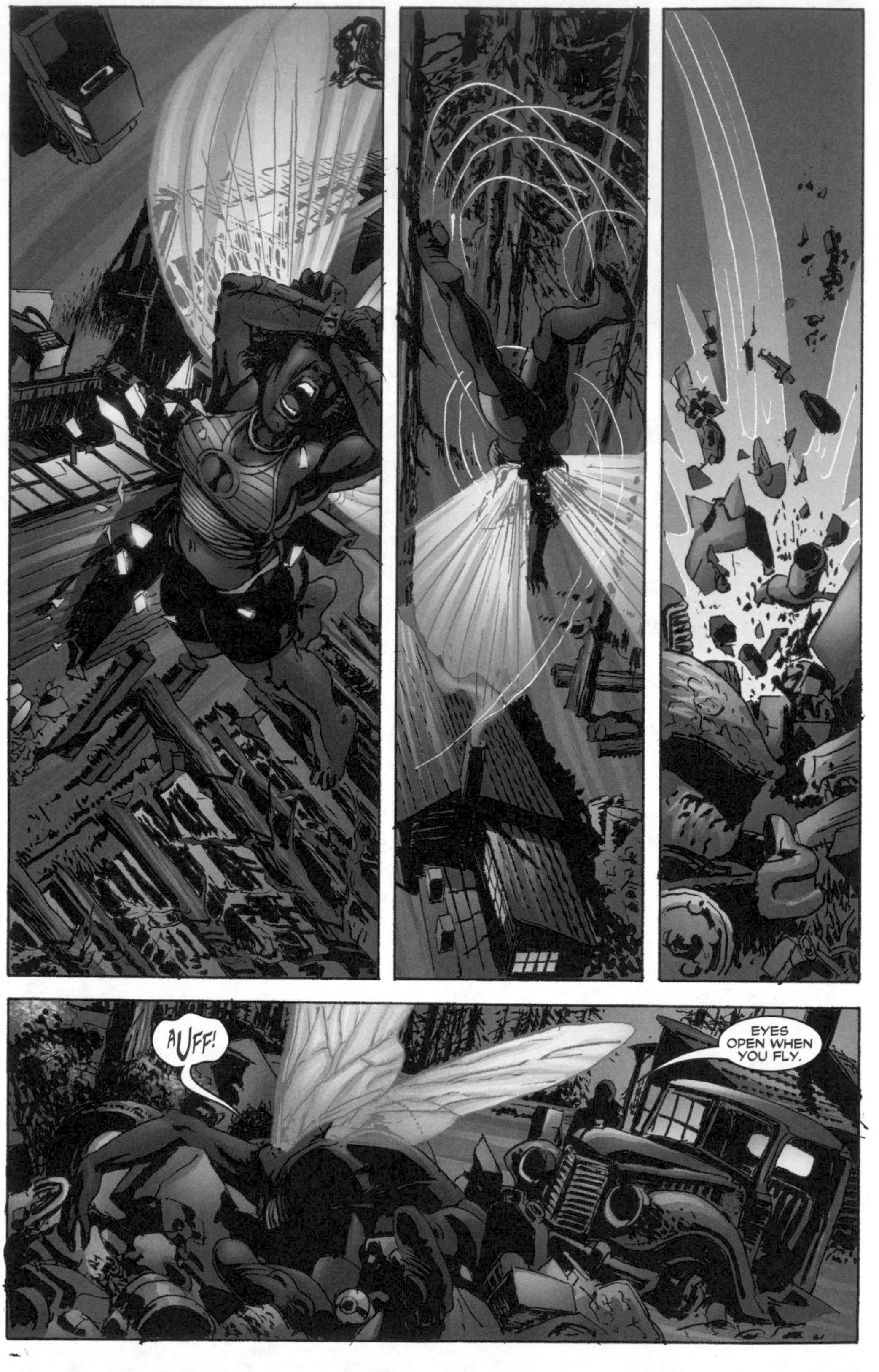
AUFF!
EYES OPEN WHEN YOU FLY.

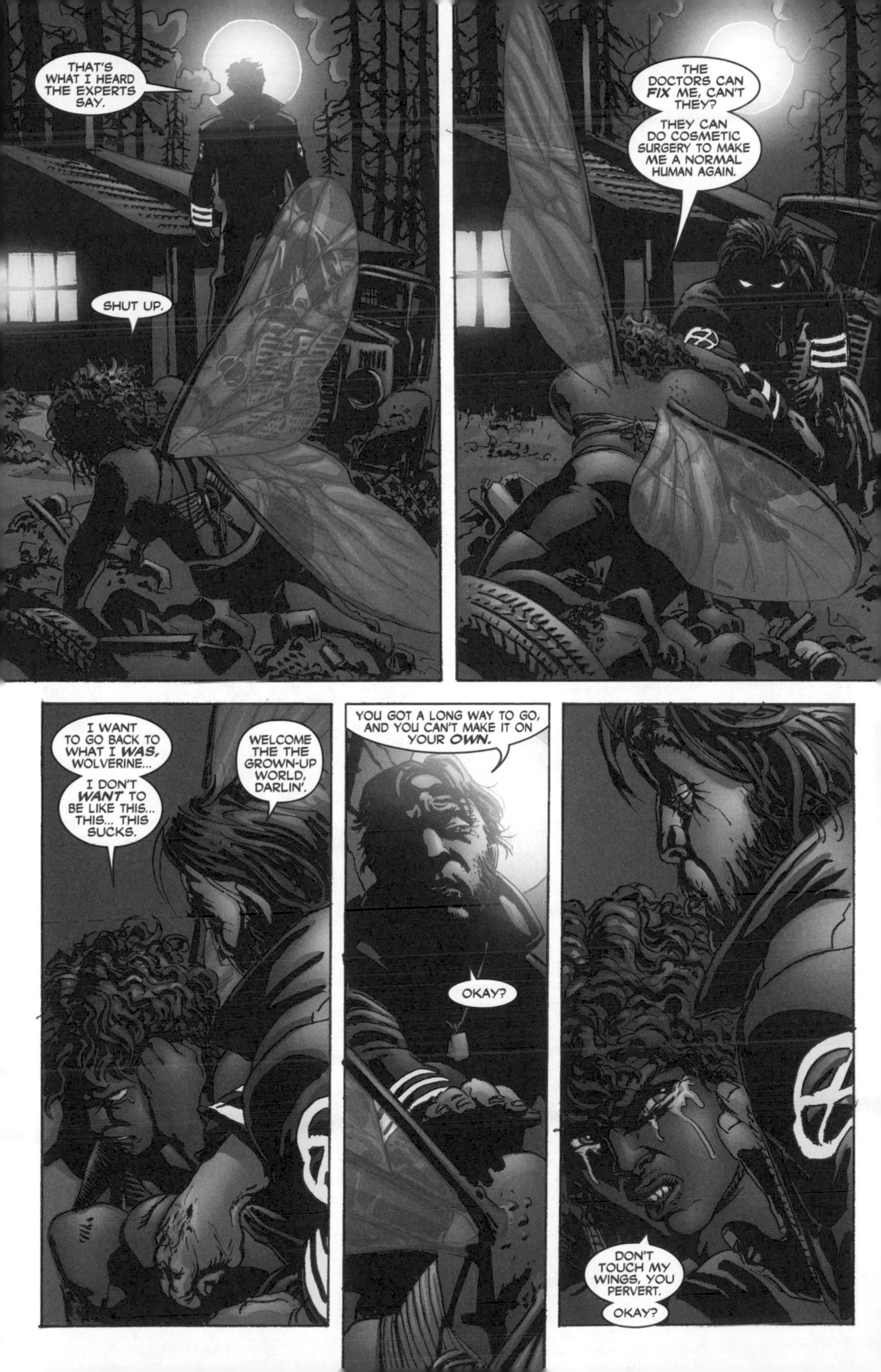
THAT'S WHAT I HEARD THE EXPERTS SAY.
SHUT UP.
THE DOCTORS CAN FIX ME, CAN'T THEY?
THEY CAN DO COSMETIC SURGERY TO MAKE ME A NORMAL HUMAN AGAIN.
I WANT TO GO BACK TO WHAT I WAS, WOLVERINE...
I DON'T WANT TO BE LIKE THIS... THIS... THIS SUCKS.
WELCOME THE THE GROWN-UP WORLD, DARLIN'.
YOU GOT A LONG WAY TO GO, AND YOU CAN'T MAKE IT ON YOUR OWN.
OKAY?
DON'T TOUCH MY WINGS, YOU PERVERT.
OKAY?

U-MAN MARZ HAD HIS MUTANT BLOOD TRANSFUSION LAST NIGHT, SO WE'RE ALL TOTALLY PSYCHED TO CUT LOOSE ON THESE FREAKS, MR. SUBLIME, SIR.

YOU SHOULD BE ABLE TO SEE THE *XAVIER INSTITUTE* UP AHEAD.

DIGITALLY PRECISE.

I LIKE IT.

DON'T GET COMPLACENT, BUT DON'T EXPECT TOO MUCH REAL RESISTANCE. WE'VE LAID OUT THEIR BEST *SOLDIERS* ON DISSECTION TABLES DOWNSTAIRS.

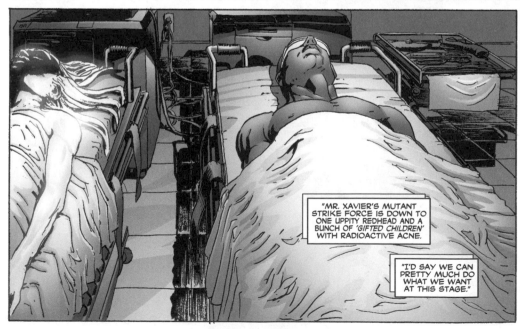

"MR. XAVIER'S MUTANT STRIKE FORCE IS DOWN TO ONE UPPITY REDHEAD AND A BUNCH OF *'GIFTED CHILDREN'* WITH RADIOACTIVE ACNE."

"I'D SAY WE CAN PRETTY MUCH DO WHAT WE WANT AT THIS STAGE."

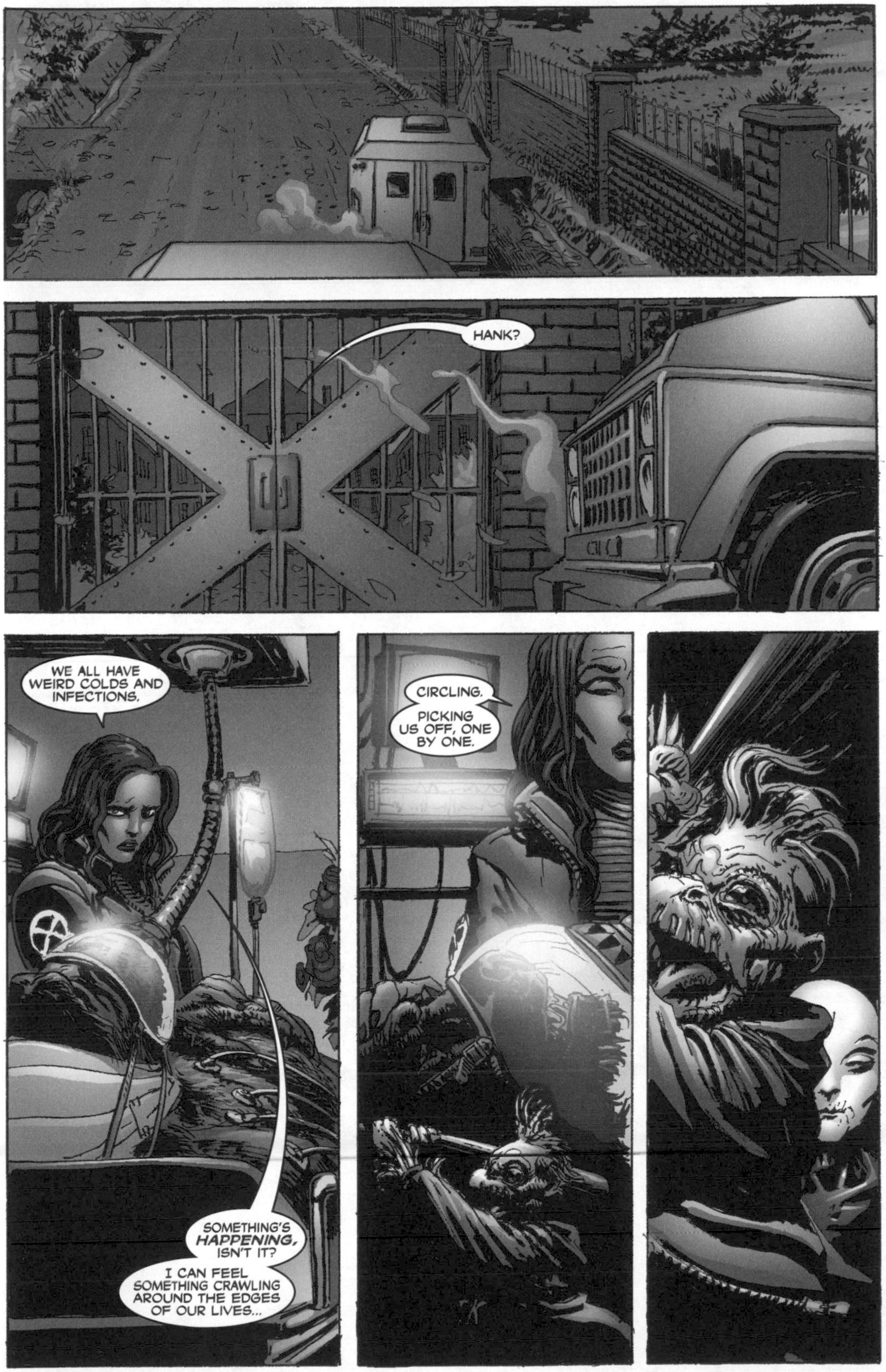
HANK?
WE ALL HAVE WEIRD COLDS AND INFECTIONS.
SOMETHING'S **HAPPENING,** ISN'T IT?
I CAN FEEL SOMETHING CRAWLING AROUND THE EDGES OF OUR LIVES...
CIRCLING.
PICKING US OFF, ONE BY ONE.

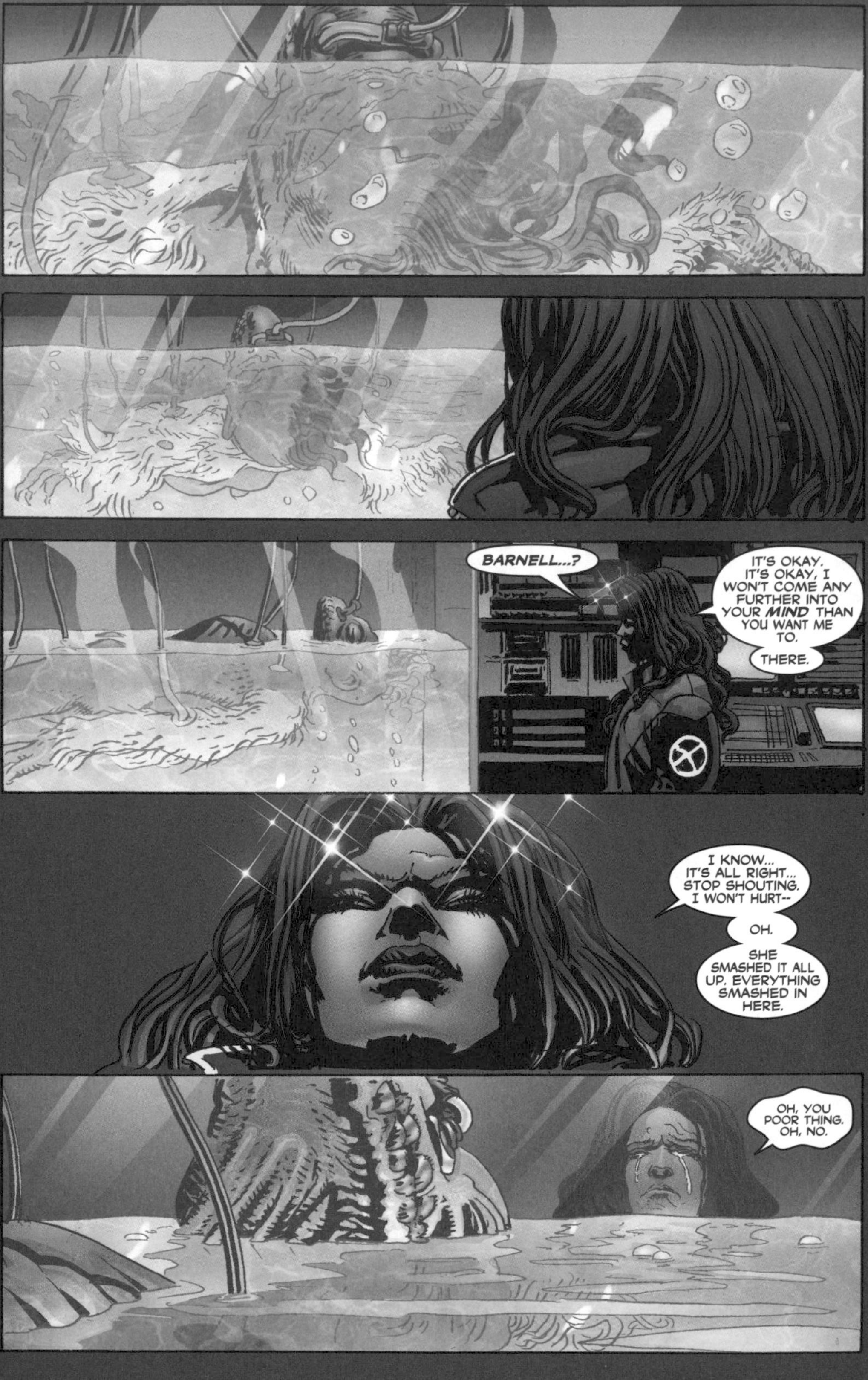
BARNELL...?
IT'S OKAY. IT'S OKAY, I WON'T COME ANY FURTHER INTO YOUR MIND THAN YOU WANT ME TO.
THERE.
I KNOW... IT'S ALL RIGHT... STOP SHOUTING. I WON'T HURT--
OH.
SHE SMASHED IT ALL UP. EVERYTHING SMASHED IN HERE.
OH, YOU POOR THING. OH, NO.

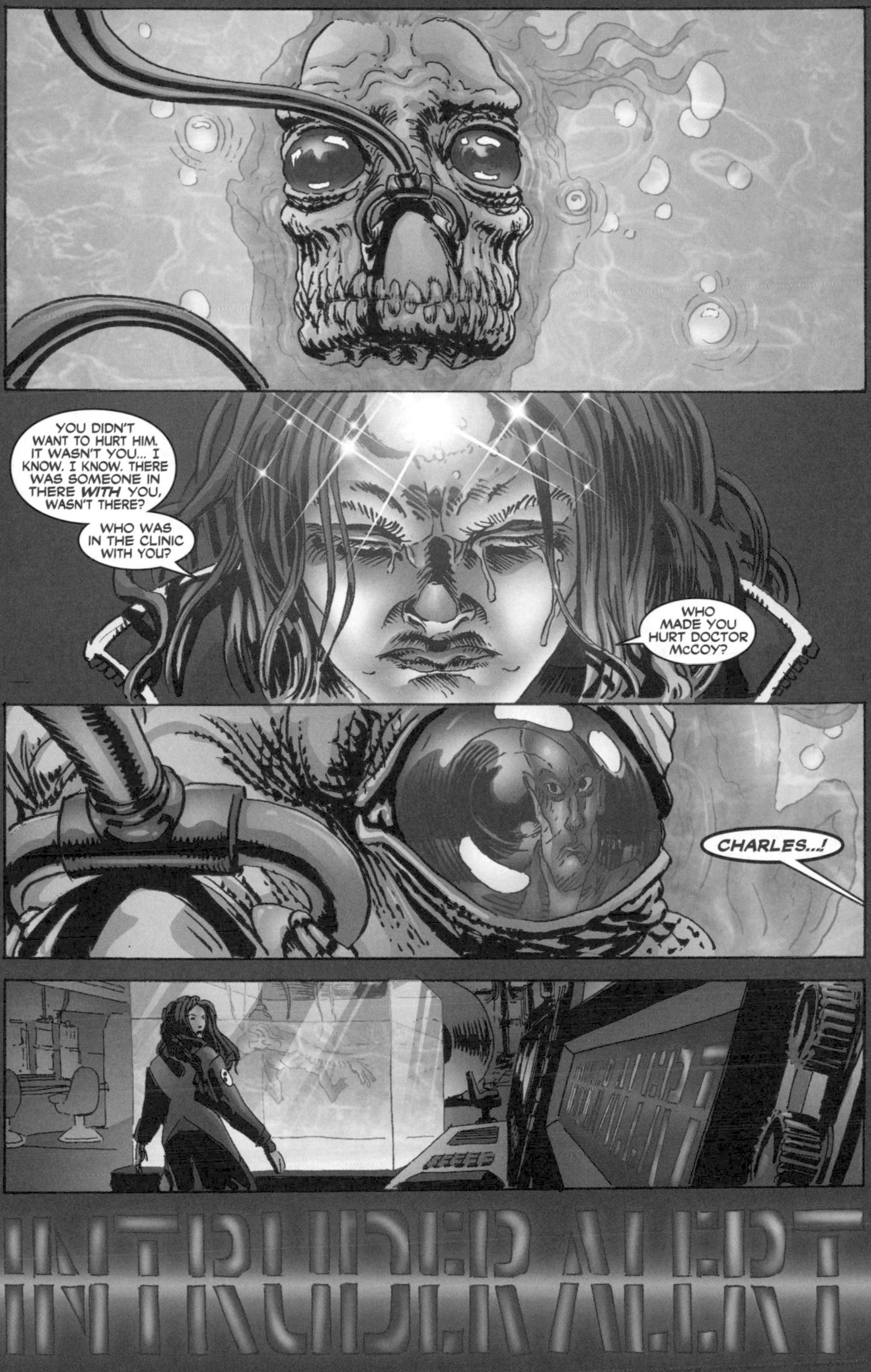
YOU DIDN'T WANT TO HURT HIM. IT WASN'T YOU... I KNOW. I KNOW. THERE WAS SOMEONE IN THERE WITH YOU, WASN'T THERE?
WHO WAS IN THE CLINIC WITH YOU?
WHO MADE YOU HURT DOCTOR McCOY?
CHARLES...!
INTRUDER ALERT

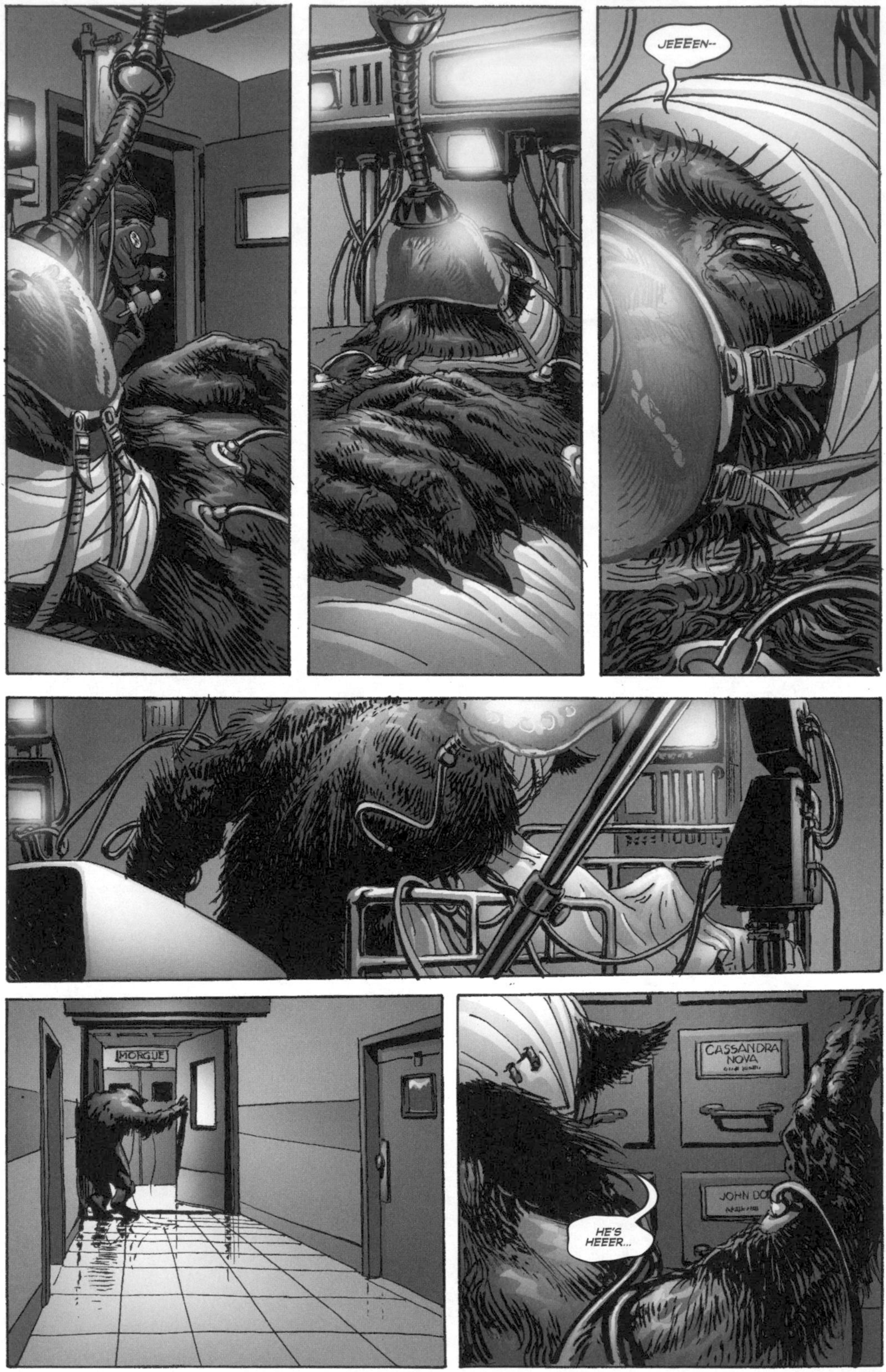
JEEEEN--
MORGUE
CASSANDRA NOVA
JOHN DO
HE'S HEEER...

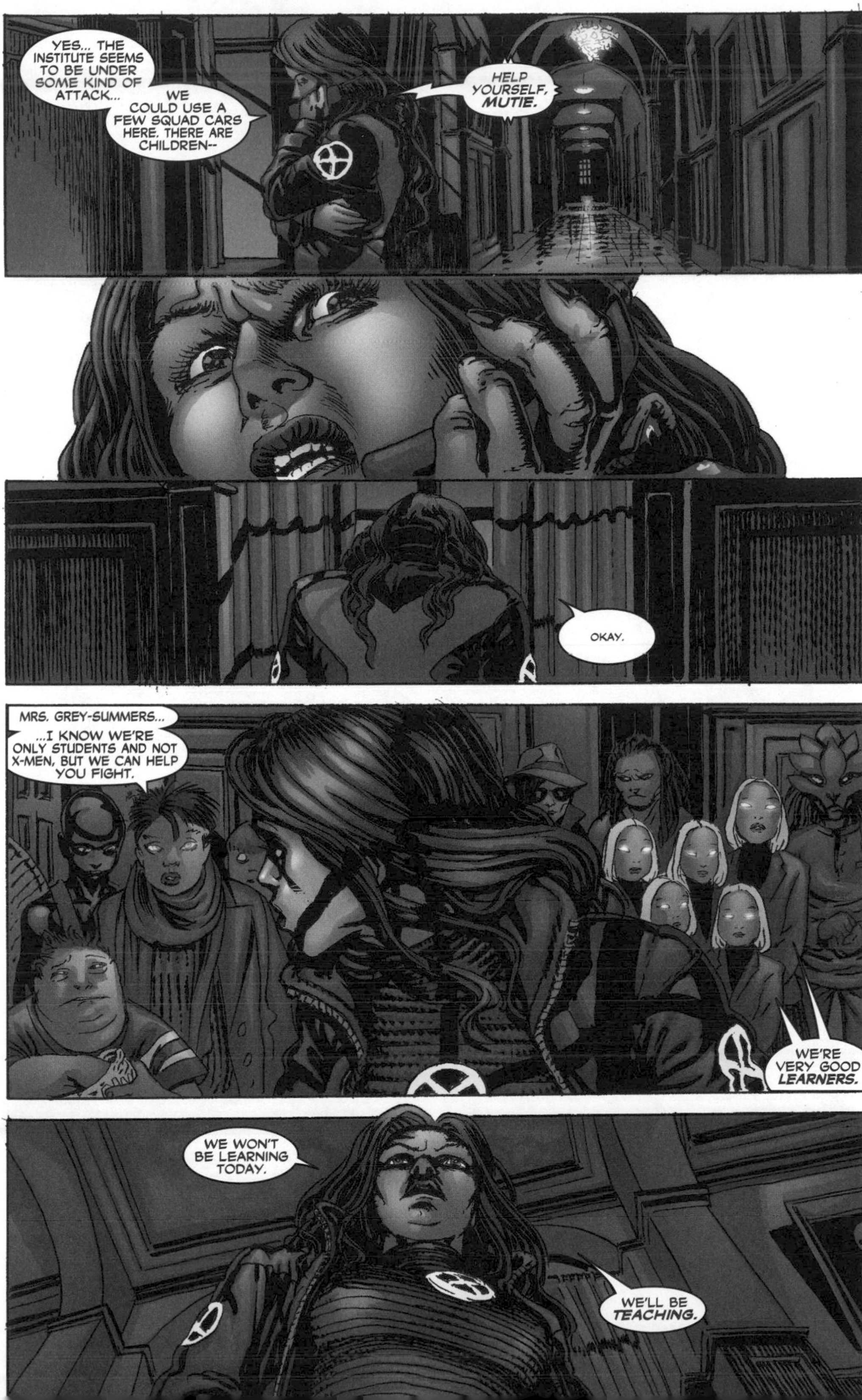
YES... THE INSTITUTE SEEMS TO BE UNDER SOME KIND OF ATTACK...
WE COULD USE A FEW SQUAD CARS HERE. THERE ARE CHILDREN--
HELP YOURSELF, MUTIE.
OKAY.
MRS. GREY-SUMMERS...
...I KNOW WE'RE ONLY STUDENTS AND NOT X-MEN, BUT WE CAN HELP YOU FIGHT.
WE'RE VERY GOOD LEARNERS.
WE WON'T BE LEARNING TODAY.
WE'LL BE TEACHING.

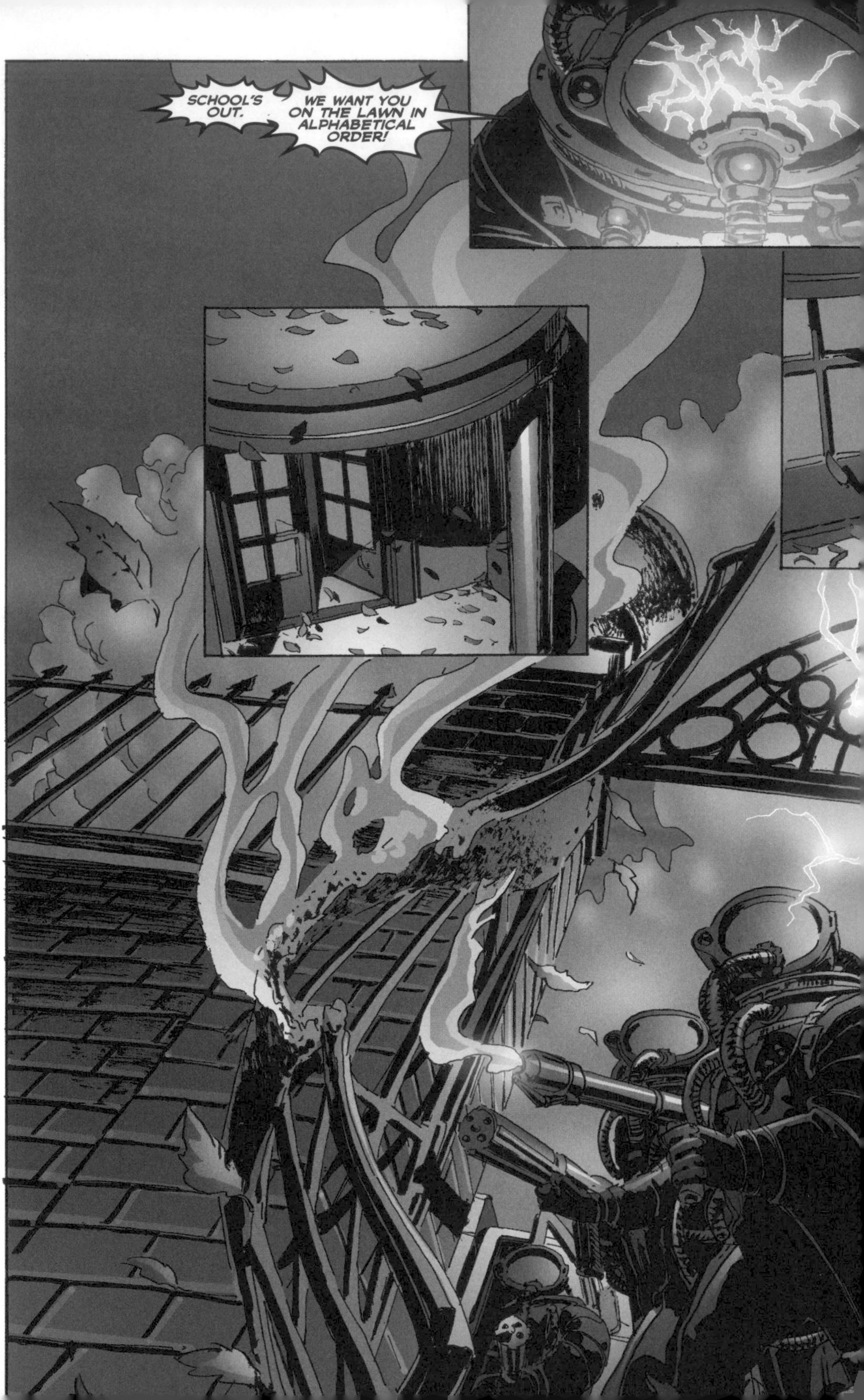
SCHOOL'S OUT.
WE WANT YOU ON THE LAWN IN ALPHABETICAL ORDER!

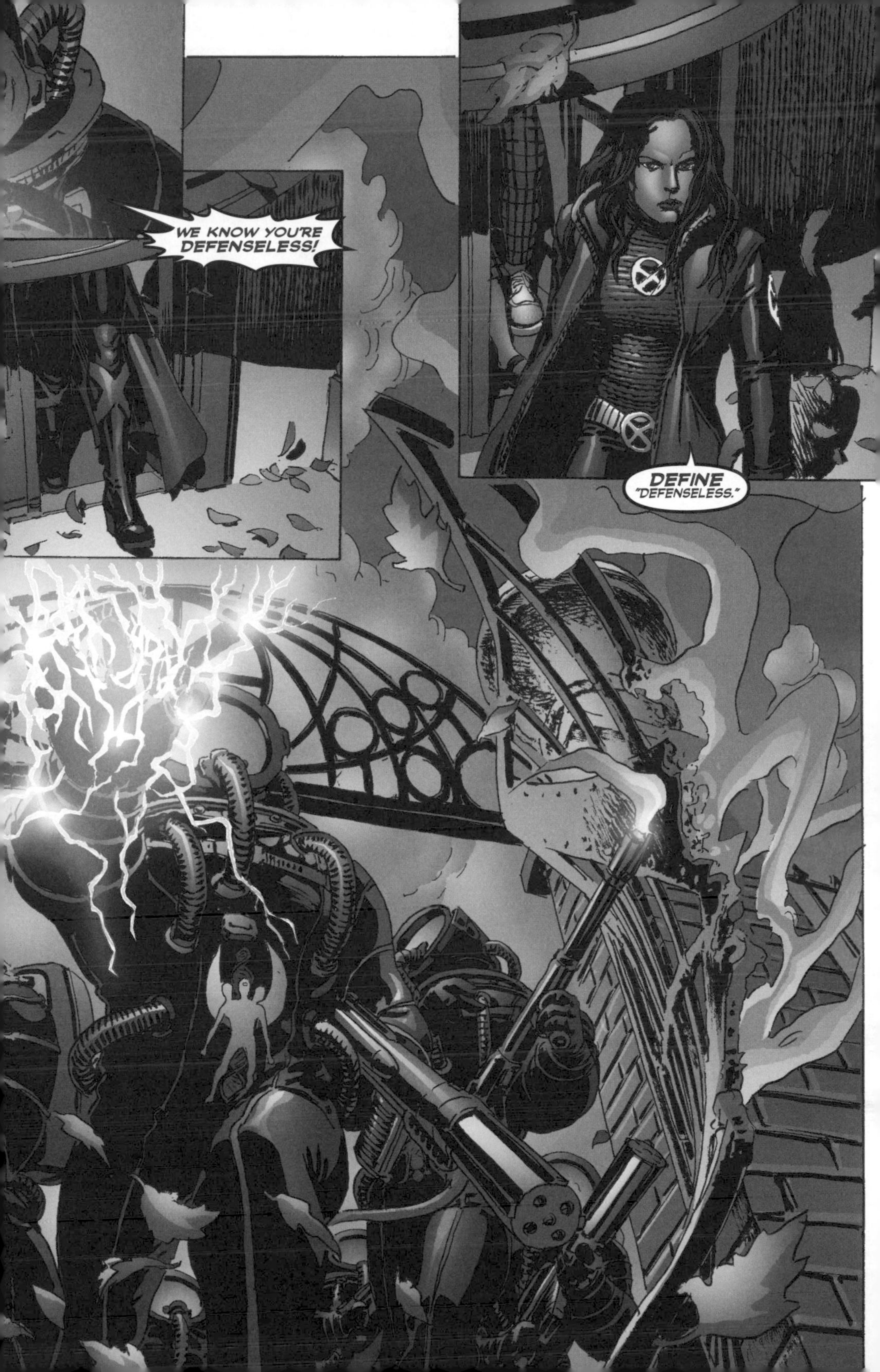
WE KNOW YOU'RE DEFENSELESS!
DEFINE "DEFENSELESS."

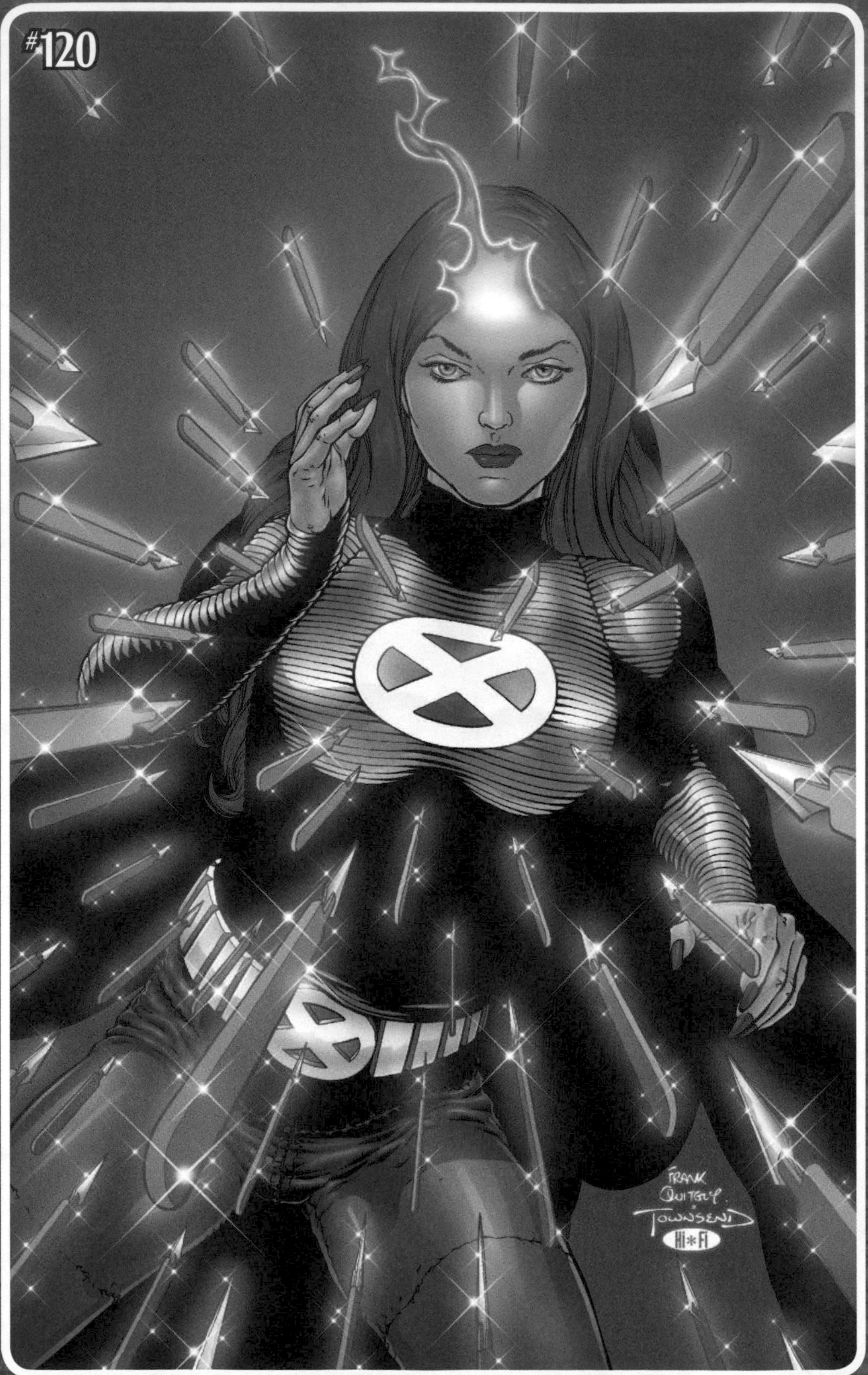
#120
FRANK QUITELY
TOWNSEND
HI*FI

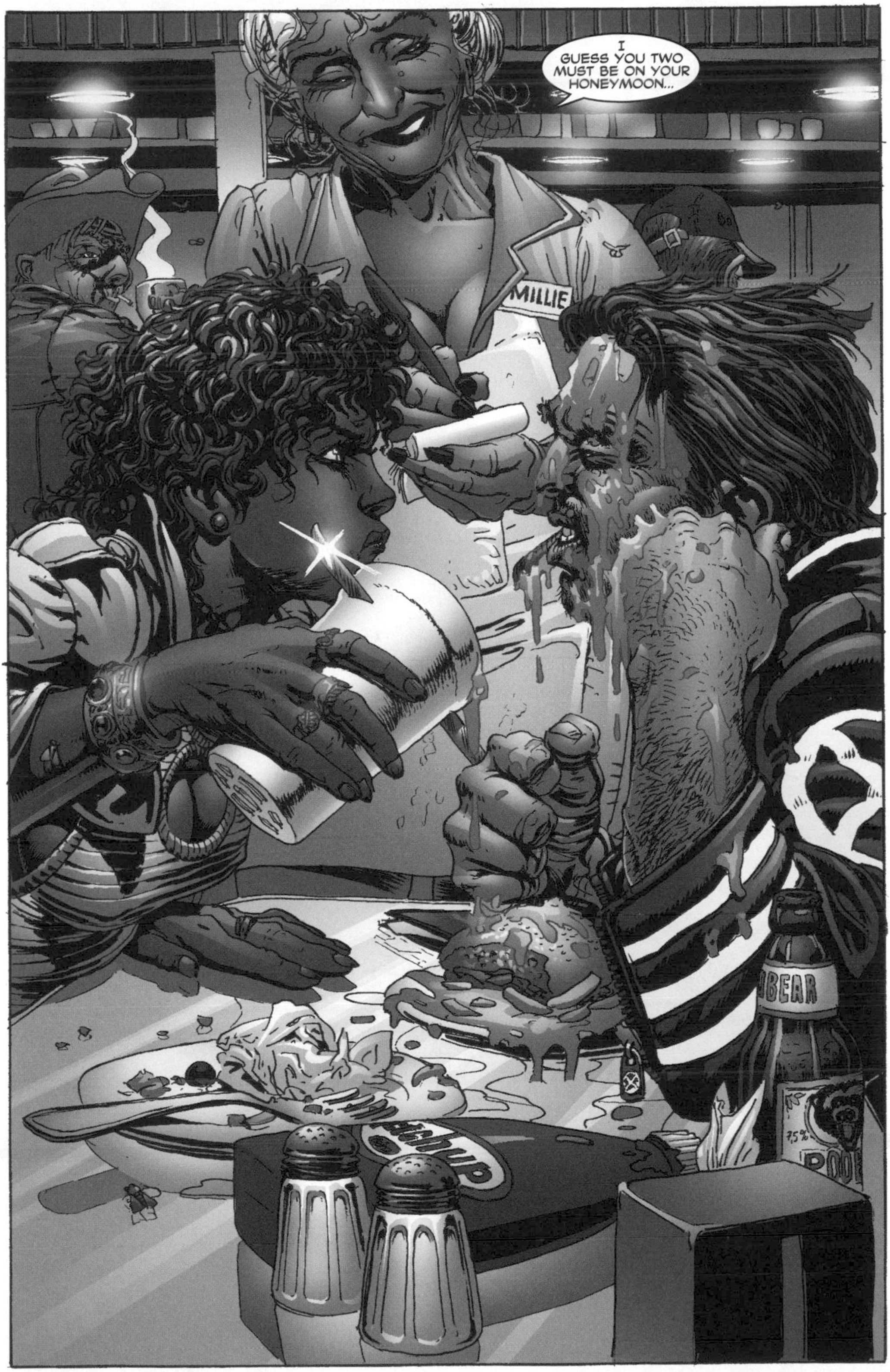
I GUESS YOU TWO MUST BE ON YOUR HONEYMOON...
MILLIE

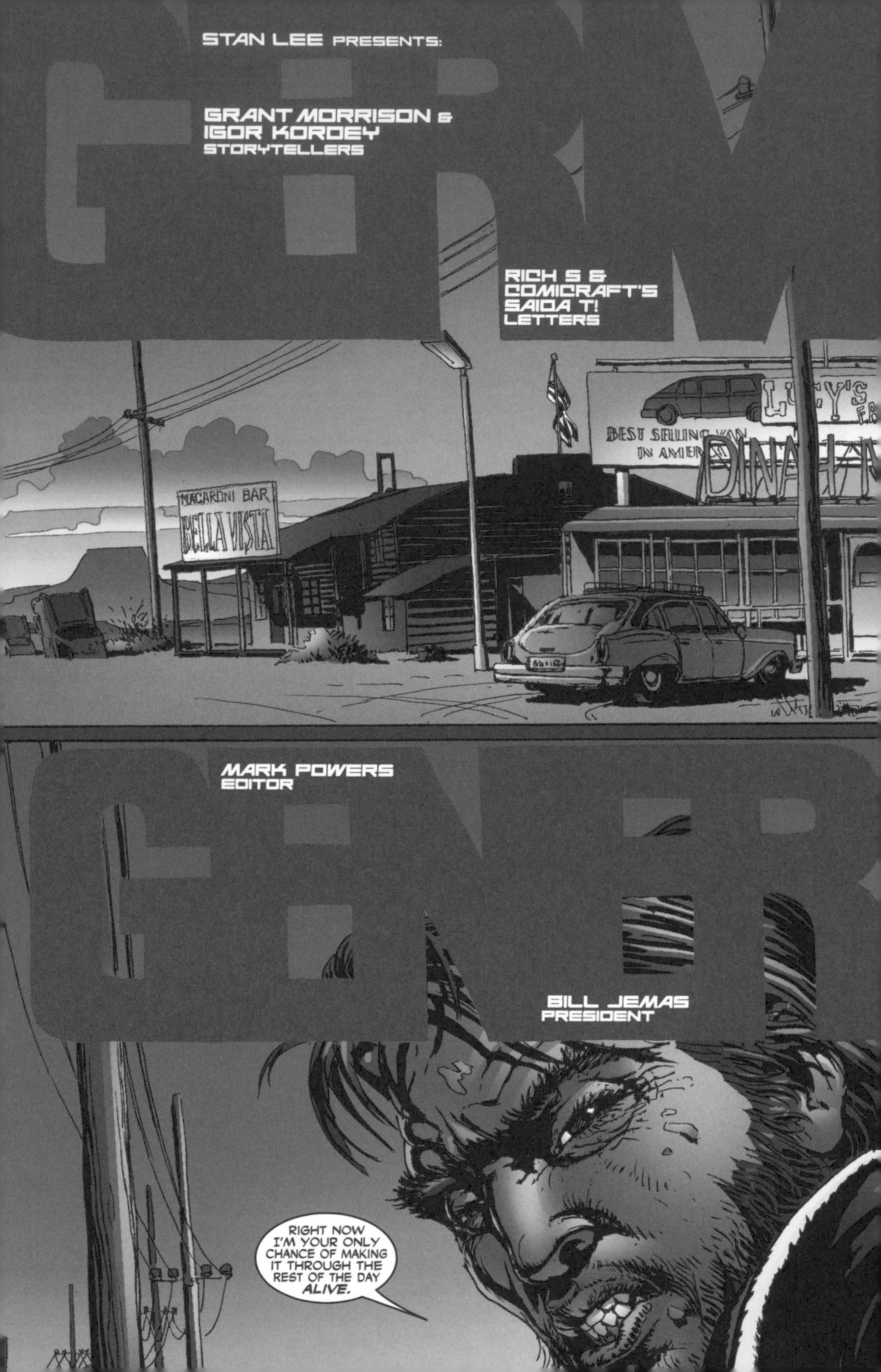
STAN LEE PRESENTS:
GRANT MORRISON & IGOR KORDEY STORYTELLERS
RICH S & COMICRAFT'S SAIDA T! LETTERS
MACARONI BAR
BELLA VISTA
BEST SELLING VAN IN AMER
MARK POWERS EDITOR
BILL JEMAS PRESIDENT
RIGHT NOW I'M YOUR ONLY CHANCE OF MAKING IT THROUGH THE REST OF THE DAY *ALIVE.*

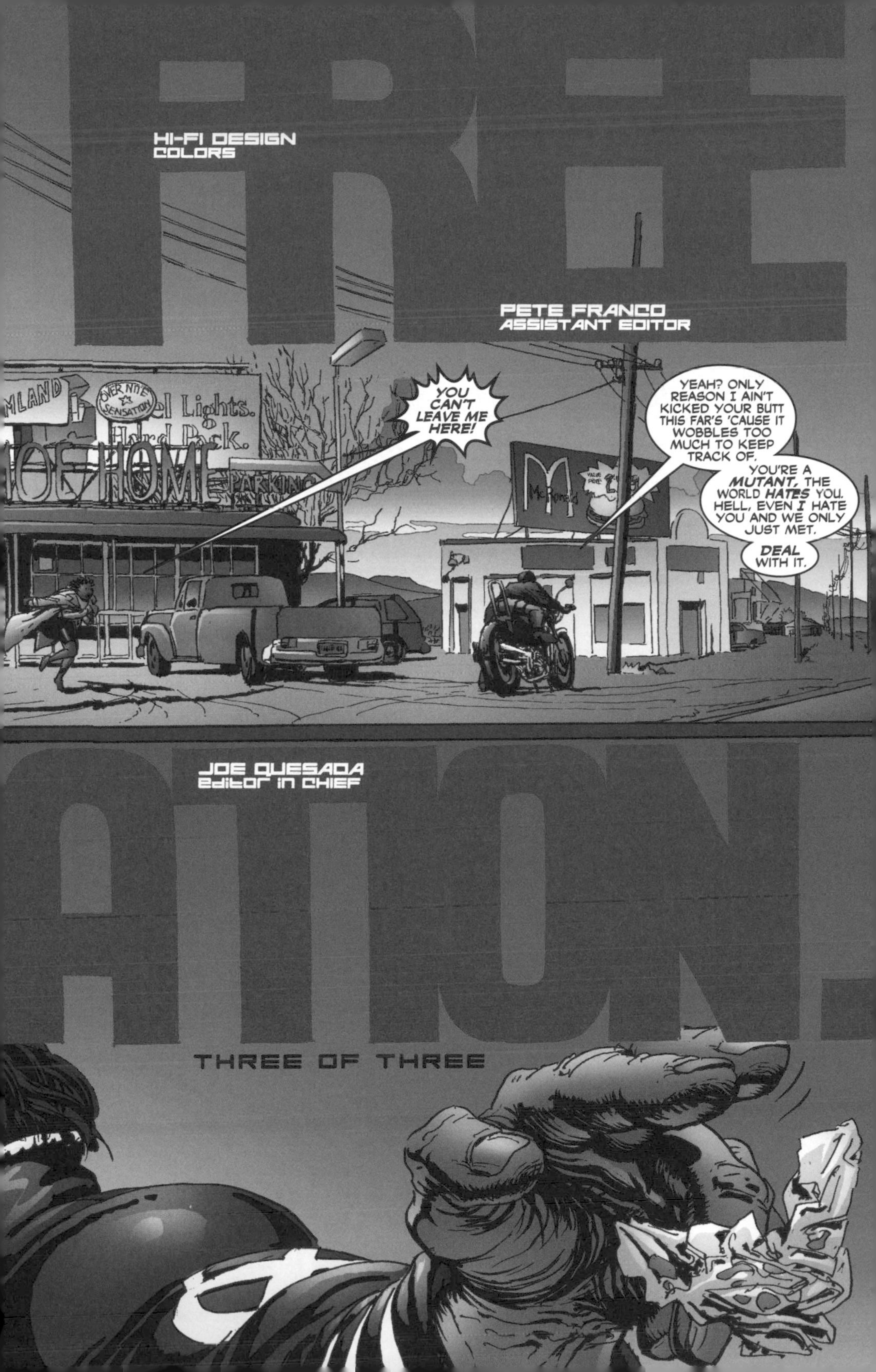
HI-FI DESIGN
COLORS
PETE FRANCO
ASSISTANT EDITOR
YOU CAN'T LEAVE ME HERE!
YEAH? ONLY REASON I AIN'T KICKED YOUR BUTT THIS FAR'S 'CAUSE IT WOBBLES TOO MUCH TO KEEP TRACK OF.
YOU'RE A MUTANT, THE WORLD HATES YOU. HELL, EVEN I HATE YOU AND WE ONLY JUST MET.
DEAL WITH IT.
JOE QUESADA
EDITOR IN CHIEF
THREE OF THREE

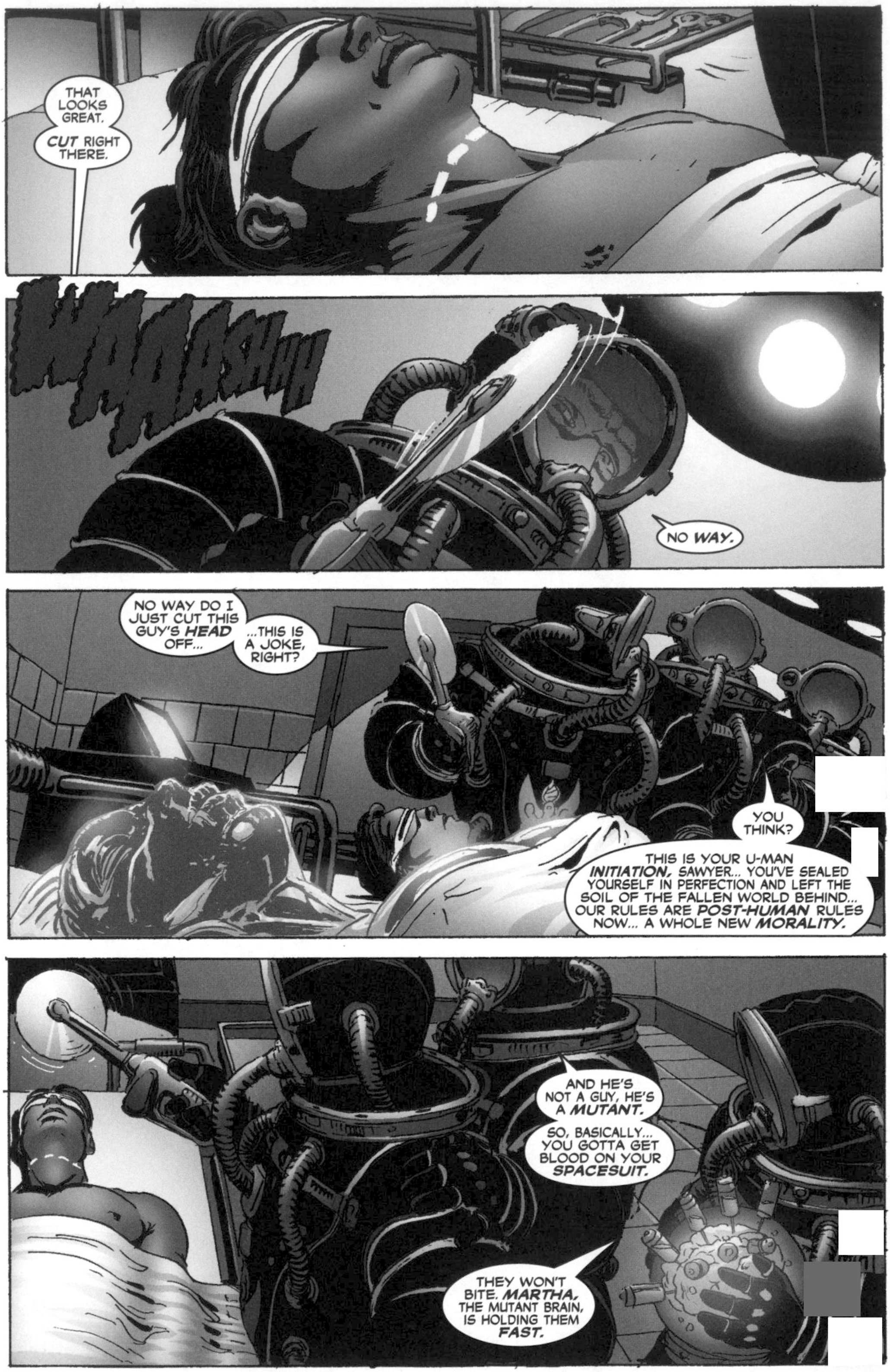

THAT LOOKS GREAT.
CUT RIGHT THERE.
WAAASHHH
NO WAY.
NO WAY DO I JUST CUT THIS GUY'S HEAD OFF...
...THIS IS A JOKE, RIGHT?
YOU THINK?
THIS IS YOUR U-MAN INITIATION, SAWYER... YOU'VE SEALED YOURSELF IN PERFECTION AND LEFT THE SOIL OF THE FALLEN WORLD BEHIND... OUR RULES ARE POST-HUMAN RULES NOW... A WHOLE NEW MORALITY.
AND HE'S NOT A GUY, HE'S A MUTANT.
SO, BASICALLY... YOU GOTTA GET BLOOD ON YOUR SPACESUIT.
THEY WON'T BITE. MARTHA, THE MUTANT BRAIN, IS HOLDING THEM FAST.

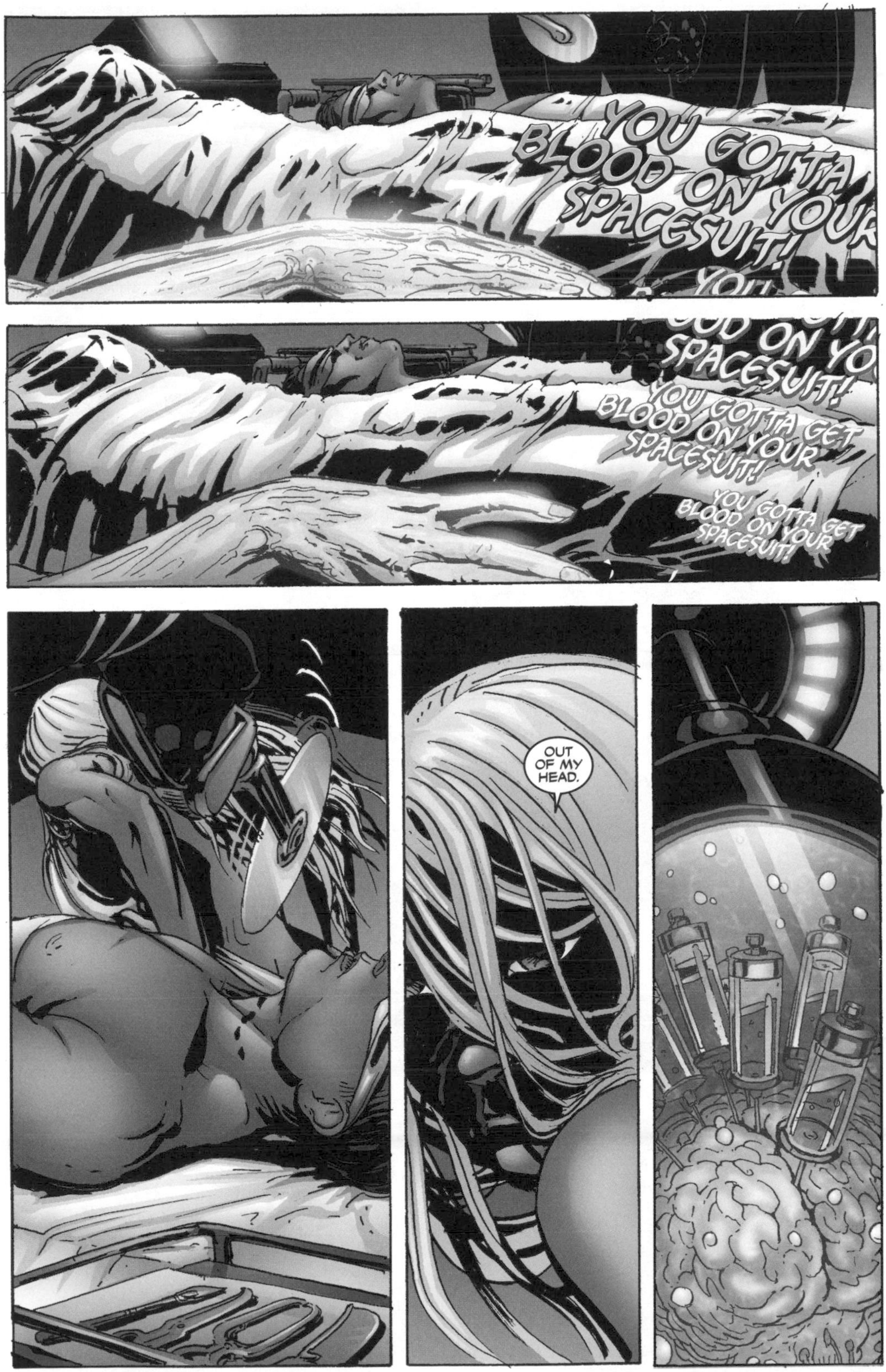
YOU GOTTA BLOOD ON YOUR SPACESUIT!
YOU
BLOOD ON YO
SPACESUIT!
YOU GOTTA GET BLOOD ON YOUR SPACESUIT!
YOU GOTTA GET BLOOD ON YOUR SPACESUIT!
OUT OF MY HEAD.

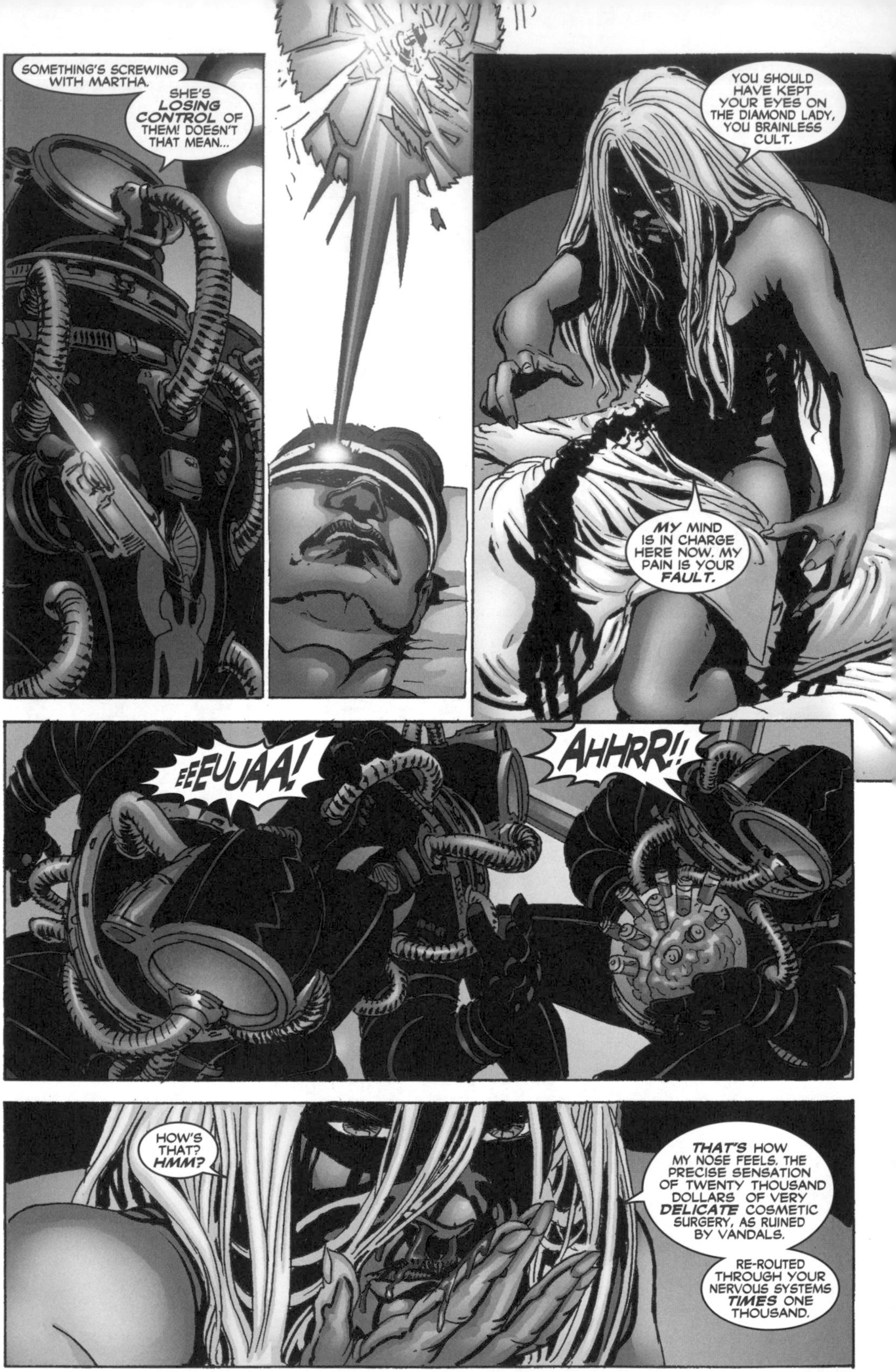
SOMETHING'S SCREWING WITH MARTHA.
SHE'S LOSING CONTROL OF THEM! DOESN'T THAT MEAN...
YOU SHOULD HAVE KEPT YOUR EYES ON THE DIAMOND LADY, YOU BRAINLESS CULT.
MY MIND IS IN CHARGE HERE NOW. MY PAIN IS YOUR FAULT.
EEEUUAA!
AHHRR!!
HOW'S THAT? HMM?
THAT'S HOW MY NOSE FEELS. THE PRECISE SENSATION OF TWENTY THOUSAND DOLLARS OF VERY DELICATE COSMETIC SURGERY, AS RUINED BY VANDALS.
RE-ROUTED THROUGH YOUR NERVOUS SYSTEMS TIMES ONE THOUSAND.

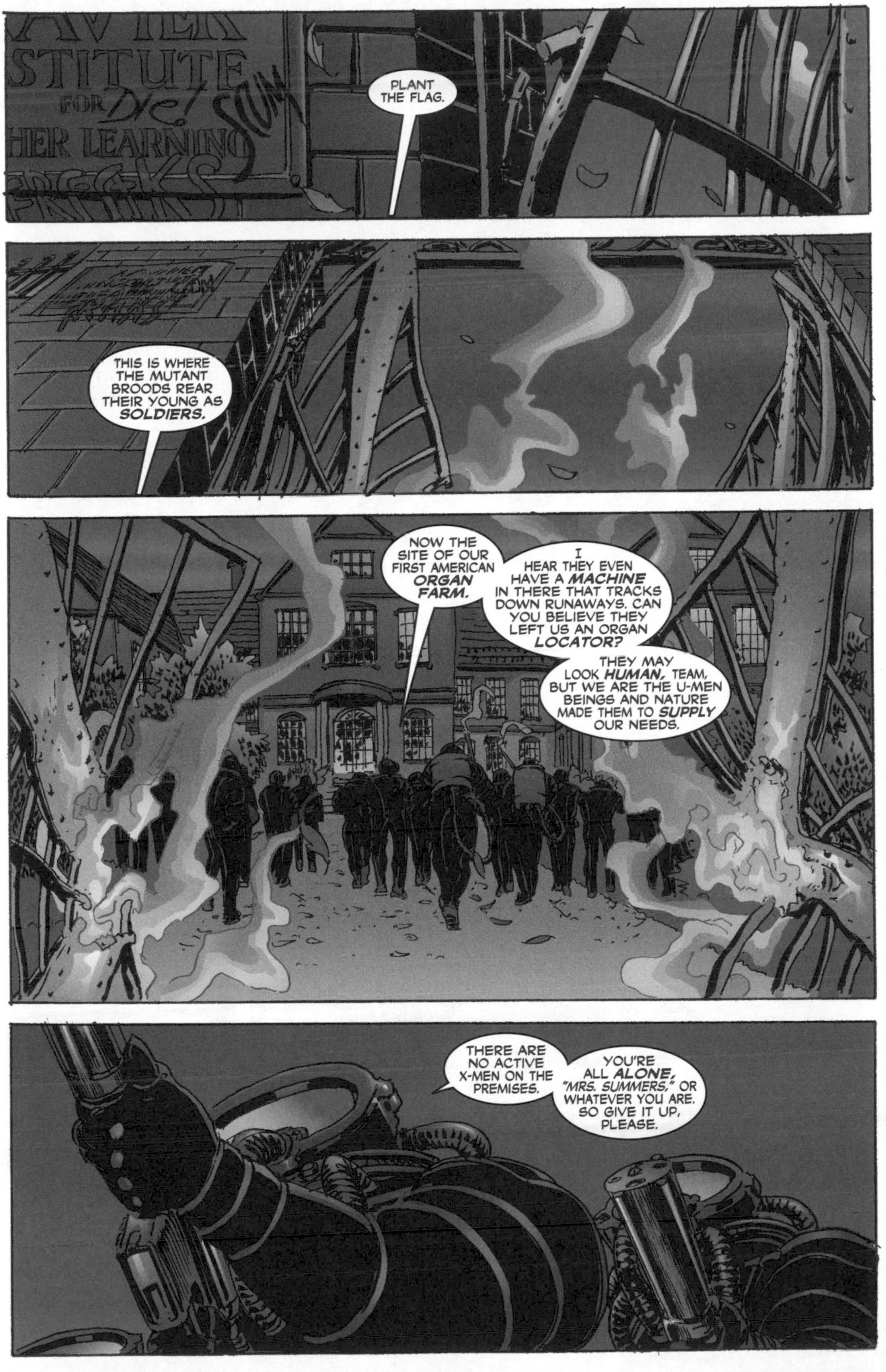
Die!
SCUM
PLANT THE FLAG.
THIS IS WHERE THE MUTANT BROODS REAR THEIR YOUNG AS **SOLDIERS.**
NOW THE SITE OF OUR FIRST AMERICAN **ORGAN FARM.**
I HEAR THEY EVEN HAVE A **MACHINE** IN THERE THAT TRACKS DOWN RUNAWAYS. CAN YOU BELIEVE THEY LEFT US AN ORGAN **LOCATOR?**
THEY MAY LOOK **HUMAN,** TEAM, BUT WE ARE THE U-MEN BEINGS AND NATURE MADE THEM TO **SUPPLY** OUR NEEDS.
THERE ARE NO ACTIVE X-MEN ON THE PREMISES.
YOU'RE ALL **ALONE,** *"MRS. SUMMERS,"* OR WHATEVER YOU ARE. SO GIVE IT UP, PLEASE.

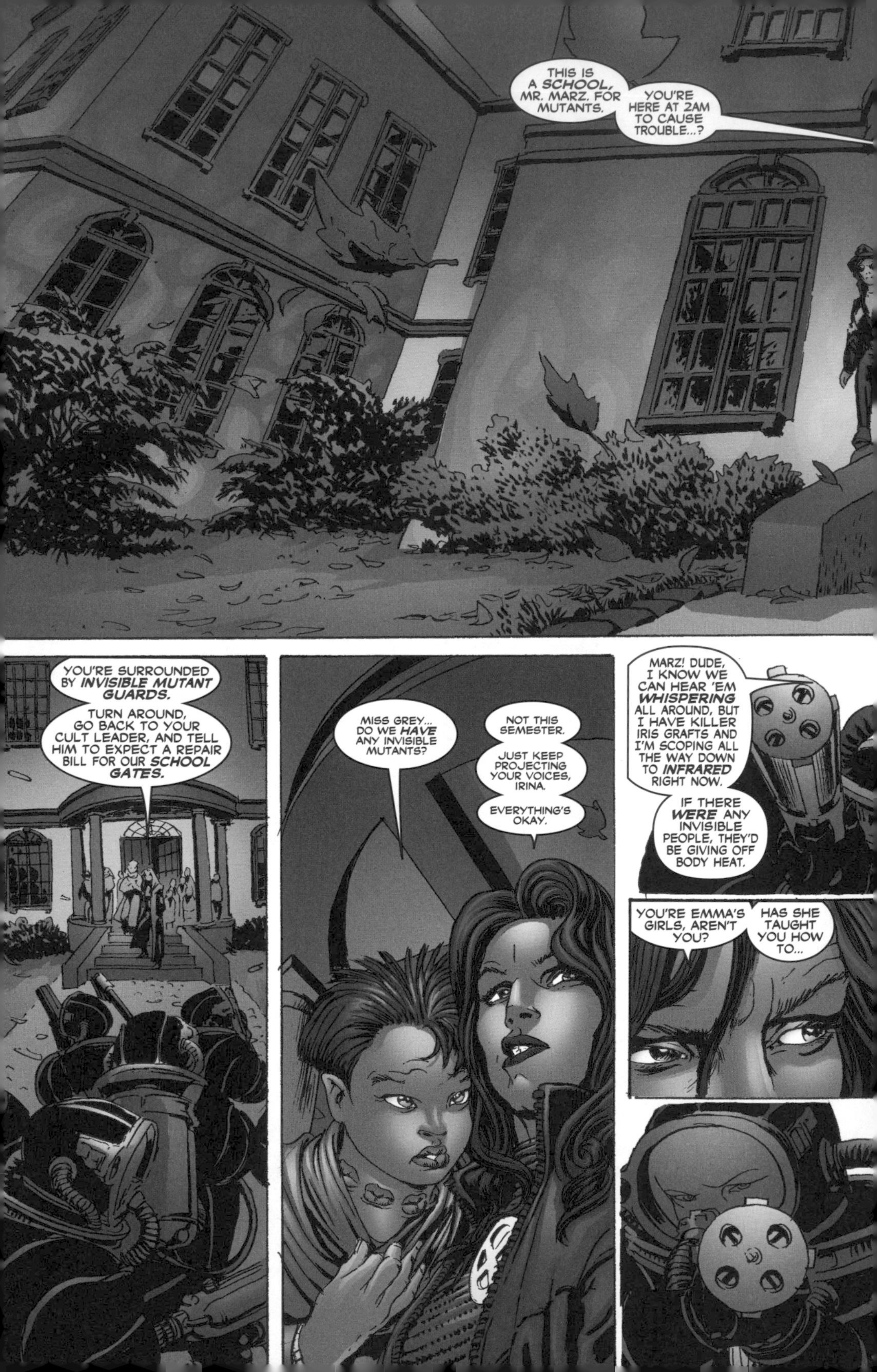
THIS IS A SCHOOL, MR. MARZ. FOR MUTANTS.
YOU'RE HERE AT 2AM TO CAUSE TROUBLE...?
YOU'RE SURROUNDED BY INVISIBLE MUTANT GUARDS.
TURN AROUND, GO BACK TO YOUR CULT LEADER, AND TELL HIM TO EXPECT A REPAIR BILL FOR OUR SCHOOL GATES.
MISS GREY... DO WE HAVE ANY INVISIBLE MUTANTS?
NOT THIS SEMESTER.
JUST KEEP PROJECTING YOUR VOICES, IRINA.
EVERYTHING'S OKAY.
MARZ! DUDE, I KNOW WE CAN HEAR 'EM WHISPERING ALL AROUND, BUT I HAVE KILLER IRIS GRAFTS AND I'M SCOPING ALL THE WAY DOWN TO INFRARED RIGHT NOW.
IF THERE WERE ANY INVISIBLE PEOPLE, THEY'D BE GIVING OFF BODY HEAT.
YOU'RE EMMA'S GIRLS, AREN'T YOU?
HAS SHE TAUGHT YOU HOW TO...

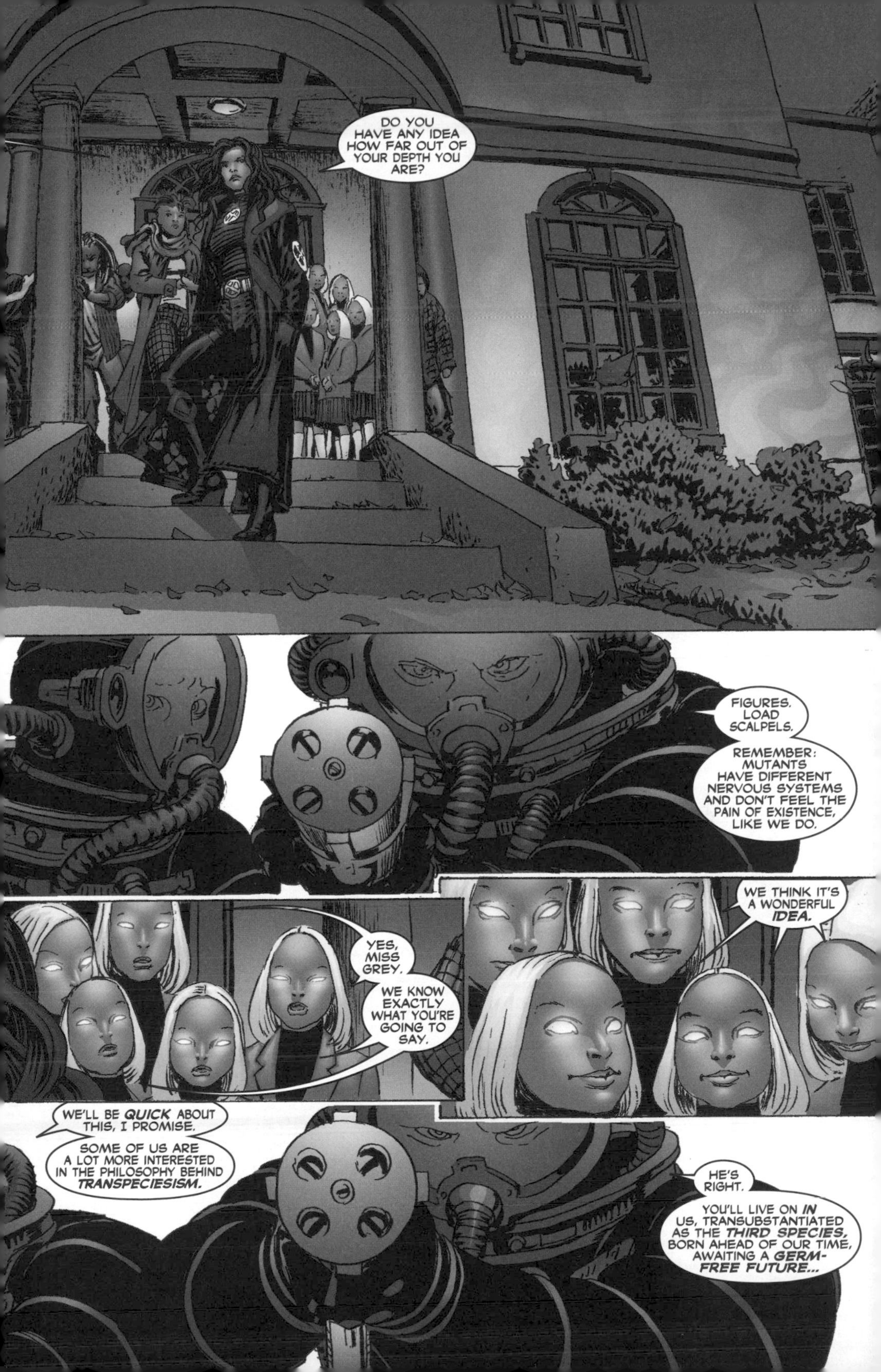
DO YOU HAVE ANY IDEA HOW FAR OUT OF YOUR DEPTH YOU ARE?
FIGURES. LOAD SCALPELS.
REMEMBER: MUTANTS HAVE DIFFERENT NERVOUS SYSTEMS AND DON'T FEEL THE PAIN OF EXISTENCE, LIKE WE DO.
YES, MISS GREY.
WE KNOW EXACTLY WHAT YOU'RE GOING TO SAY.
WE THINK IT'S A WONDERFUL IDEA.
WE'LL BE QUICK ABOUT THIS, I PROMISE.
SOME OF US ARE A LOT MORE INTERESTED IN THE PHILOSOPHY BEHIND TRANSPECIESISM.
HE'S RIGHT.
YOU'LL LIVE ON IN US, TRANSUBSTANTIATED AS THE THIRD SPECIES, BORN AHEAD OF OUR TIME, AWAITING A GERM-FREE FUTURE...

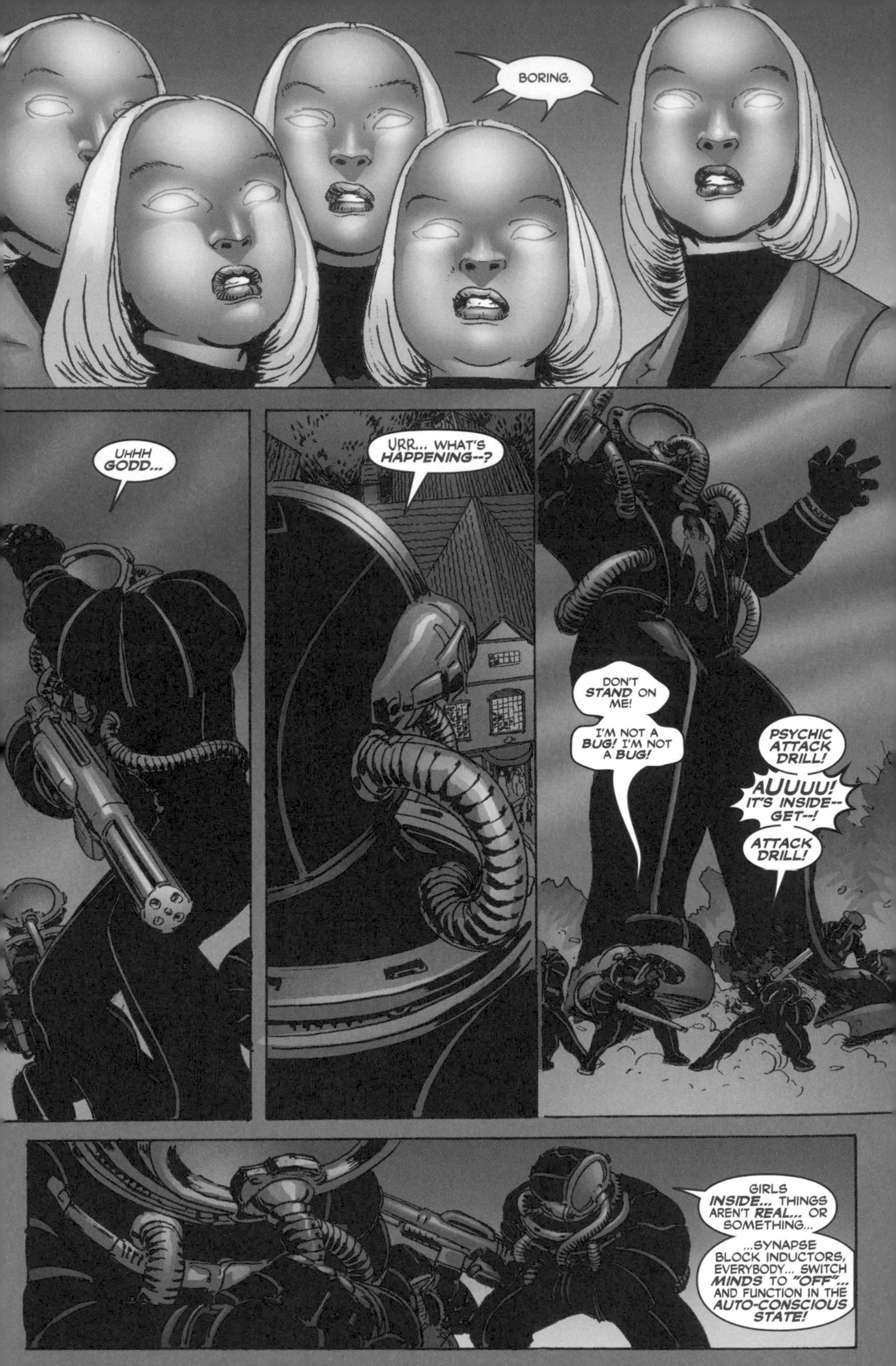
BORING.
UHHH GODD...
URR... WHAT'S HAPPENING--?
DON'T STAND ON ME!
I'M NOT A BUG! I'M NOT A BUG!
PSYCHIC ATTACK DRILL!
AUUUU! IT'S INSIDE-- GET--!
ATTACK DRILL!
GIRLS INSIDE... THINGS AREN'T REAL... OR SOMETHING...
...SYNAPSE BLOCK INDUCTORS, EVERYBODY... SWITCH MINDS TO "OFF"... AND FUNCTION IN THE AUTO-CONSCIOUS STATE!

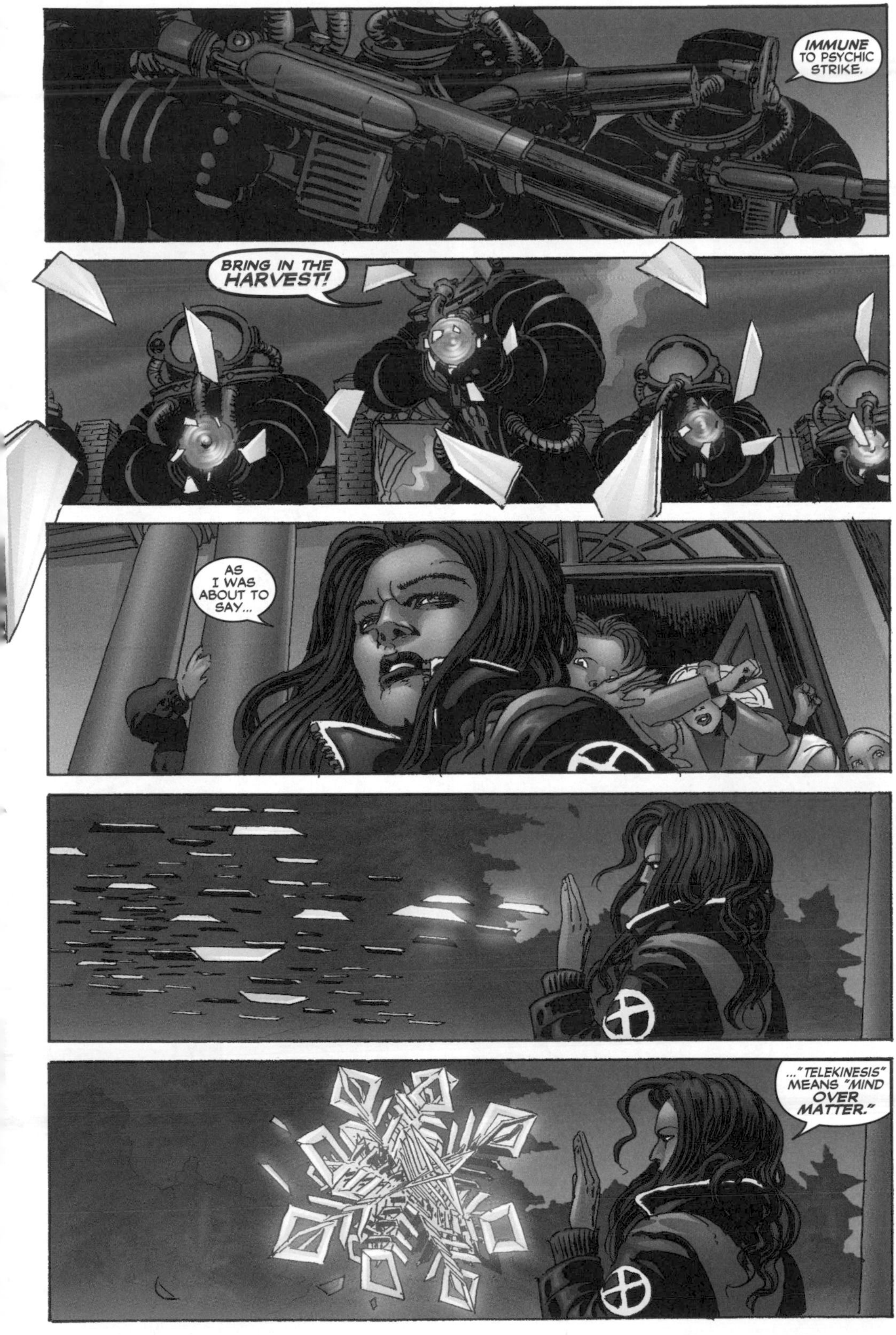
IMMUNE TO PSYCHIC STRIKE.
BRING IN THE HARVEST!
AS I WAS ABOUT TO SAY...
..."TELEKINESIS" MEANS "MIND OVER MATTER."

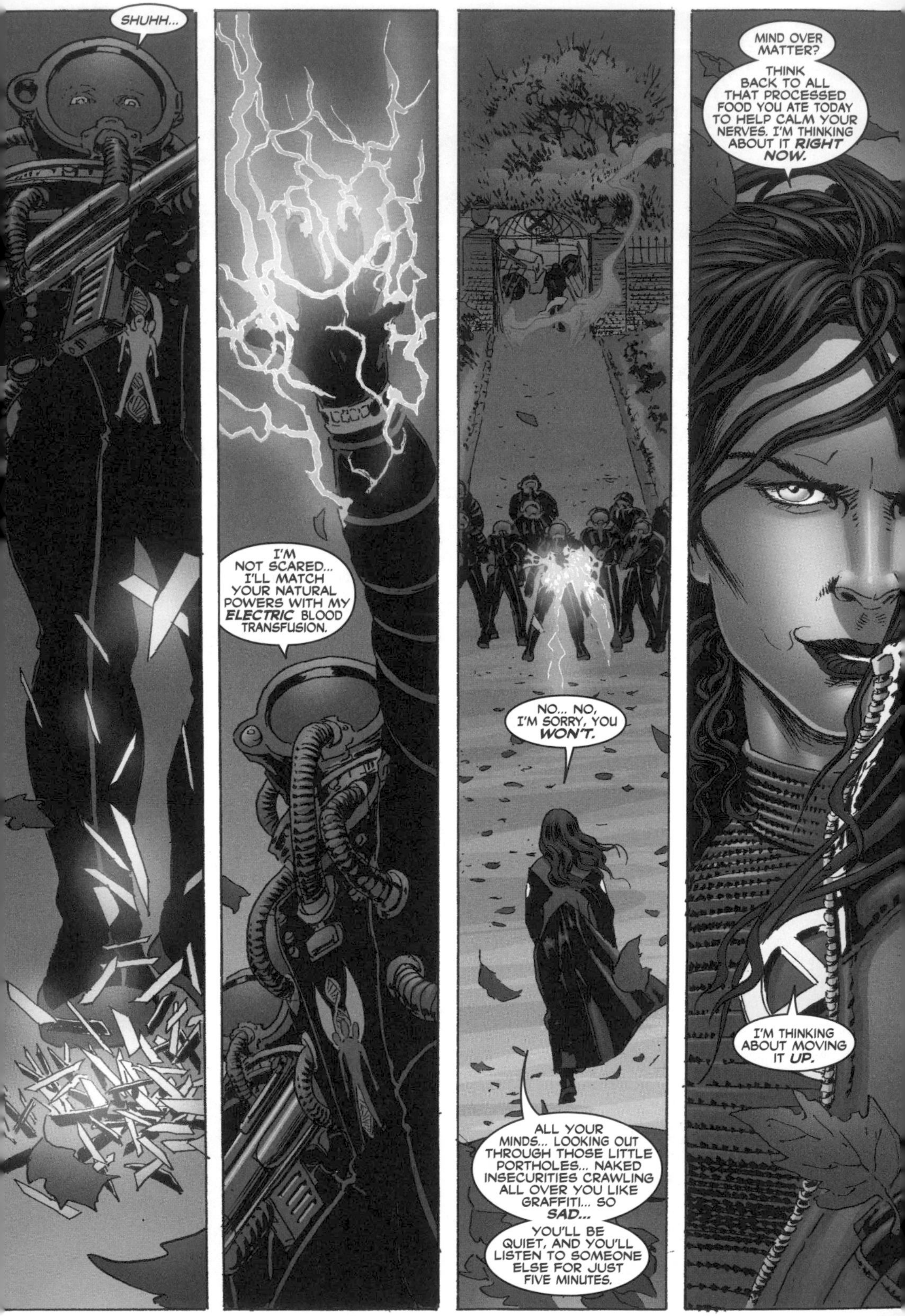
SHUHH...
I'M NOT SCARED... I'LL MATCH YOUR NATURAL POWERS WITH MY ELECTRIC BLOOD TRANSFUSION.
NO... NO, I'M SORRY, YOU WON'T.
ALL YOUR MINDS... LOOKING OUT THROUGH THOSE LITTLE PORTHOLES... NAKED INSECURITIES CRAWLING ALL OVER YOU LIKE GRAFFITI... SO SAD...
YOU'LL BE QUIET, AND YOU'LL LISTEN TO SOMEONE ELSE FOR JUST FIVE MINUTES.
MIND OVER MATTER?
THINK BACK TO ALL THAT PROCESSED FOOD YOU ATE TODAY TO HELP CALM YOUR NERVES. I'M THINKING ABOUT IT RIGHT NOW.
I'M THINKING ABOUT MOVING IT UP.

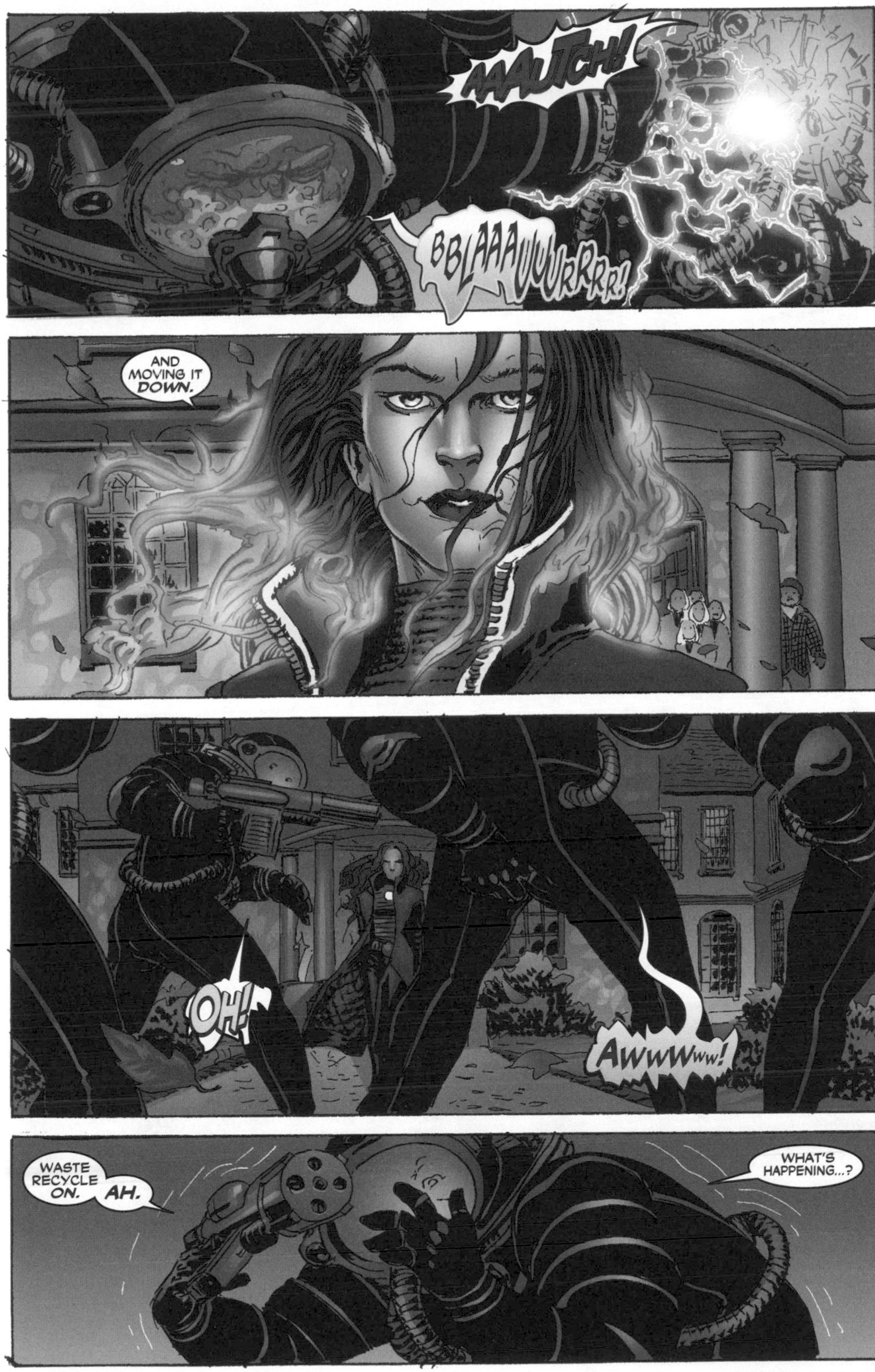
AAAUTCH!
BBLAAAUUURRRR!
AND MOVING IT DOWN.
OH!
AWWWWW!
WASTE RECYCLE ON.
AH.
WHAT'S HAPPENING...?

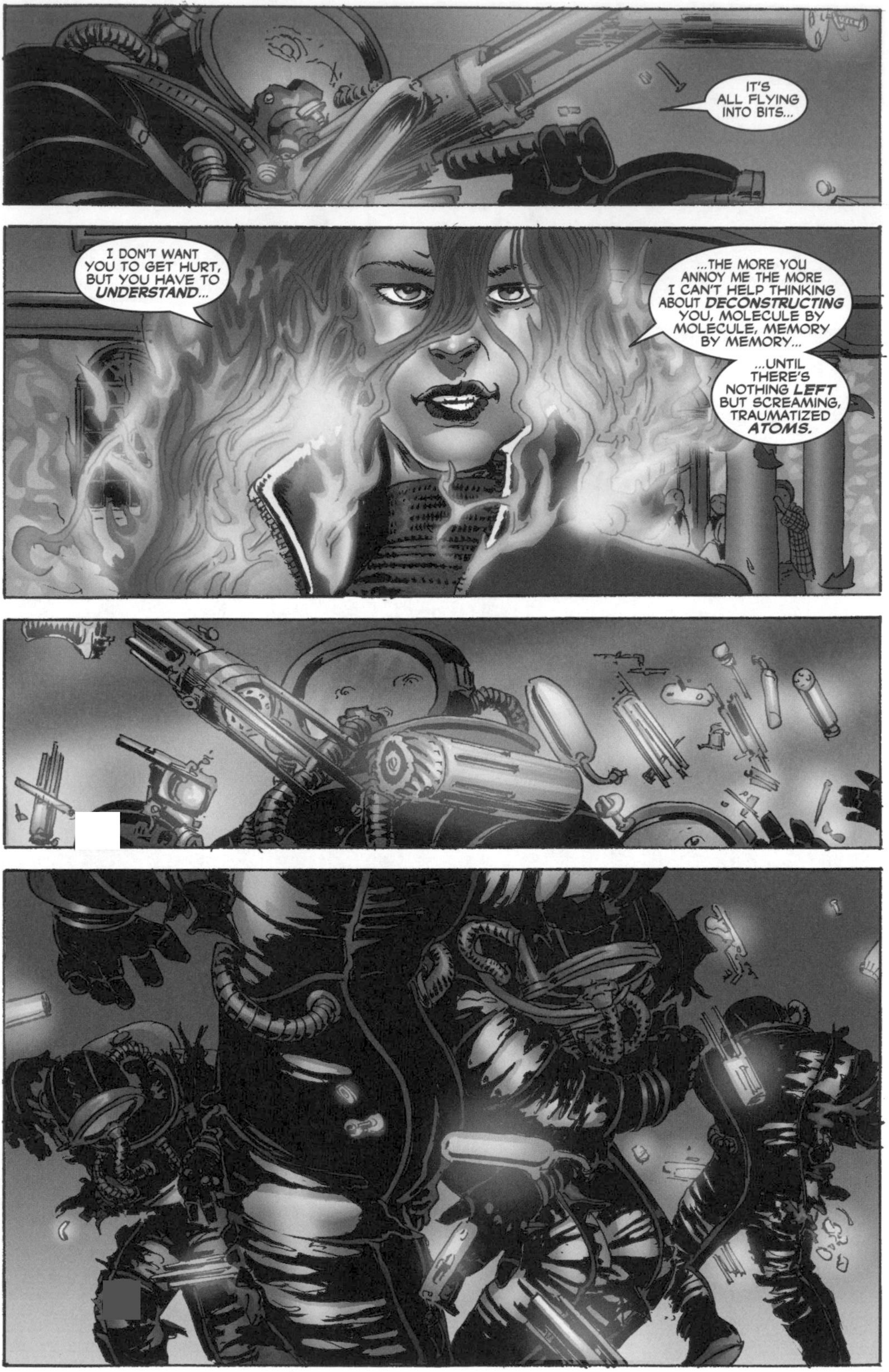
IT'S ALL FLYING INTO BITS...
I DON'T WANT YOU TO GET HURT, BUT YOU HAVE TO UNDERSTAND...
...THE MORE YOU ANNOY ME THE MORE I CAN'T HELP THINKING ABOUT DECONSTRUCTING YOU, MOLECULE BY MOLECULE, MEMORY BY MEMORY...
...UNTIL THERE'S NOTHING LEFT BUT SCREAMING, TRAUMATIZED ATOMS.

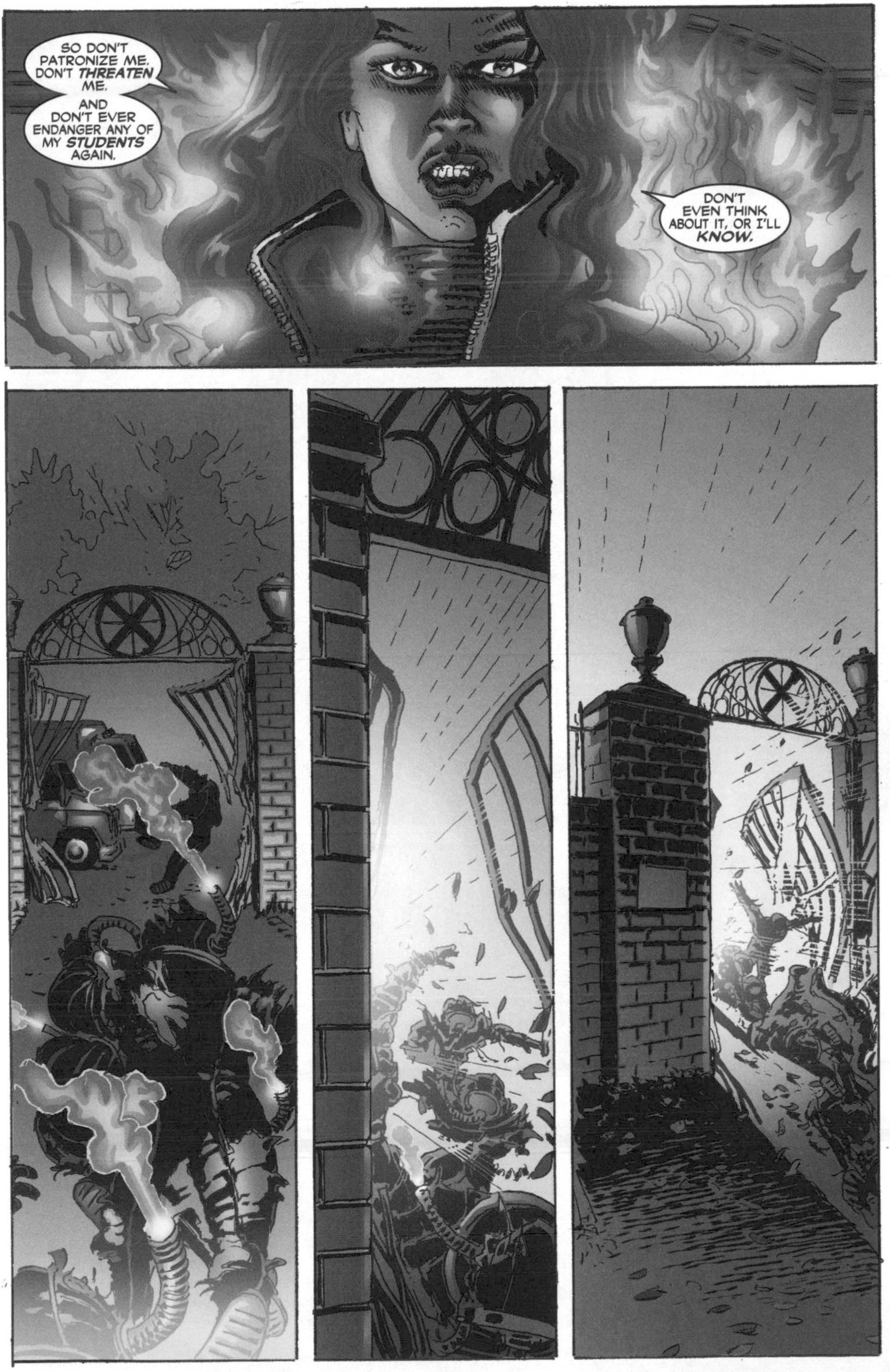
SO DON'T PATRONIZE ME. DON'T *THREATEN* ME.
AND DON'T EVER ENDANGER ANY OF MY *STUDENTS* AGAIN.
DON'T EVEN THINK ABOUT IT, OR I'LL *KNOW.*

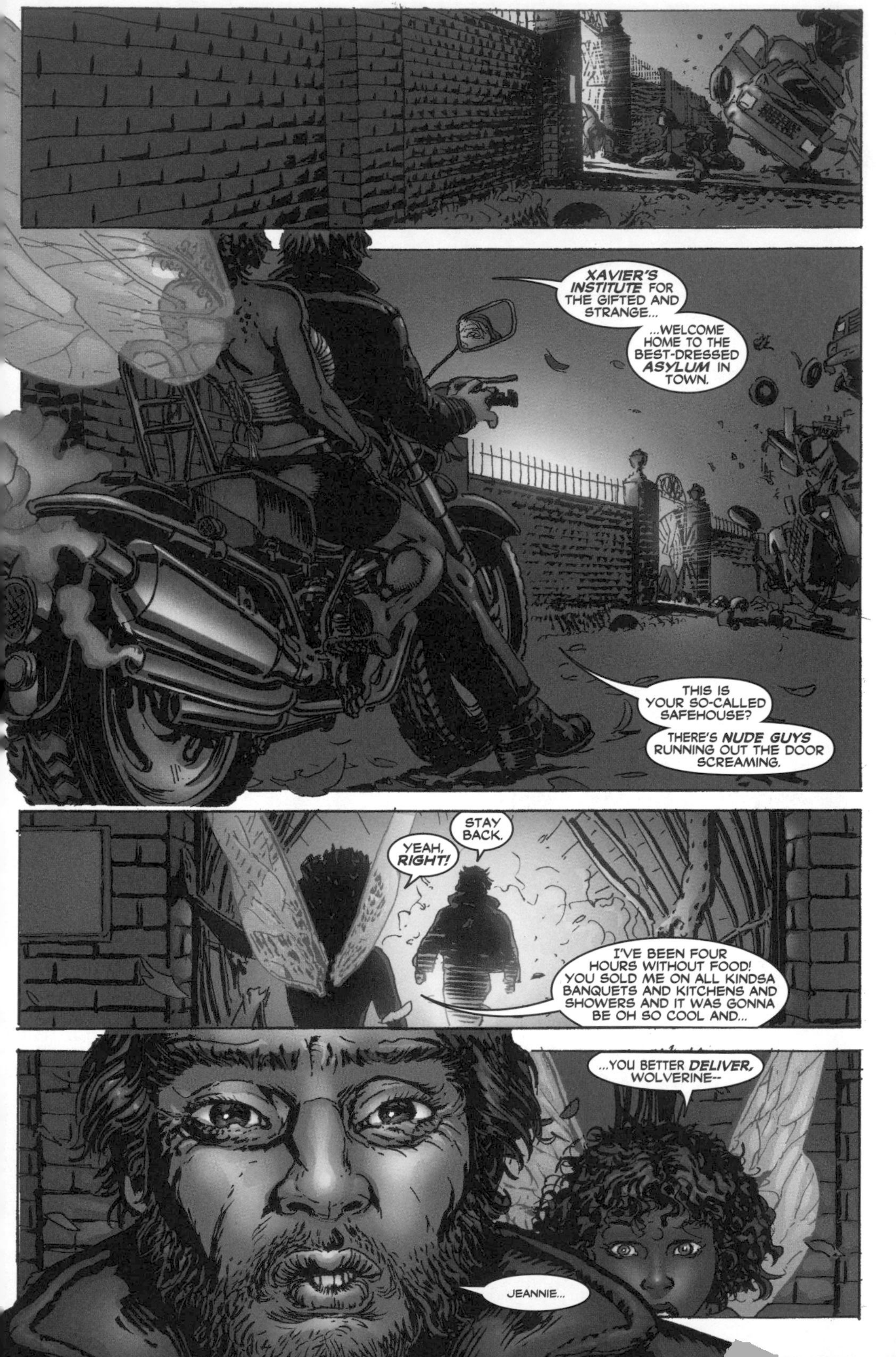
XAVIER'S INSTITUTE FOR THE GIFTED AND STRANGE...
...WELCOME HOME TO THE BEST-DRESSED ASYLUM IN TOWN.
THIS IS YOUR SO-CALLED SAFEHOUSE?
THERE'S NUDE GUYS RUNNING OUT THE DOOR SCREAMING.
STAY BACK.
YEAH, RIGHT!
I'VE BEEN FOUR HOURS WITHOUT FOOD! YOU SOLD ME ON ALL KINDSA BANQUETS AND KITCHENS AND SHOWERS AND IT WAS GONNA BE OH SO COOL AND...
...YOU BETTER DELIVER, WOLVERINE--
JEANNIE...

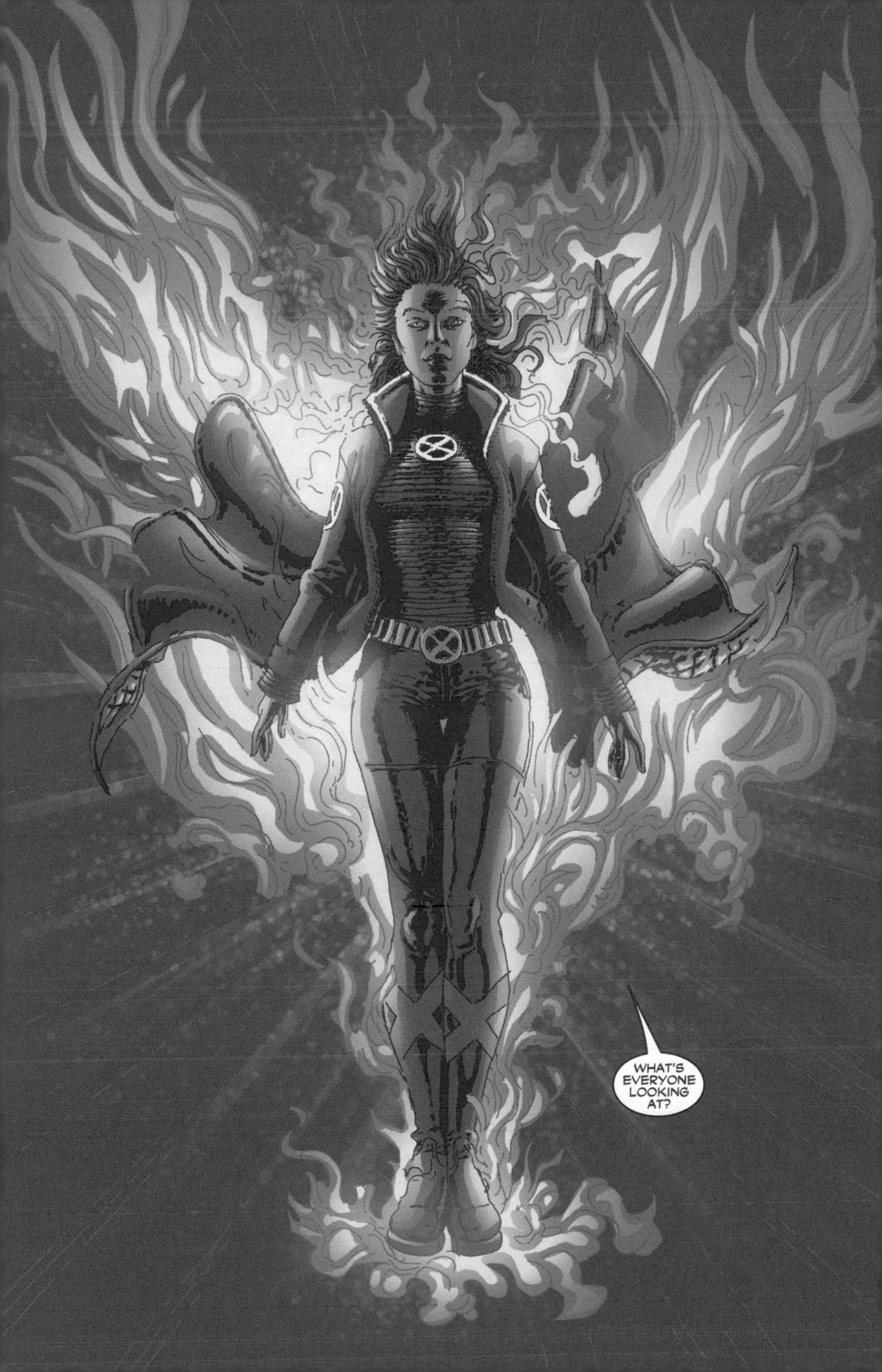
WHAT'S EVERYONE LOOKING AT?

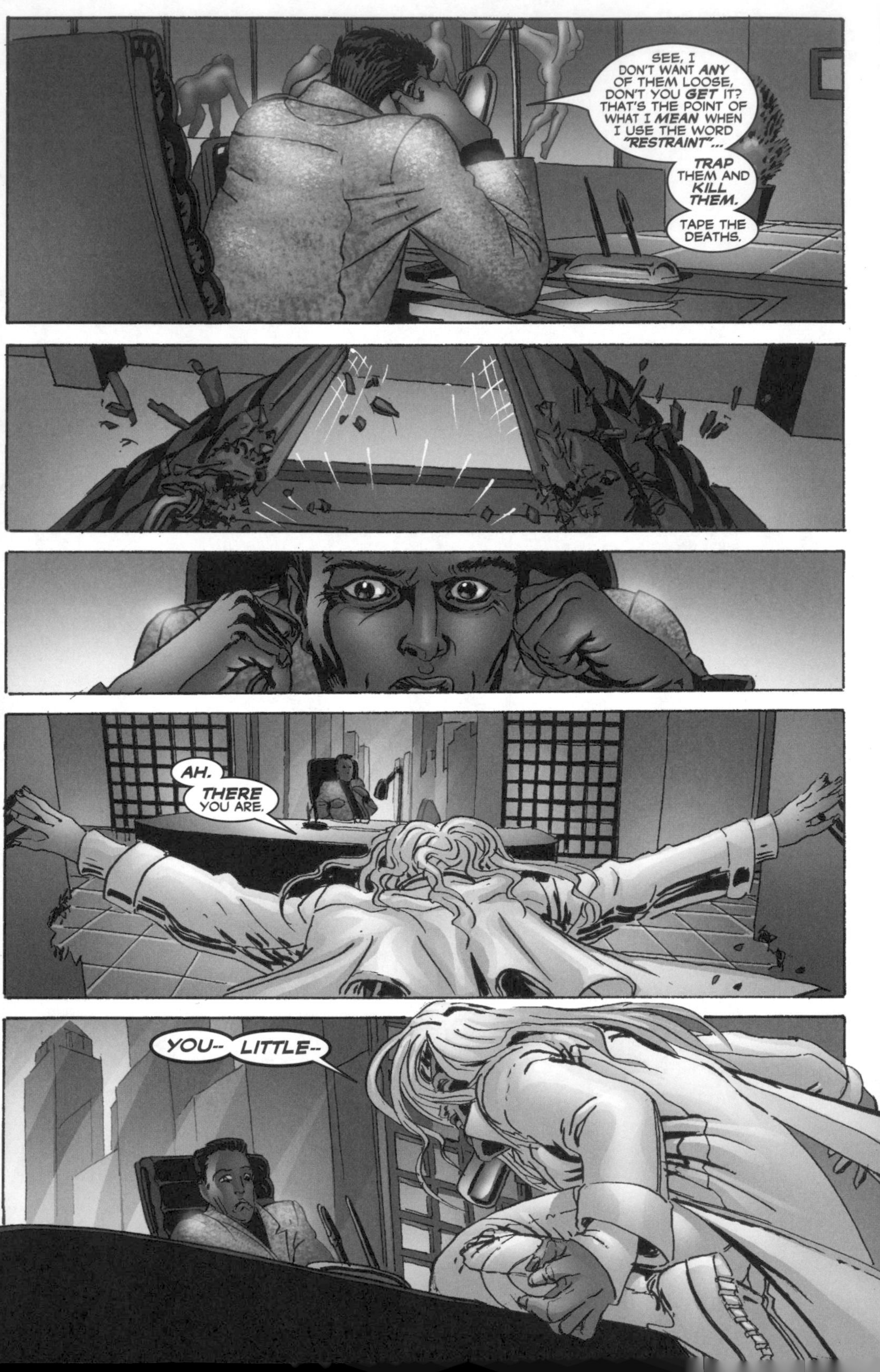
SEE, I DON'T WANT ANY OF THEM LOOSE, DON'T YOU GET IT? THAT'S THE POINT OF WHAT I MEAN WHEN I USE THE WORD "RESTRAINT"...
TRAP THEM AND KILL THEM.
TAPE THE DEATHS.
AH. THERE YOU ARE.
YOU--
LITTLE--

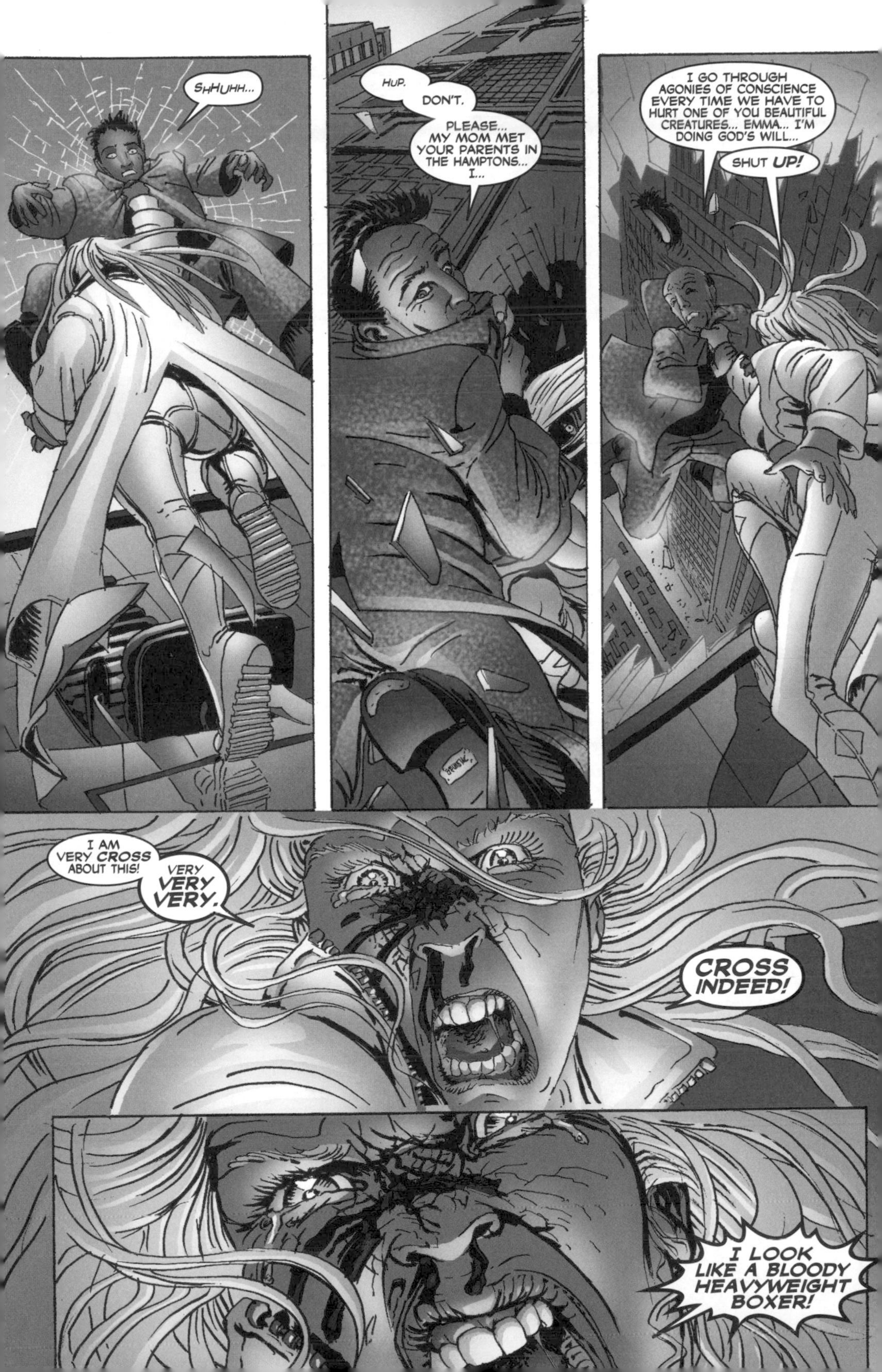
SHHUHH...
HUP.
DON'T.
PLEASE... MY MOM MET YOUR PARENTS IN THE HAMPTONS... I...
I GO THROUGH AGONIES OF CONSCIENCE EVERY TIME WE HAVE TO HURT ONE OF YOU BEAUTIFUL CREATURES... EMMA... I'M DOING GOD'S WILL...
SHUT UP!
I AM VERY CROSS ABOUT THIS!
VERY VERY VERY.
CROSS INDEED!
I LOOK LIKE A BLOODY HEAVYWEIGHT BOXER!

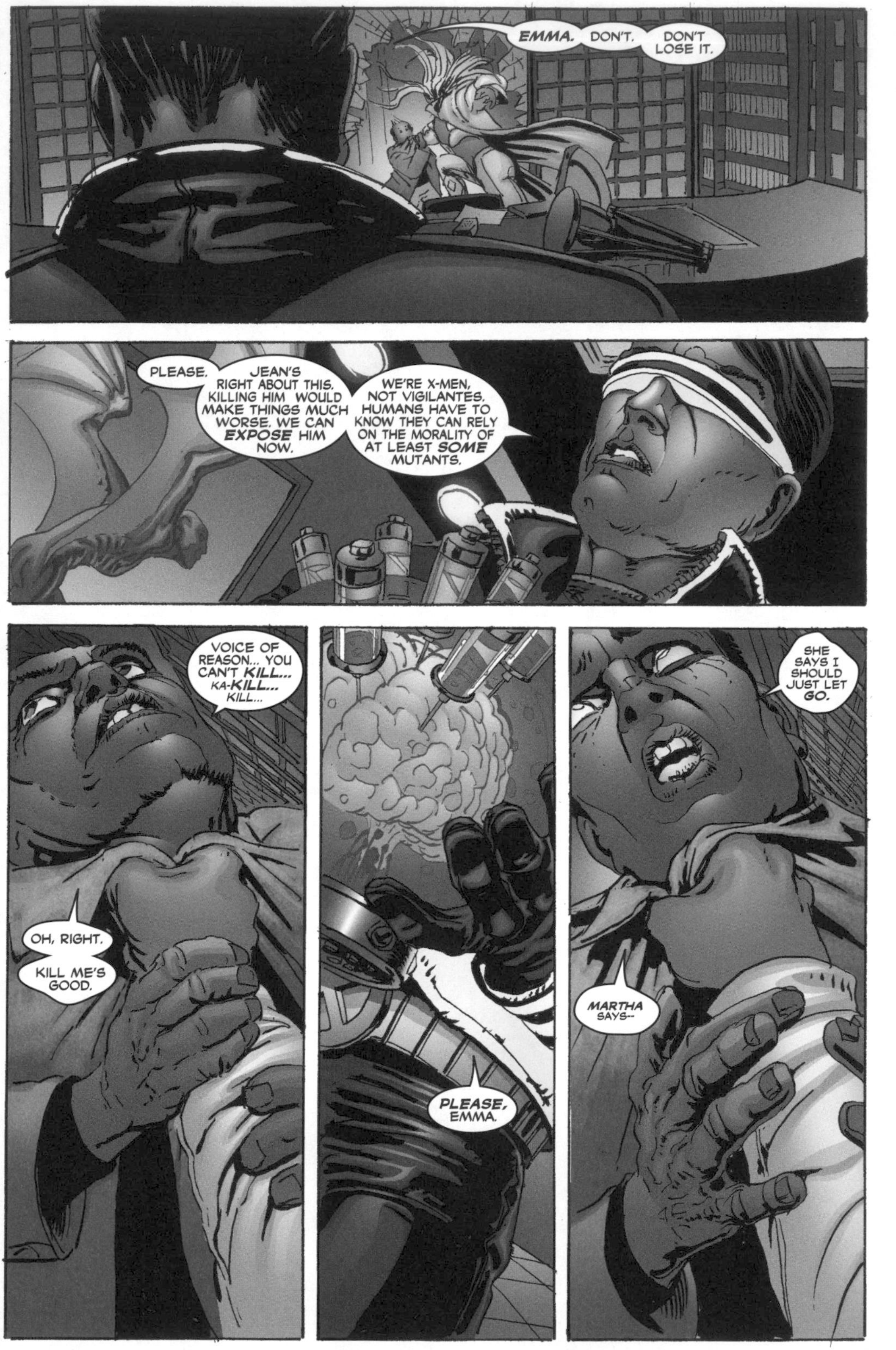
EMMA. DON'T. DON'T LOSE IT.
PLEASE. JEAN'S RIGHT ABOUT THIS. KILLING HIM WOULD MAKE THINGS MUCH WORSE. WE CAN EXPOSE HIM NOW.
WE'RE X-MEN, NOT VIGILANTES. HUMANS HAVE TO KNOW THEY CAN RELY ON THE MORALITY OF AT LEAST SOME MUTANTS.
VOICE OF REASON... YOU CAN'T KILL... KA-KILL... KILL...
OH, RIGHT.
KILL ME'S GOOD.
PLEASE, EMMA.
SHE SAYS I SHOULD JUST LET GO.
MARTHA SAYS--

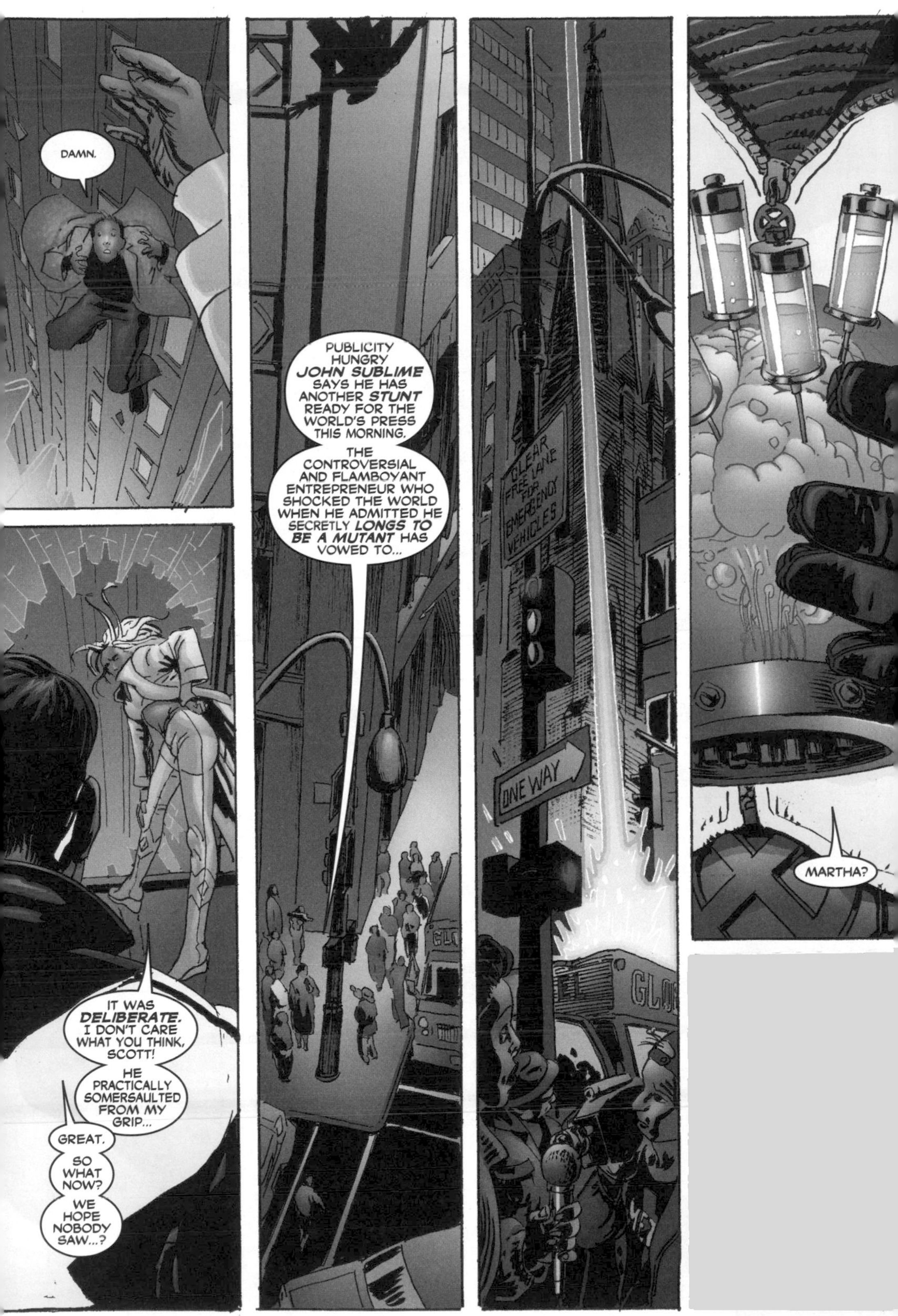

DAMN.
IT WAS **DELIBERATE.** I DON'T CARE WHAT YOU THINK, SCOTT!
HE PRACTICALLY SOMERSAULTED FROM MY GRIP...
GREAT.
SO WHAT NOW?
WE HOPE NOBODY SAW...?
PUBLICITY HUNGRY **JOHN SUBLIME** SAYS HE HAS ANOTHER **STUNT** READY FOR THE WORLD'S PRESS THIS MORNING.
THE CONTROVERSIAL AND FLAMBOYANT ENTREPRENEUR WHO SHOCKED THE WORLD WHEN HE ADMITTED HE SECRETLY **LONGS TO BE A MUTANT** HAS VOWED TO...
CLEAR FIRE LANE FOR EMERGENCY VEHICLES
ONE WAY
MARTHA?

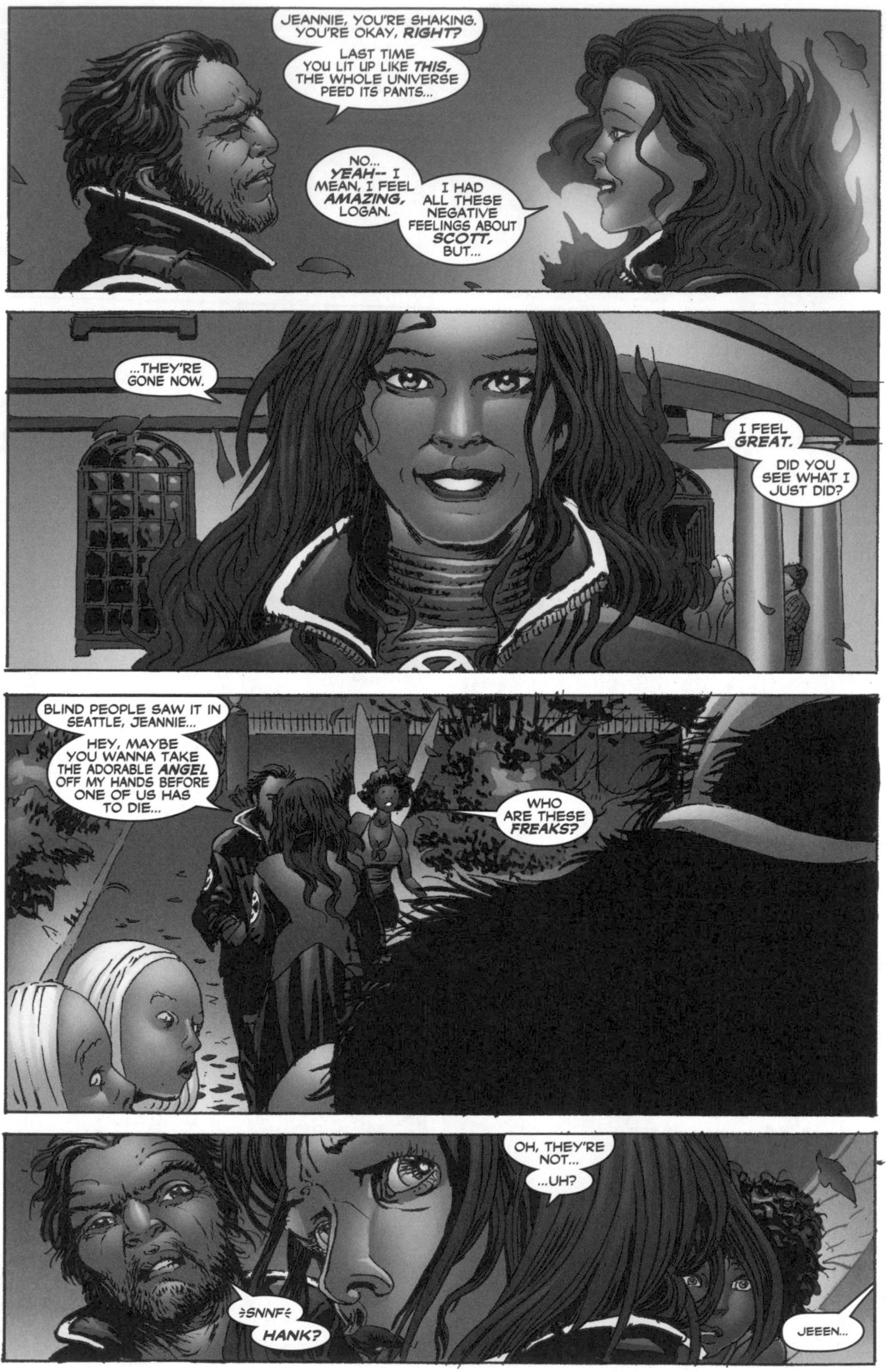
JEANNIE, YOU'RE SHAKING. YOU'RE OKAY, RIGHT?
LAST TIME YOU LIT UP LIKE THIS, THE WHOLE UNIVERSE PEED ITS PANTS...
NO... YEAH-- I MEAN, I FEEL AMAZING, LOGAN.
I HAD ALL THESE NEGATIVE FEELINGS ABOUT SCOTT, BUT...
...THEY'RE GONE NOW.
I FEEL GREAT.
DID YOU SEE WHAT I JUST DID?
BLIND PEOPLE SAW IT IN SEATTLE, JEANNIE...
HEY, MAYBE YOU WANNA TAKE THE ADORABLE ANGEL OFF MY HANDS BEFORE ONE OF US HAS TO DIE...
WHO ARE THESE FREAKS?
OH, THEY'RE NOT...
...UH?
SNNF
HANK?
JEEEN...

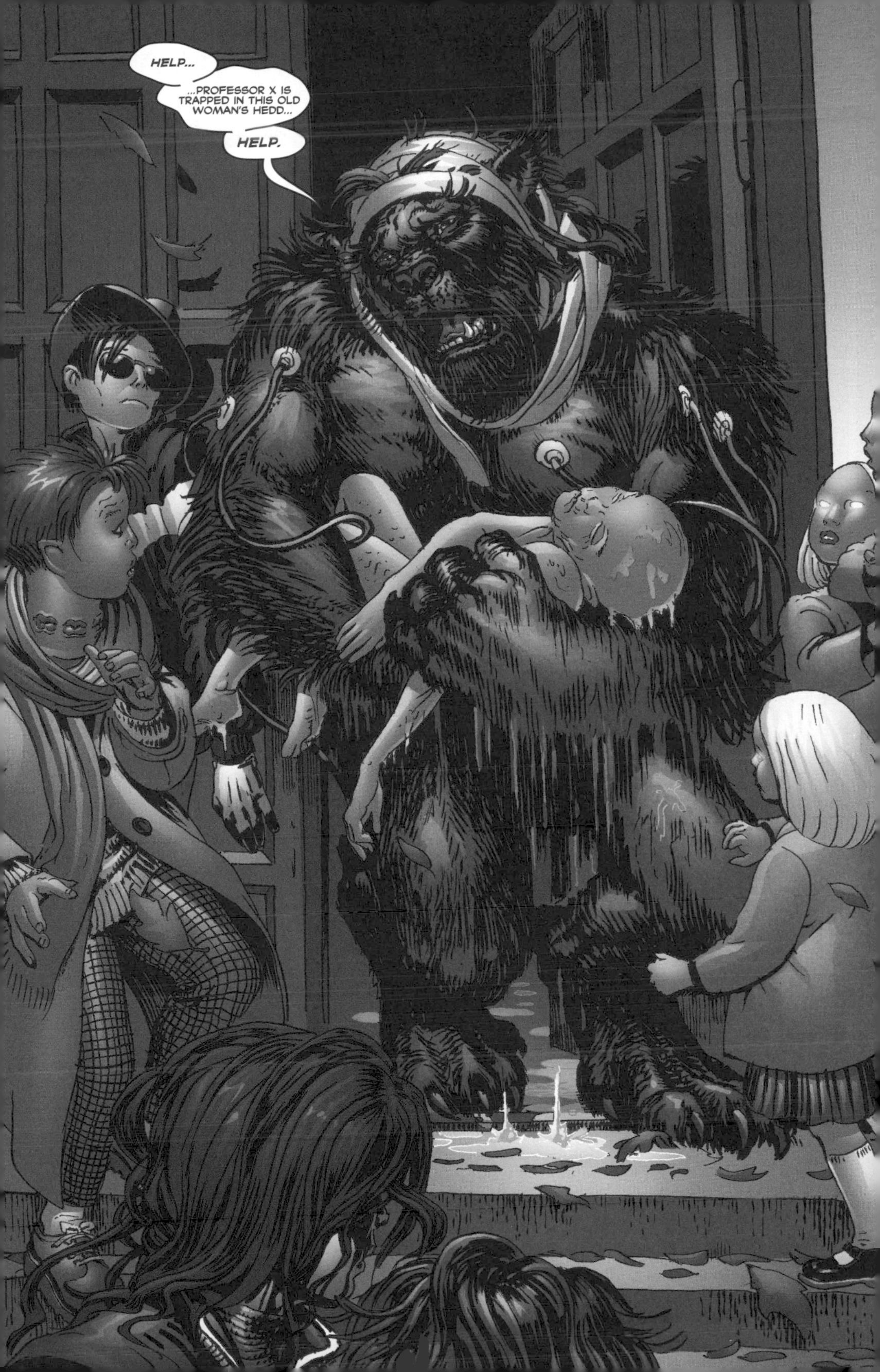
HELP...
...PROFESSOR X IS TRAPPED IN THIS OLD WOMAN'S HEDD...
HELP.

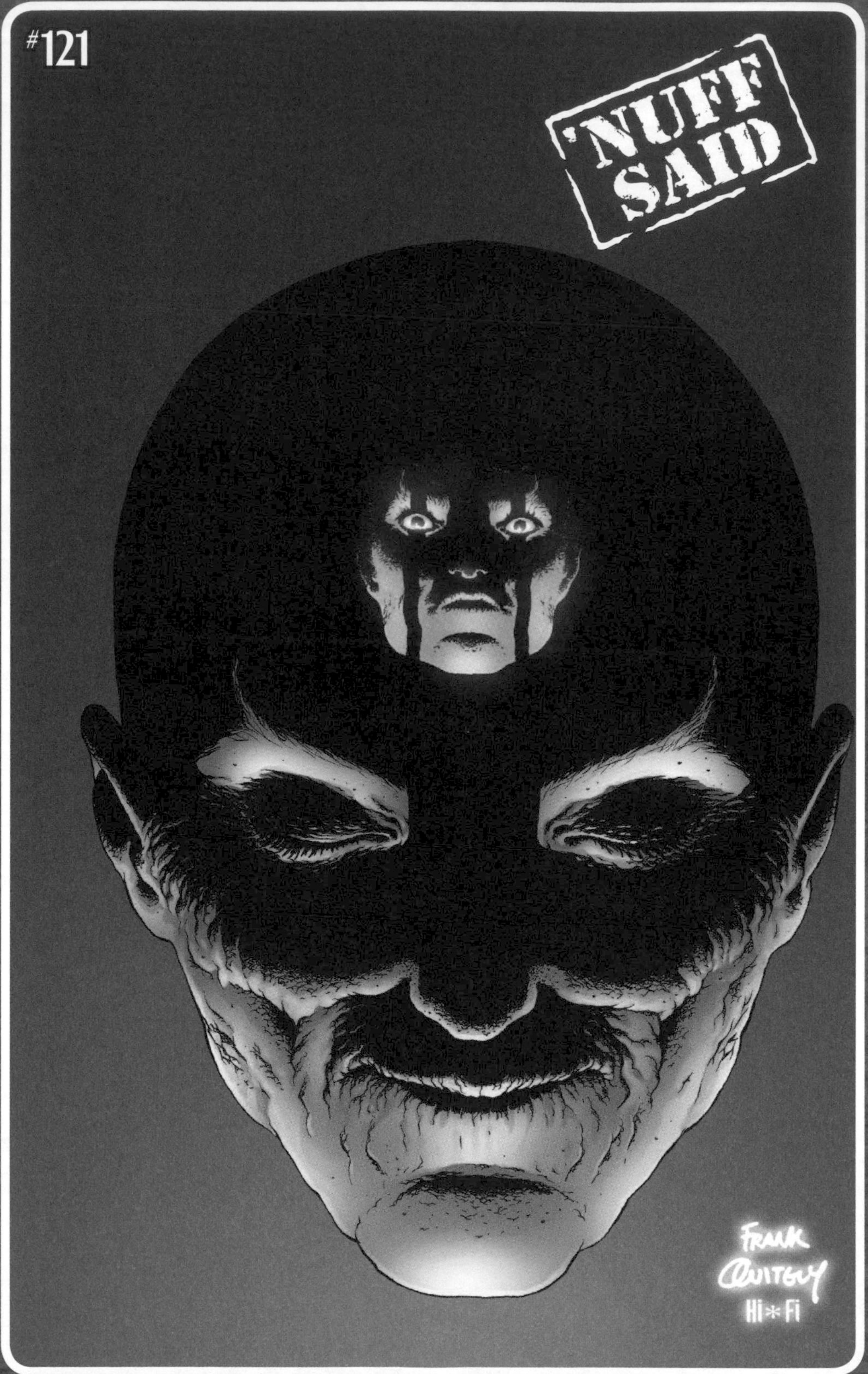
#121
'NUFF SAID
FRANK QUITELY
Hi*Fi

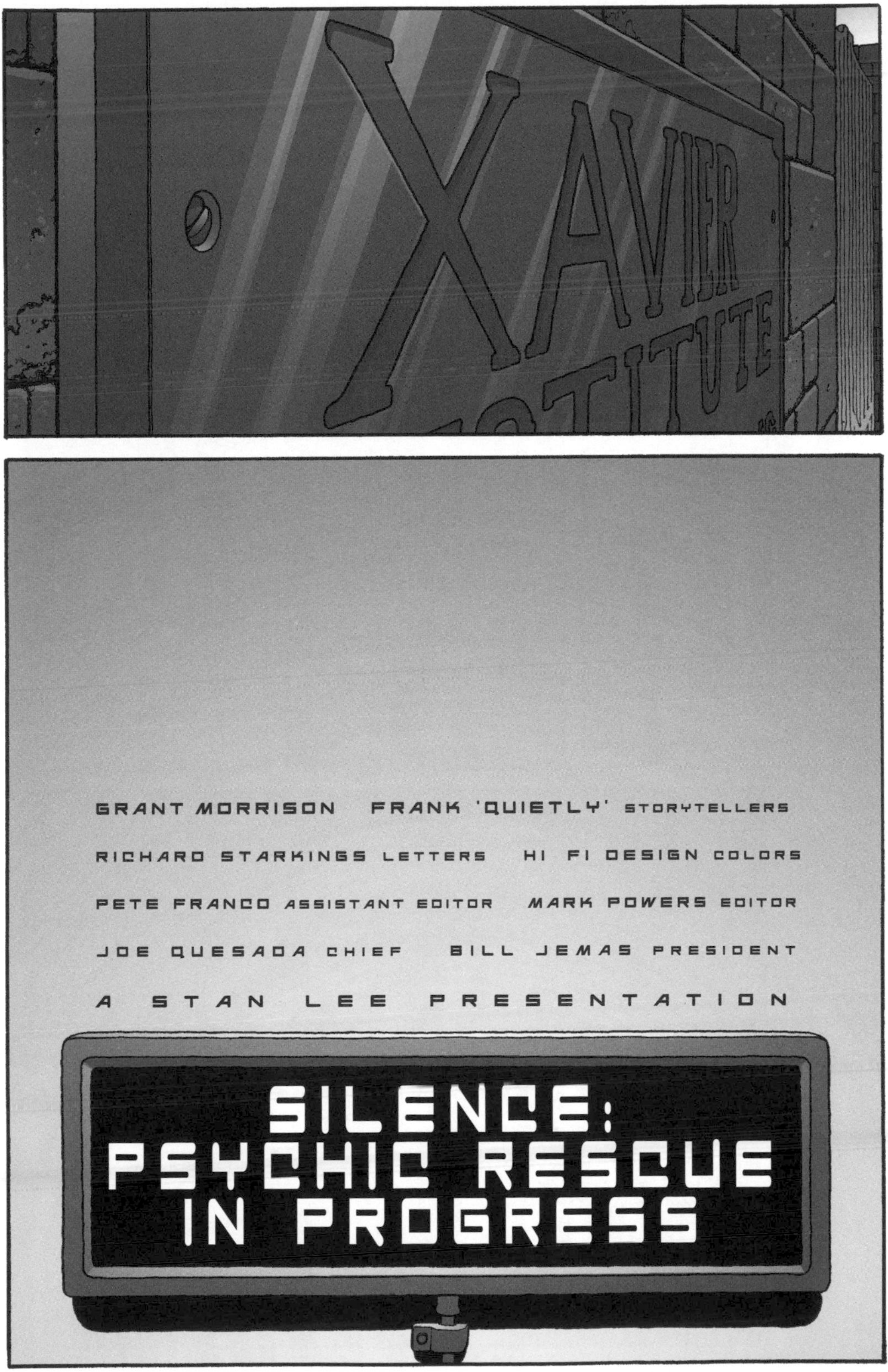
XAVIER
INSTITUTE
GRANT MORRISON FRANK 'QUIETLY' STORYTELLERS
RICHARD STARKINGS LETTERS HI FI DESIGN COLORS
PETE FRANCO ASSISTANT EDITOR MARK POWERS EDITOR
JOE QUESADA CHIEF BILL JEMAS PRESIDENT
A STAN LEE PRESENTATION
SILENCE:
PSYCHIC RESCUE
IN PROGRESS

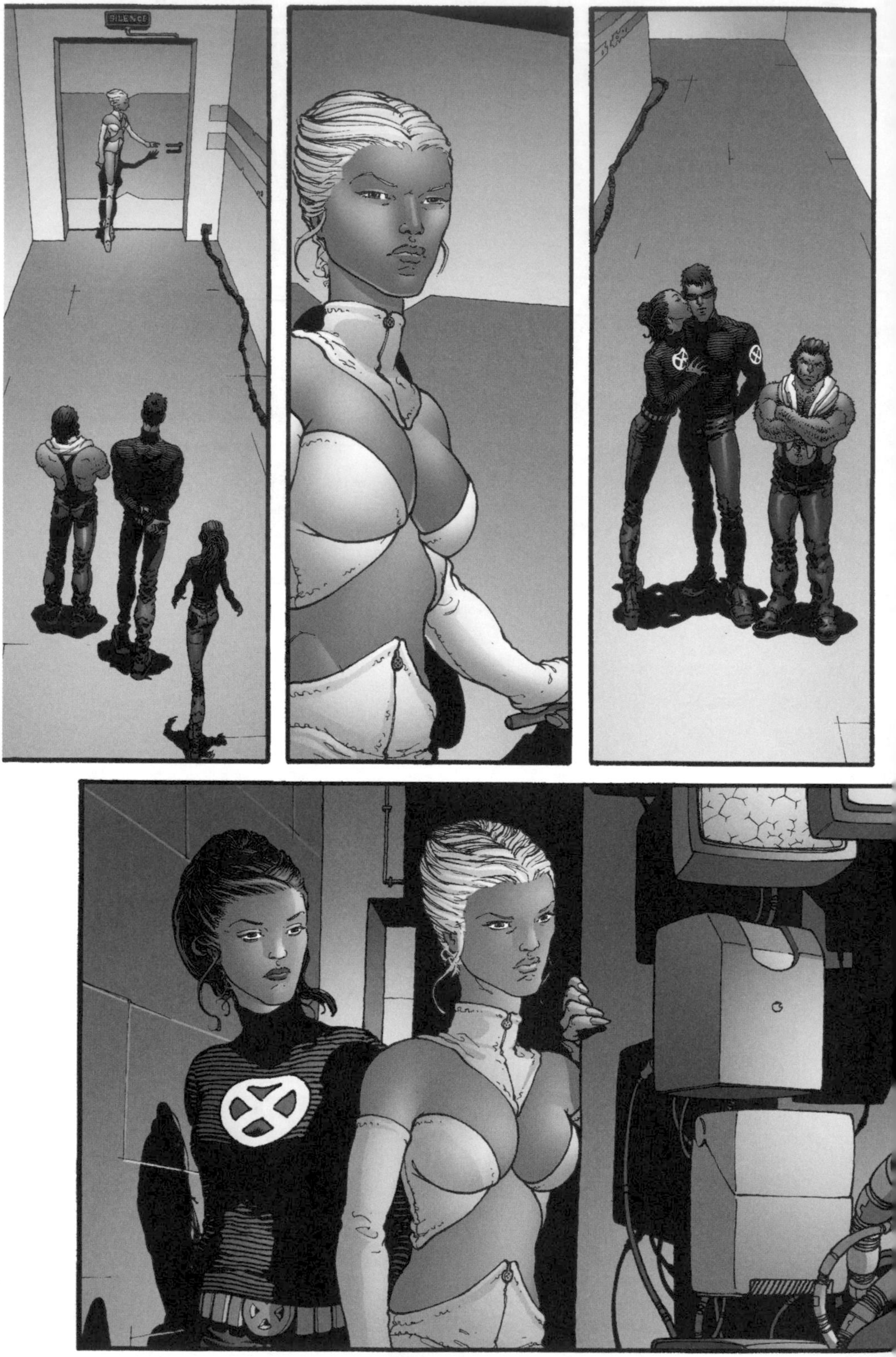
SILENCE

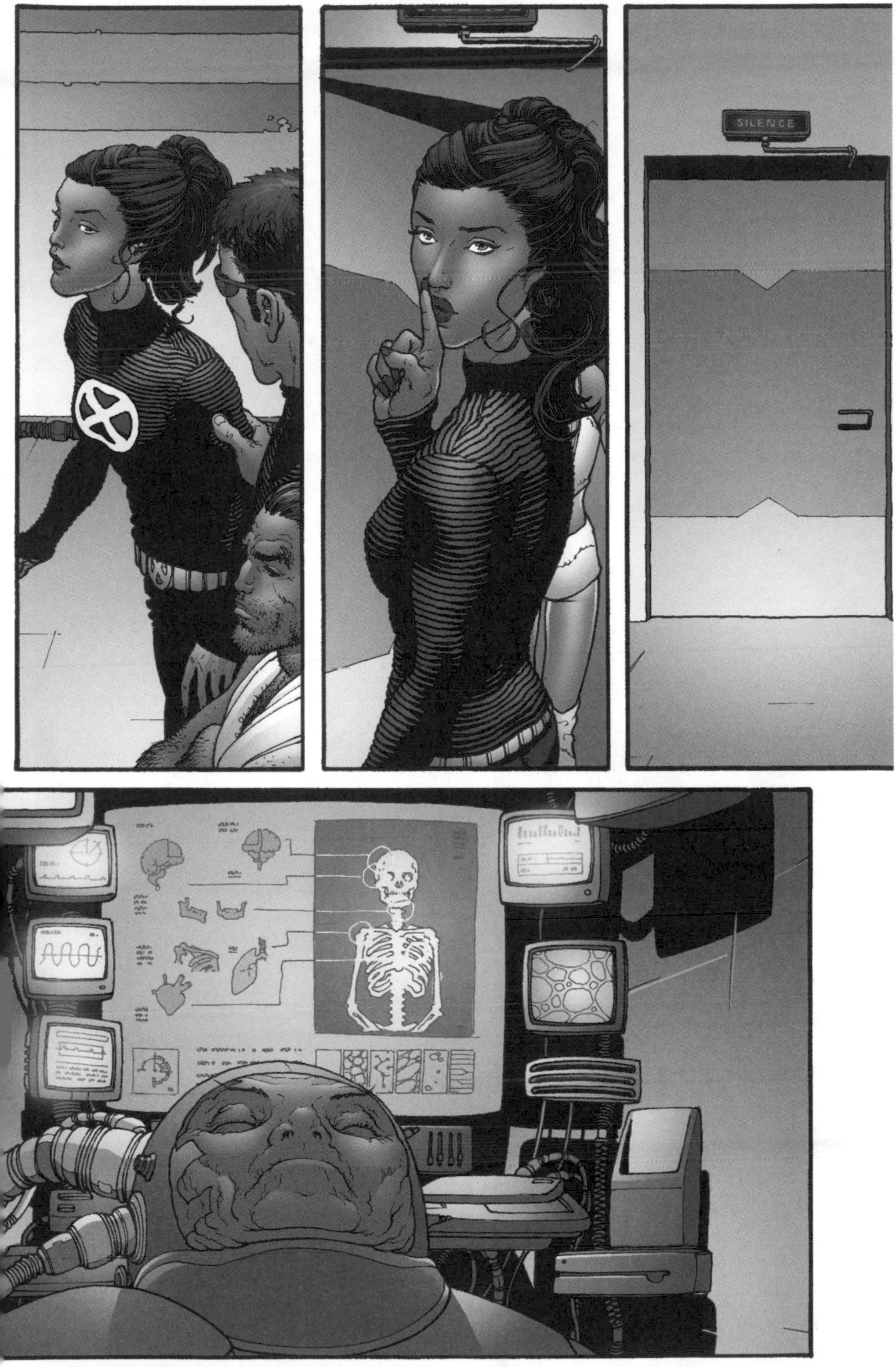
SILENCE

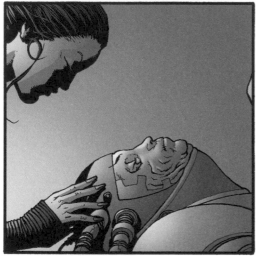

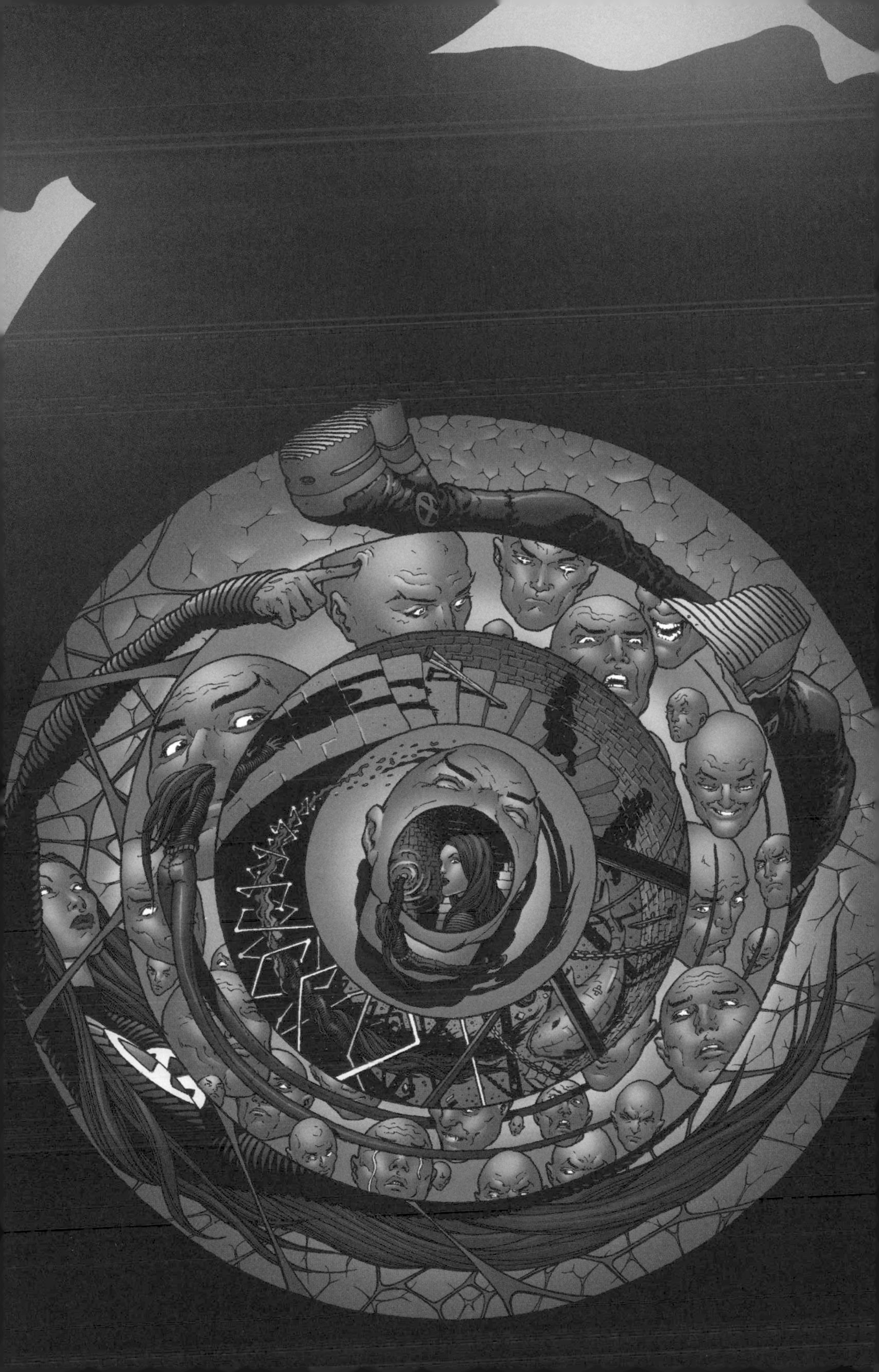

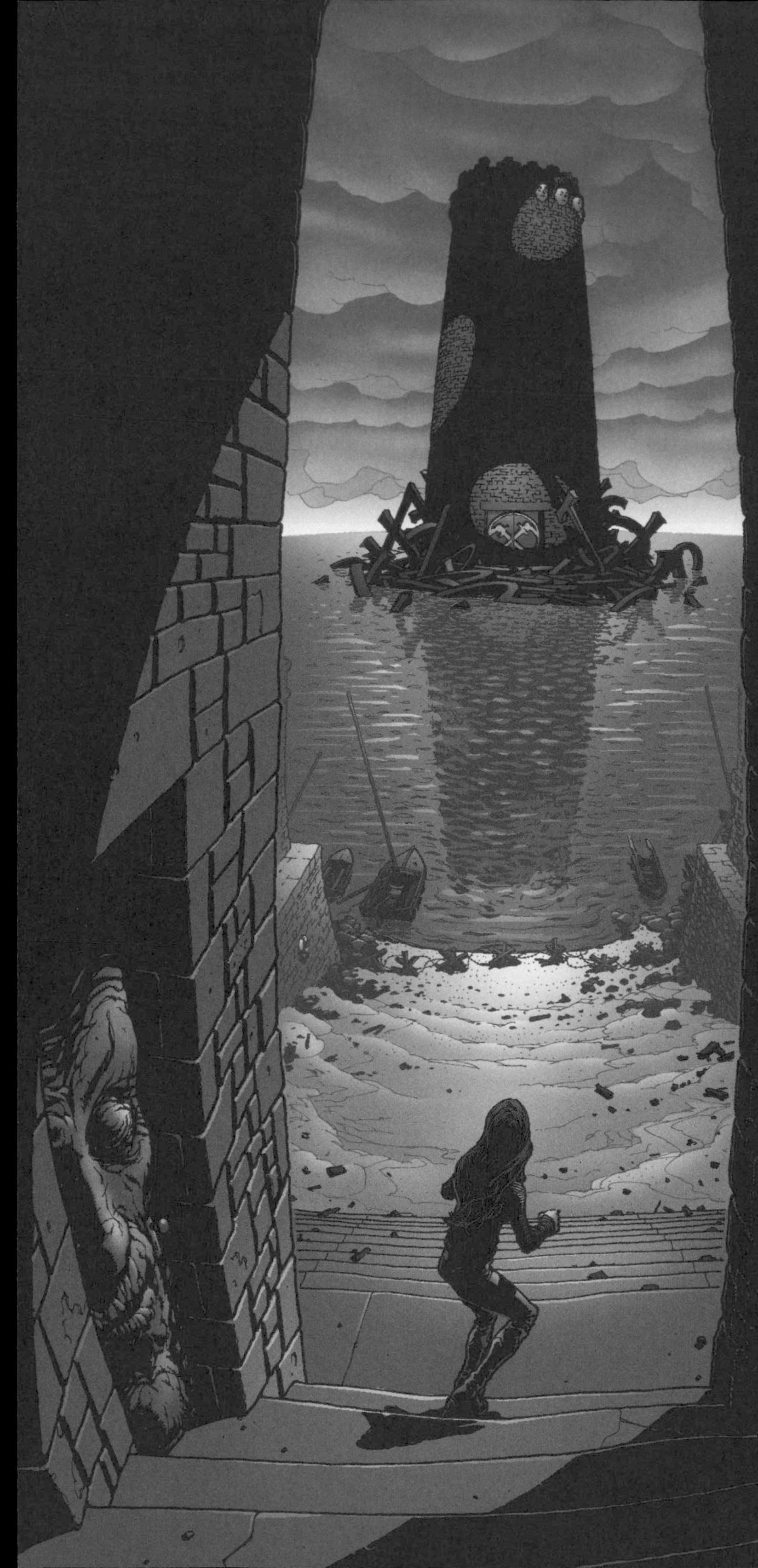

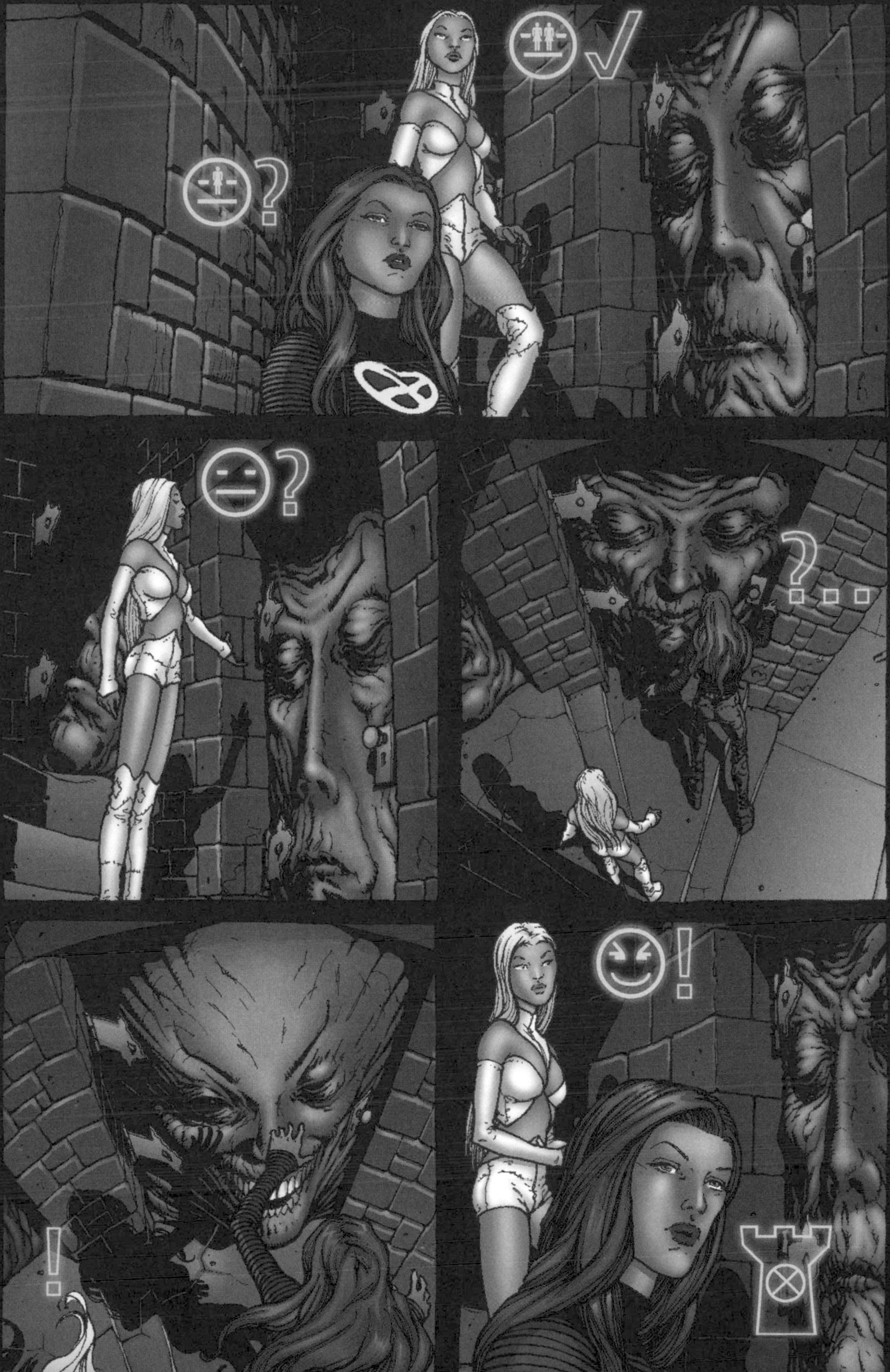
✓
?
?
?...
!
!

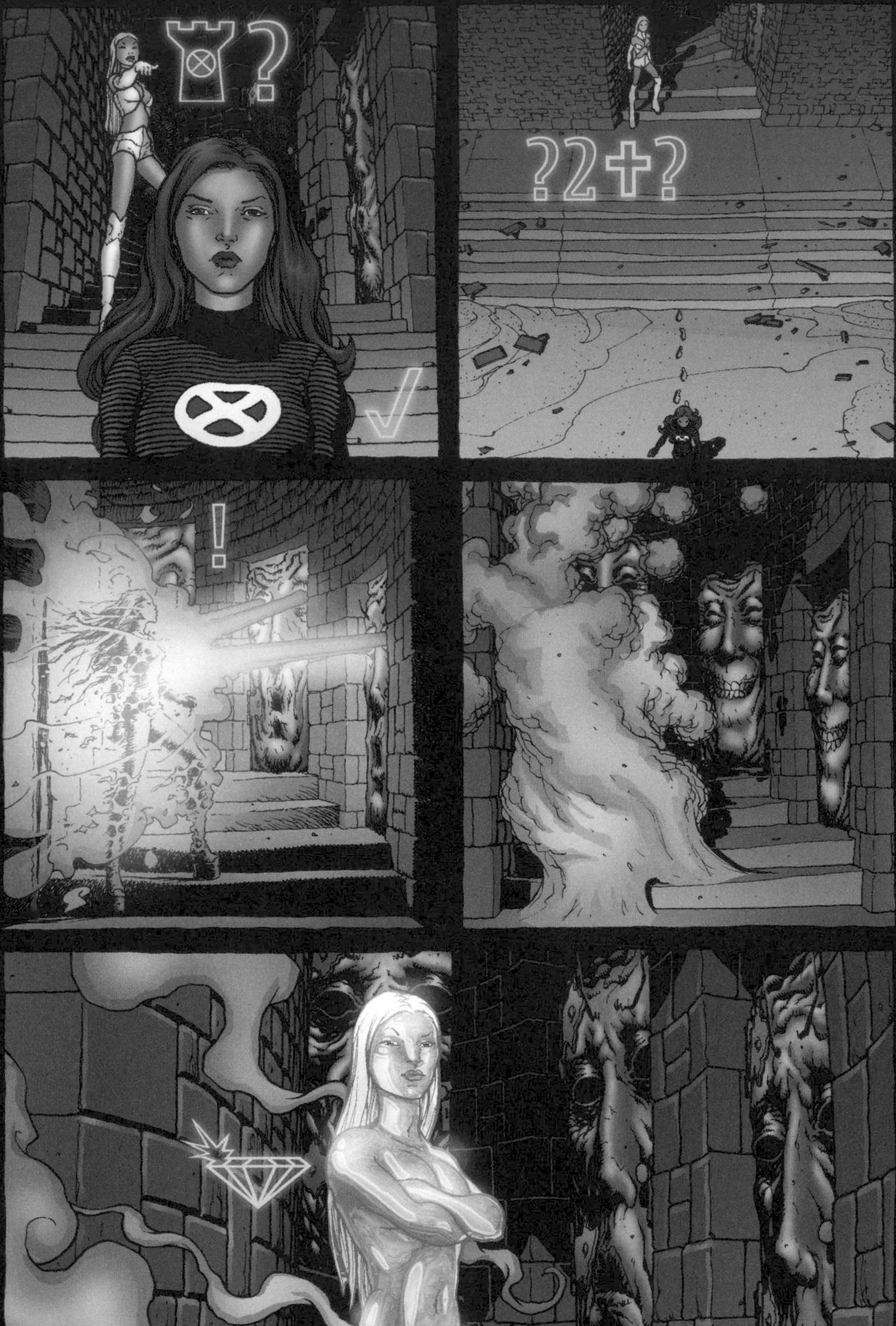
?
?2+?
!

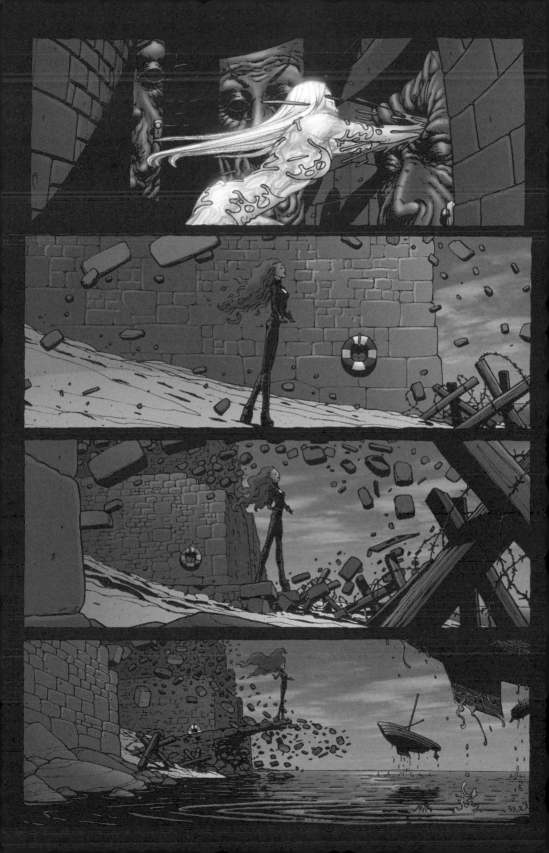

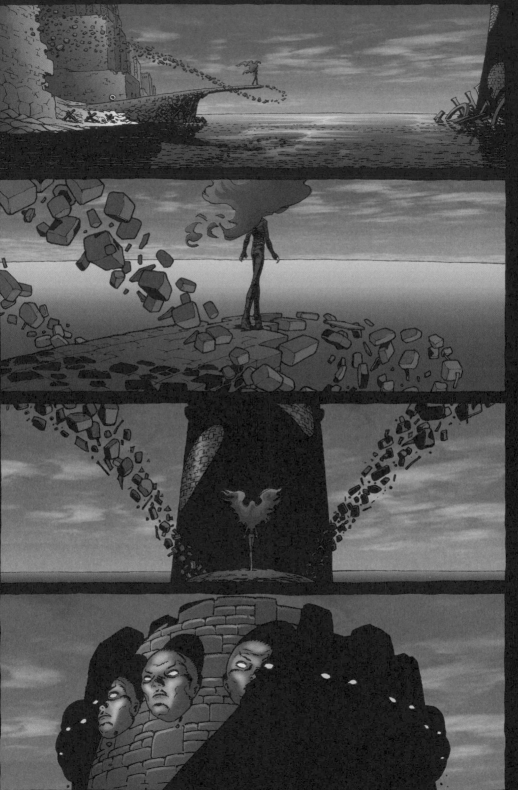

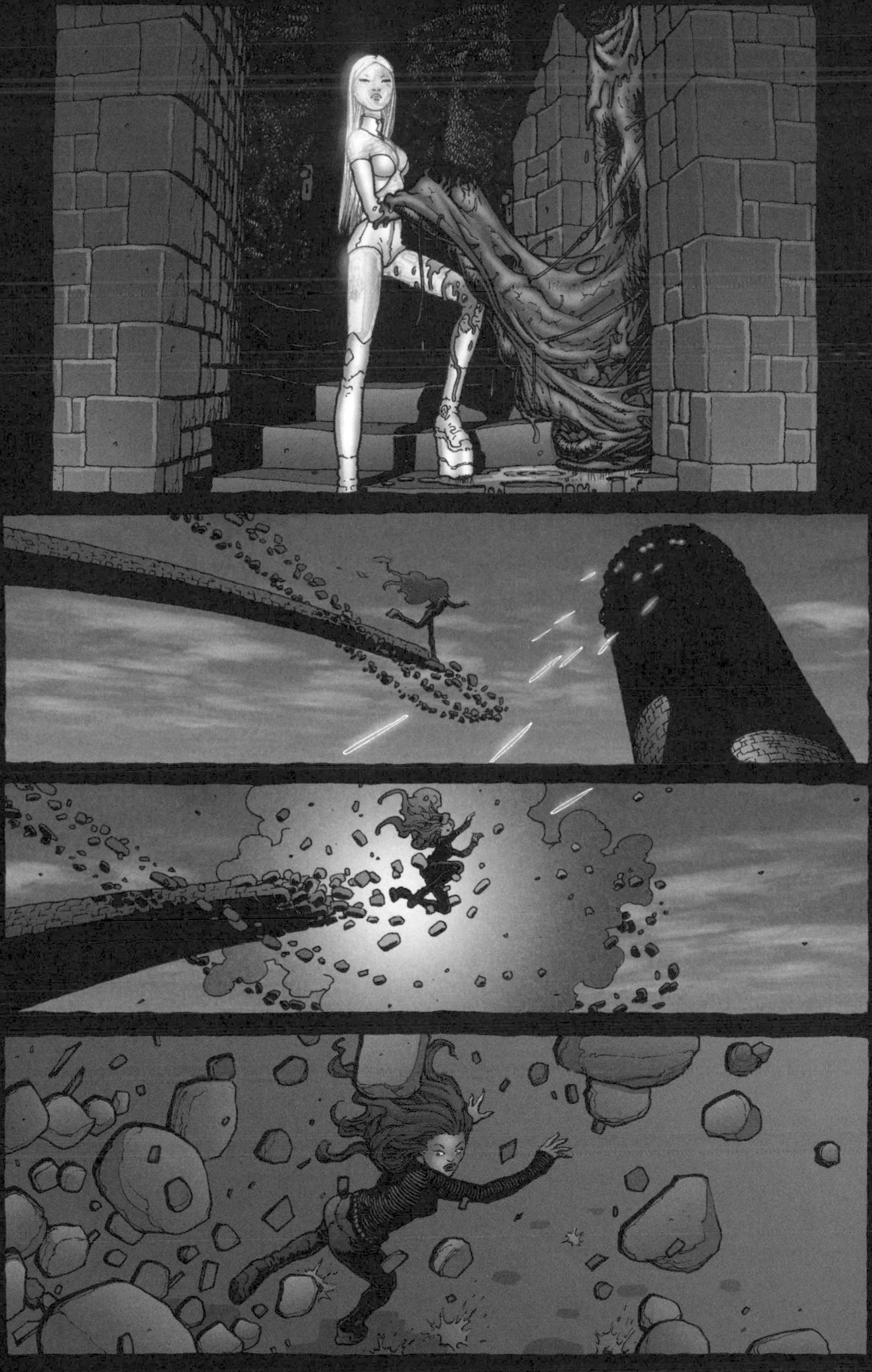

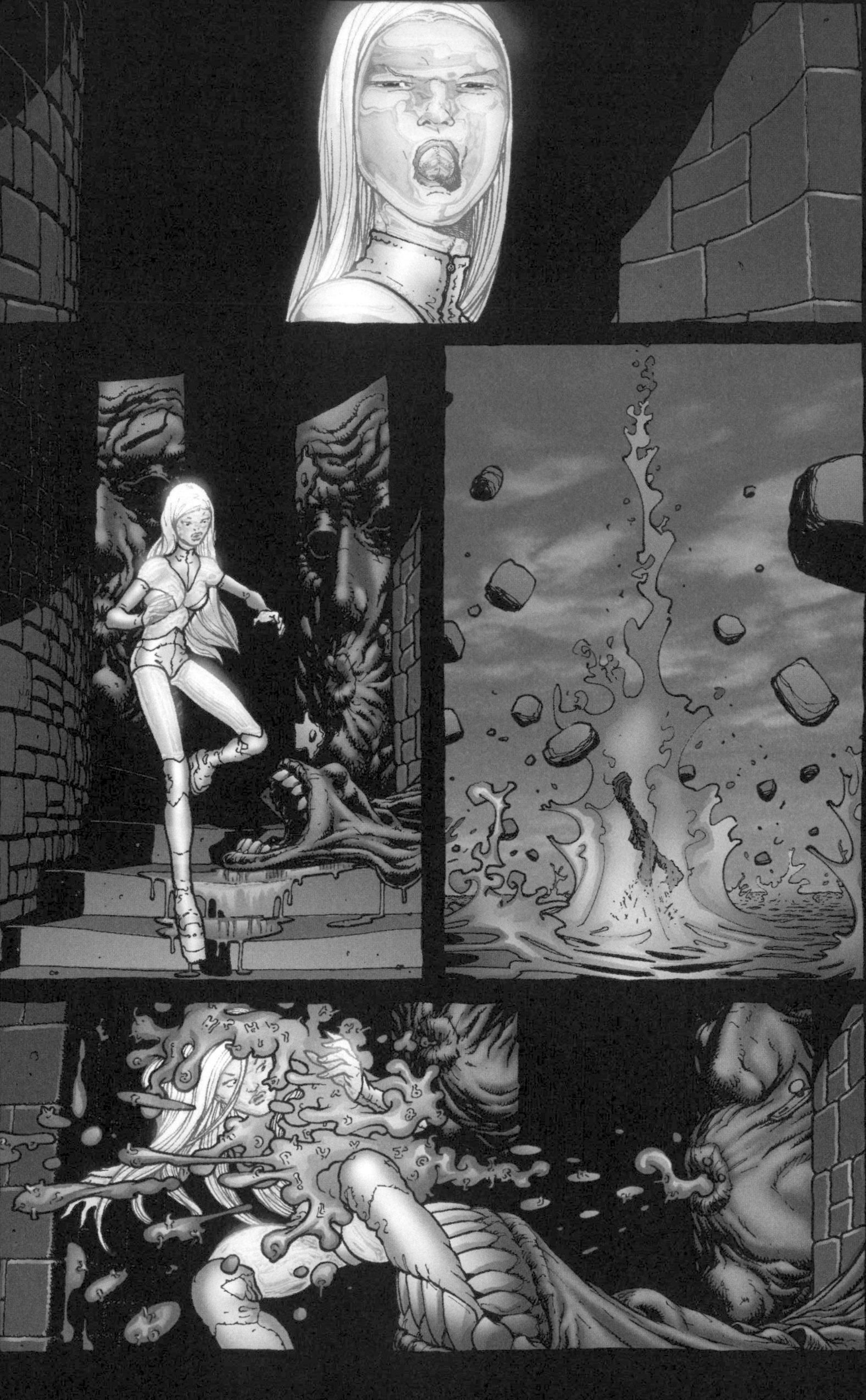

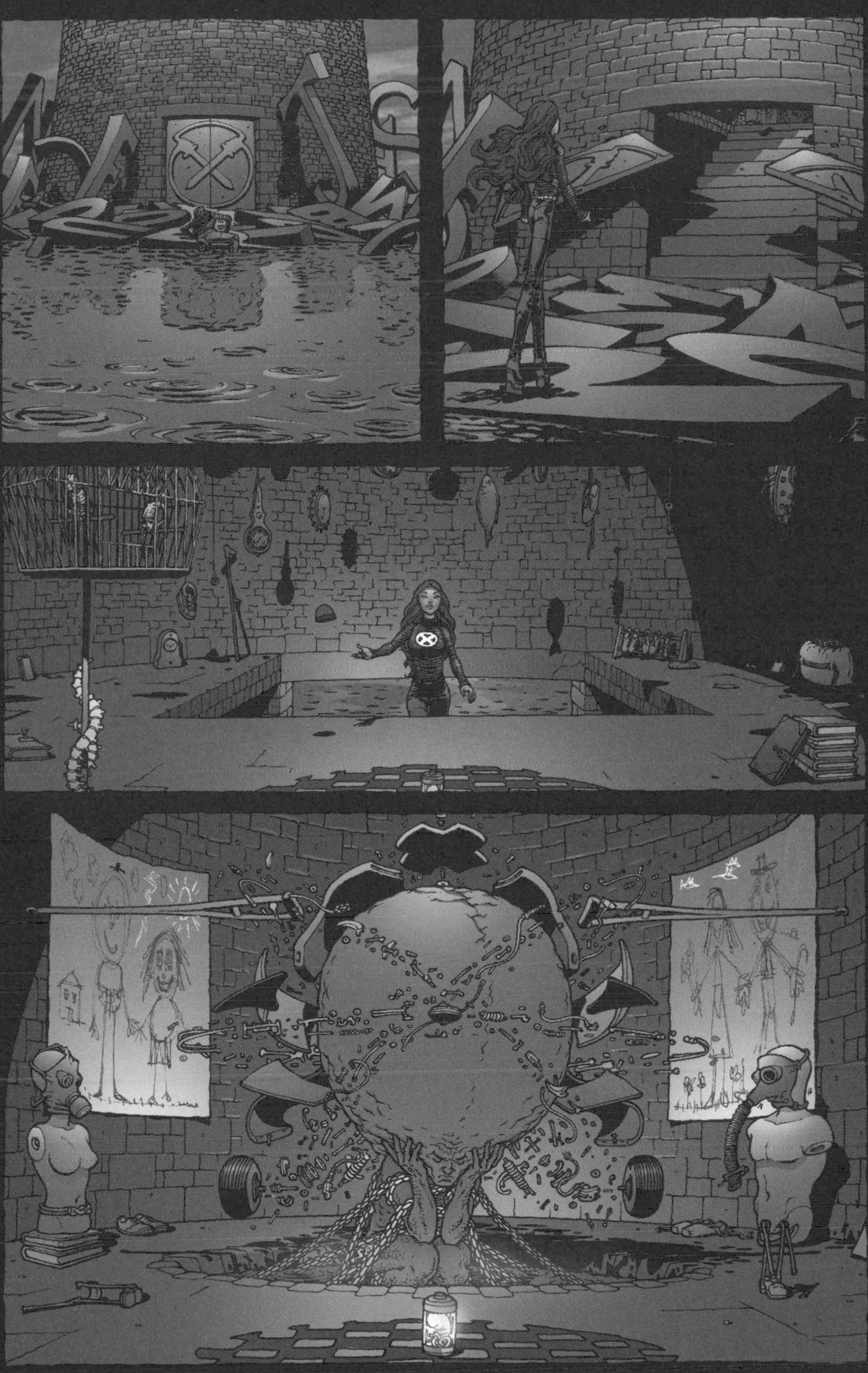

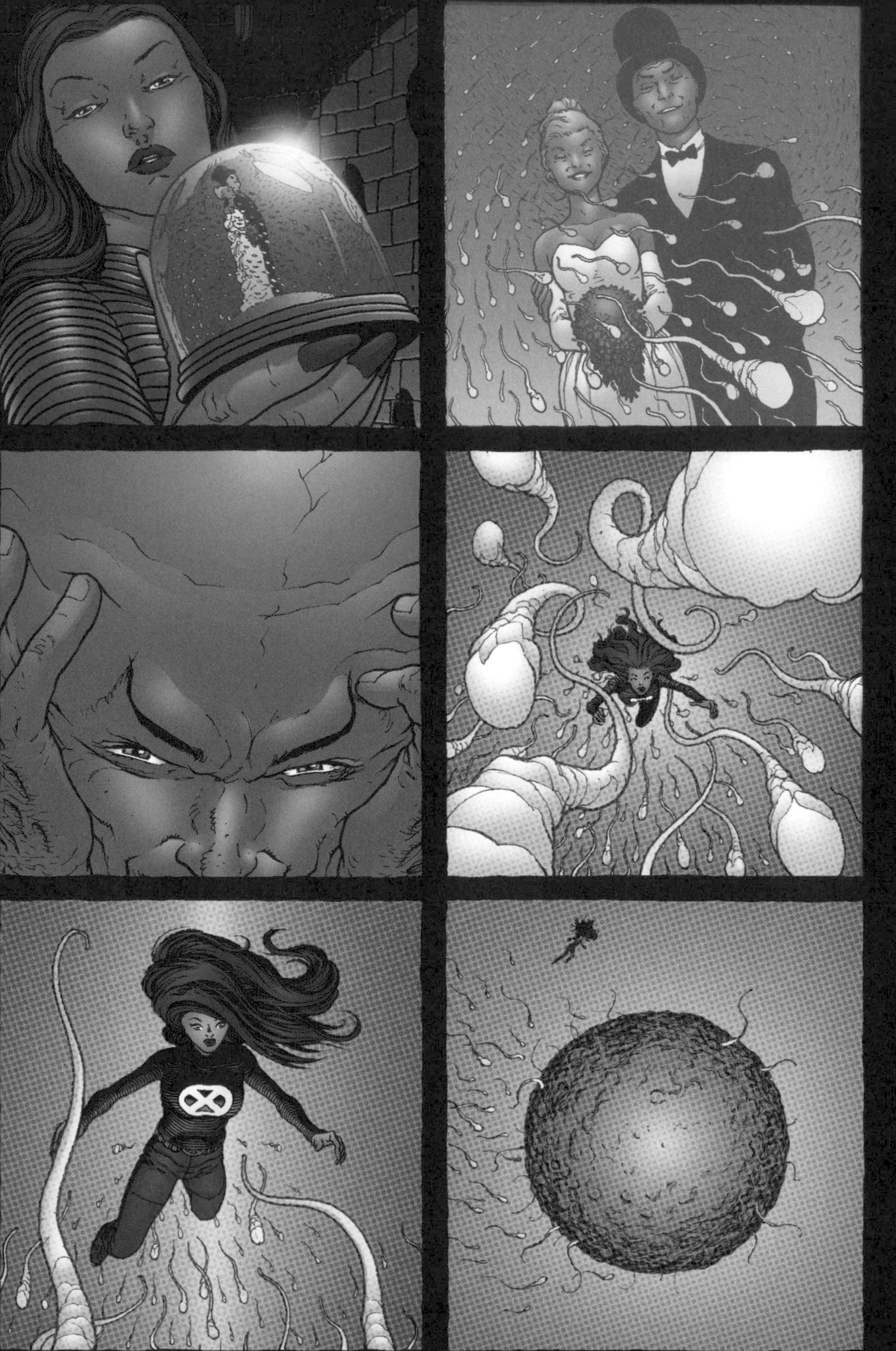

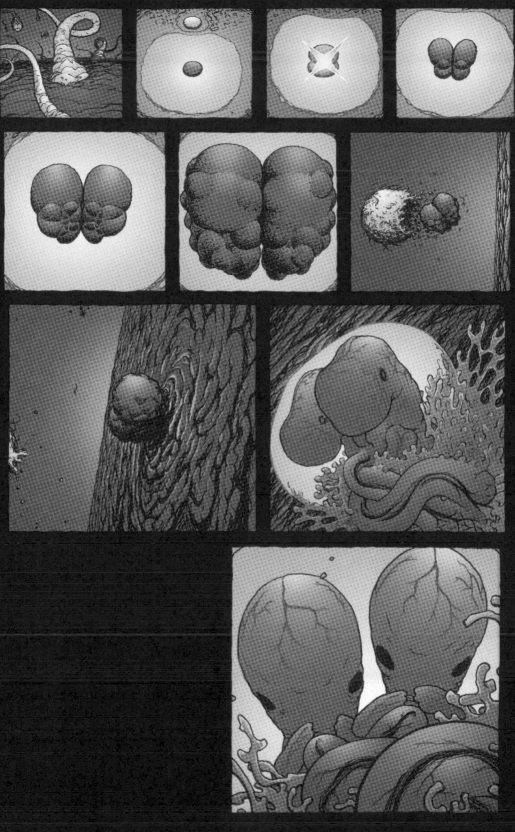

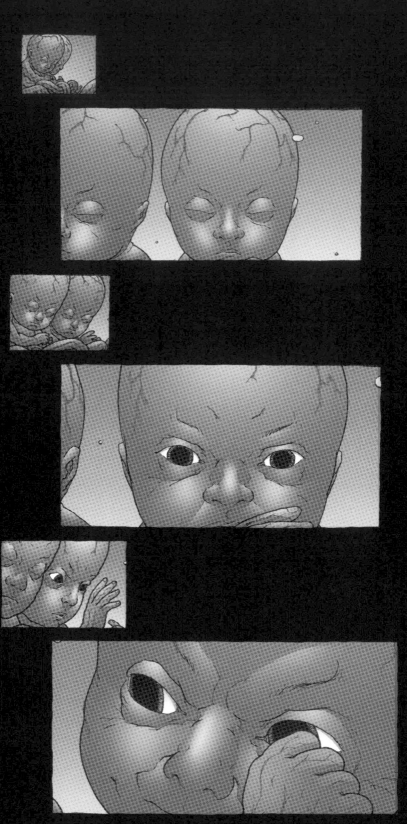

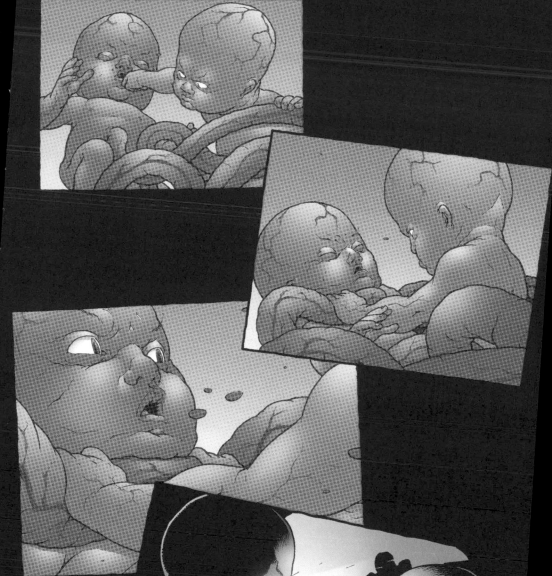

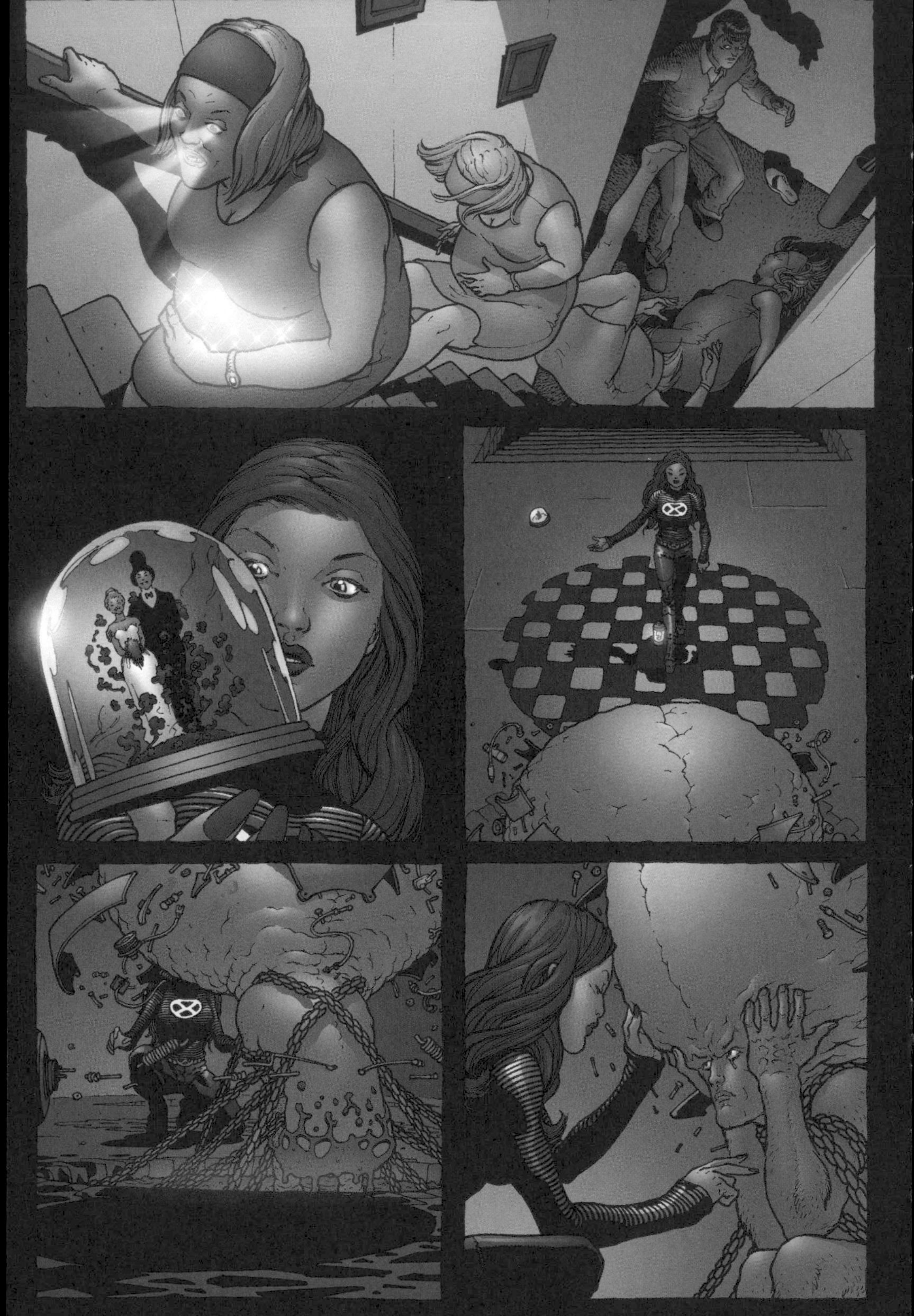

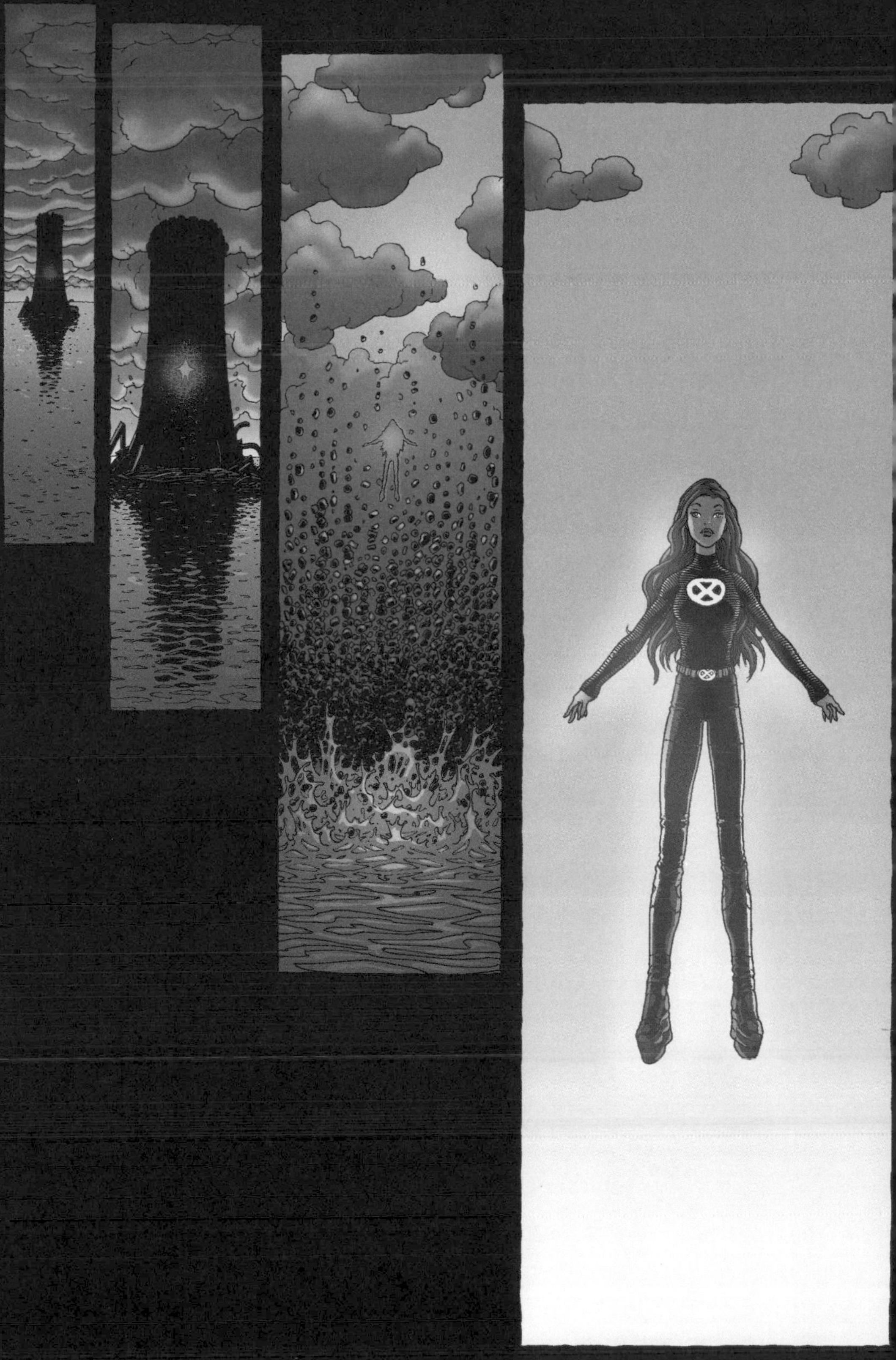

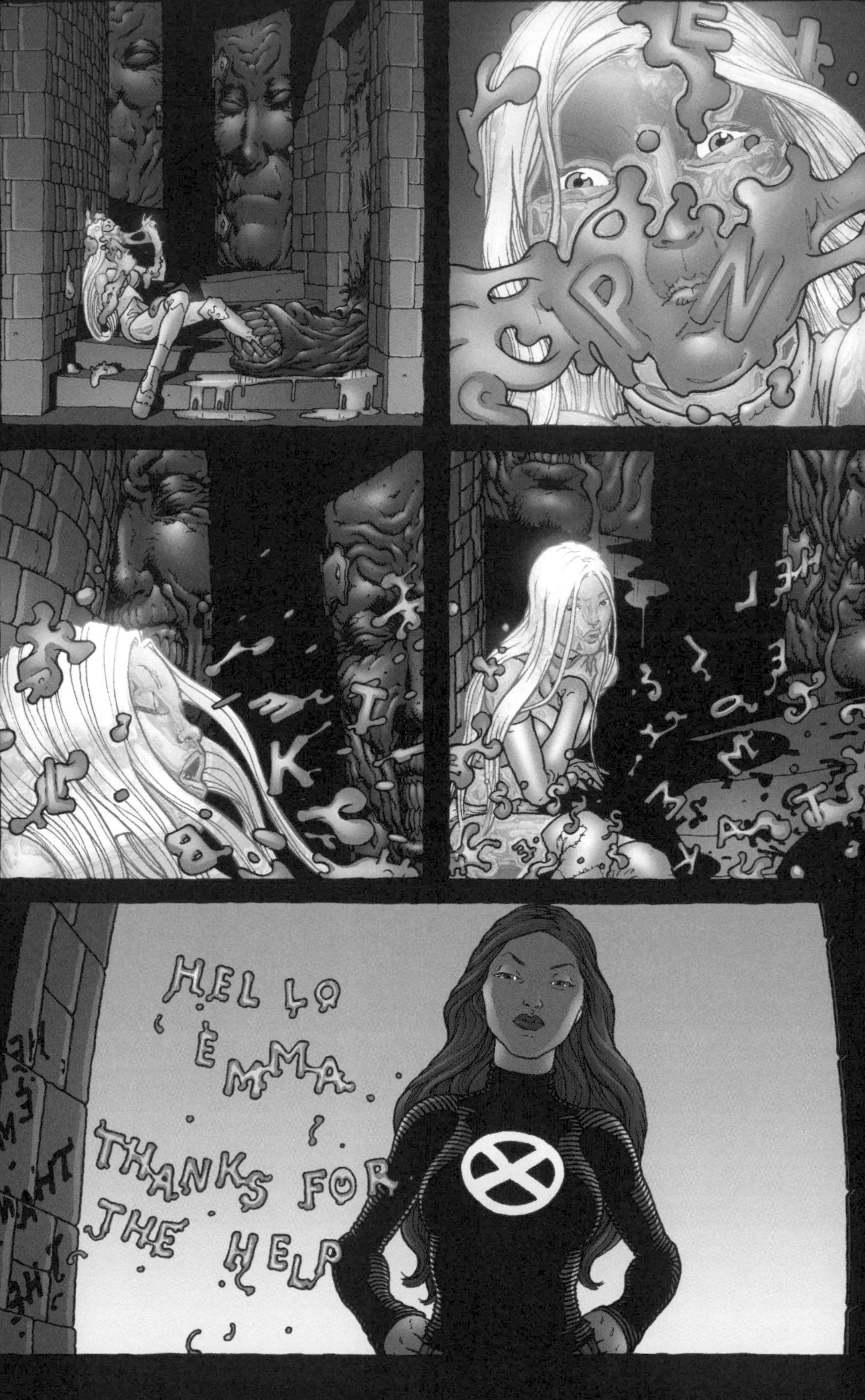
HELLO
EMMA
THANKS FOR
THE HELP

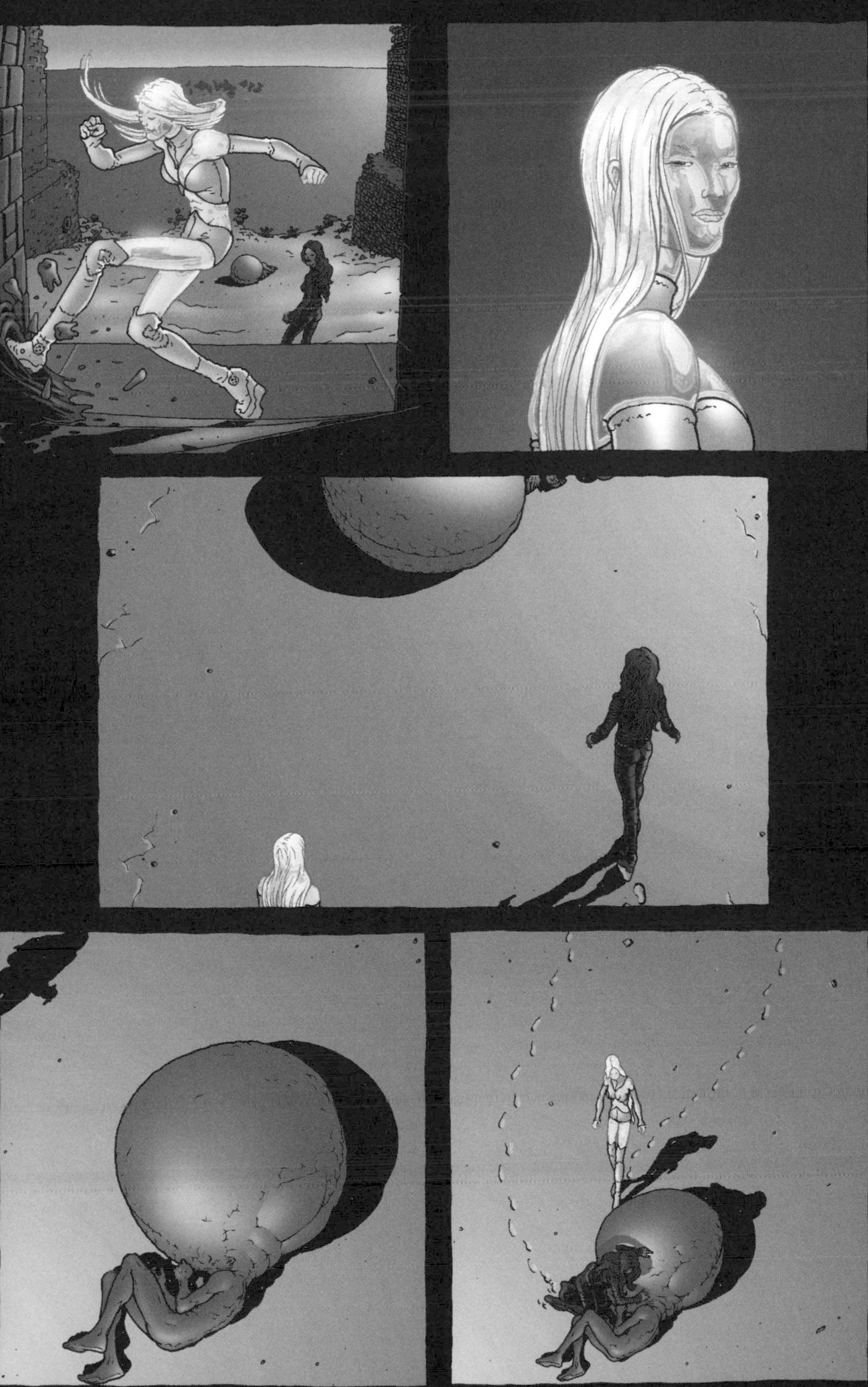

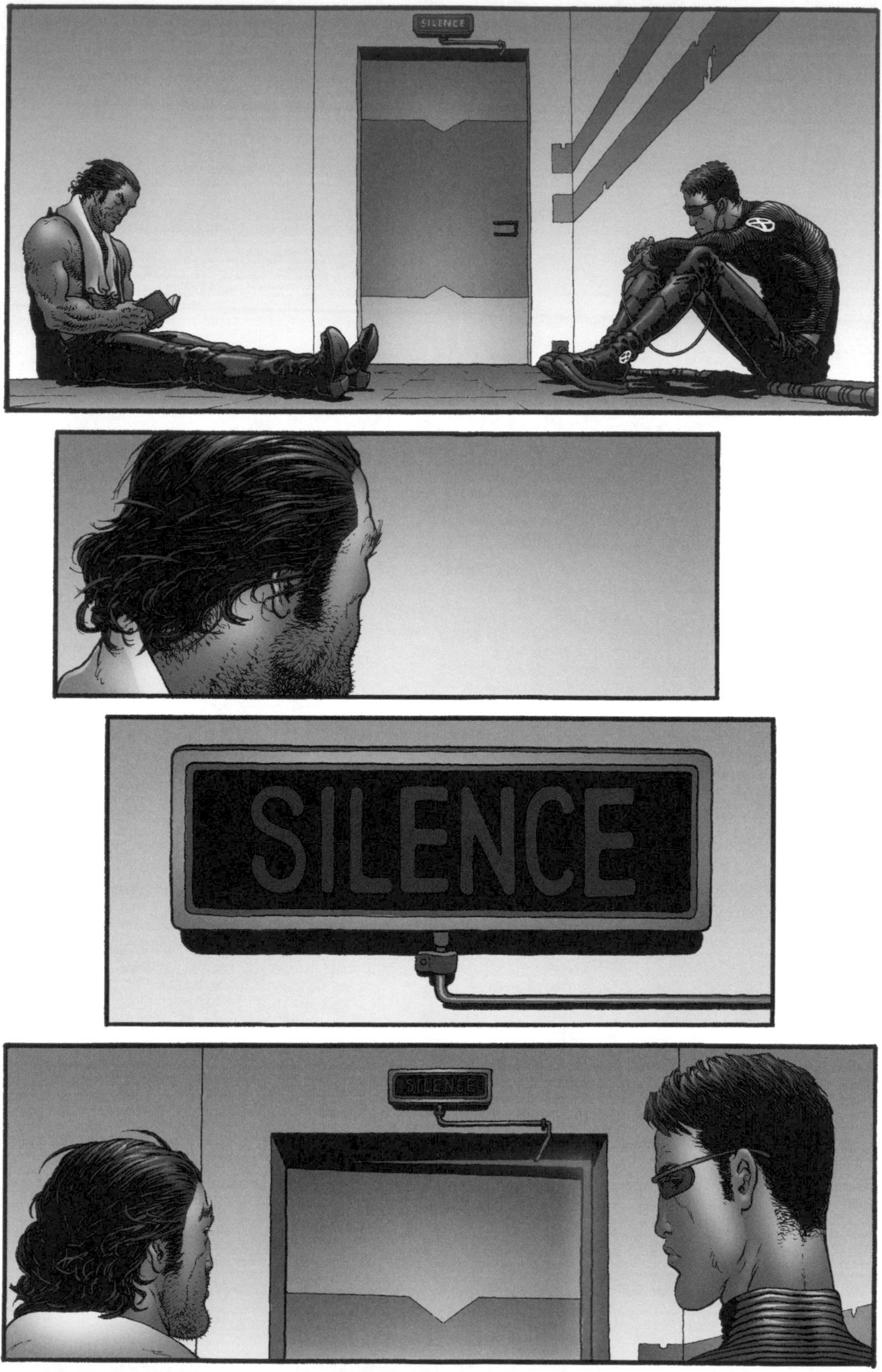
SILENCE
SILENCE
SILENCE

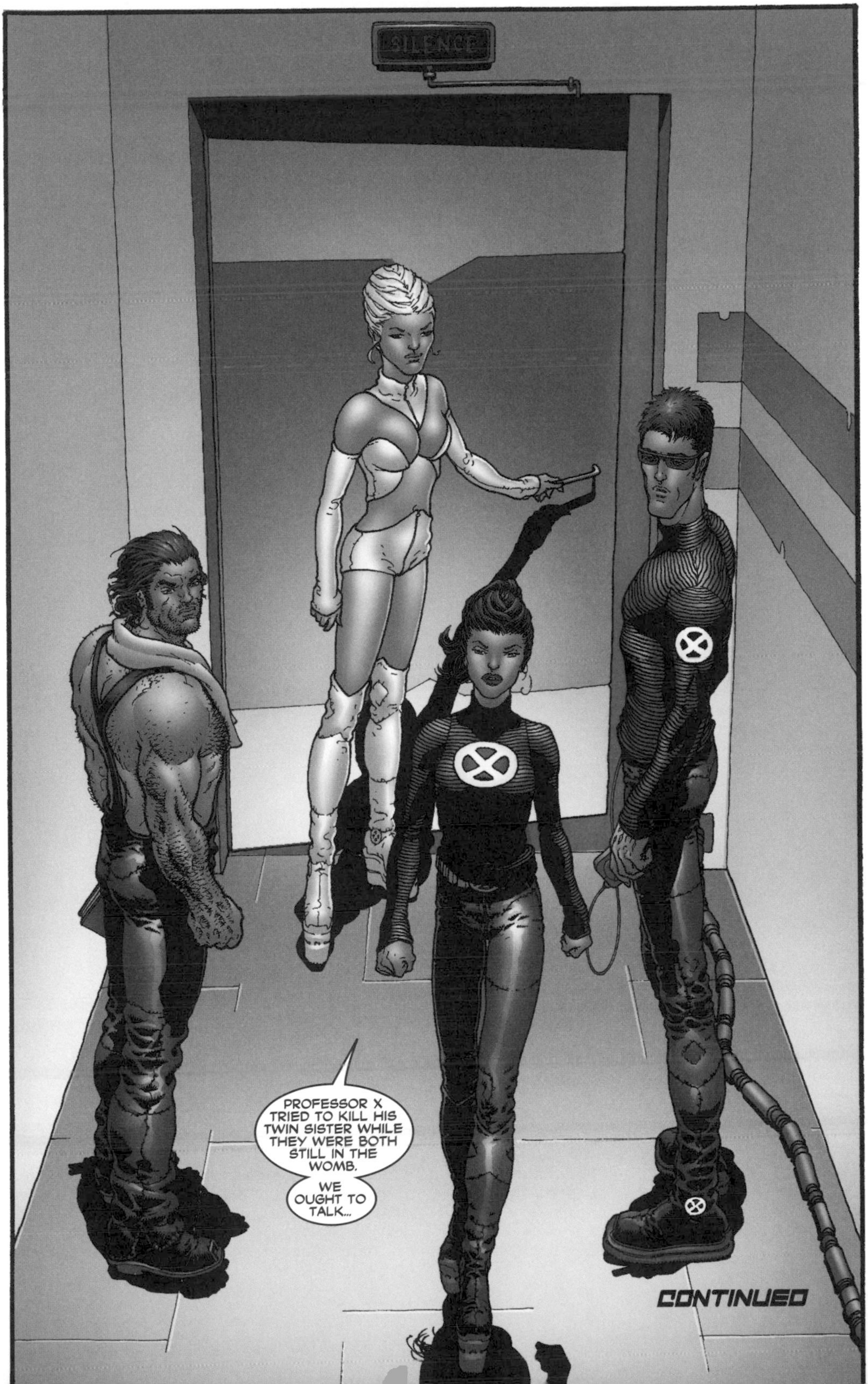

SILENCE
PROFESSOR X TRIED TO KILL HIS TWIN SISTER WHILE THEY WERE BOTH STILL IN THE WOMB.
WE OUGHT TO TALK...
CONTINUED

'NUFF SAID

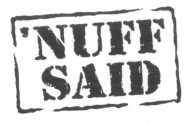

We dared them.

That's right, Marvel Prez Bill Jemas and EIC Joe Quesada hatched a test for the Mighty Marvel Maestros: Since you are the best artists and writers in the biz, we challenge you to tell a story using visuals only. After all, if a picture is worth a thousand words, then a comic book filled with images only would be worth... well, more words than the Collector could count!

And if you think creating a story with no words is half the work, think again, True Believer! The writer has to craft a story using no dialogue or caption boxes to communicate information – and pencilers have to make sure their storytelling is so clear that text isn't needed to explain what's going on.

Just to show you how our Mighty Marvel Maestros met the challenge, and to give you a unique peek behind the curtain, here's the plot to the very story you just read! Just compare it to the art and you'll see how the dare was done!

ISSUE #121
WRITER: GRANT MORRISON
ARTIST: FRANK QUIETLY
COLORS: HI-FI DESIGN

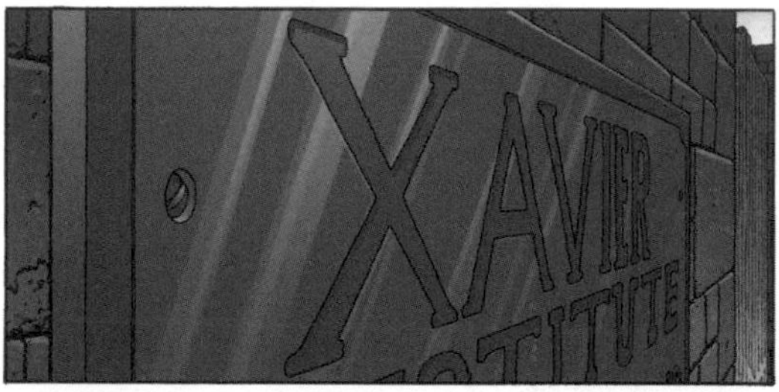
XAVIER

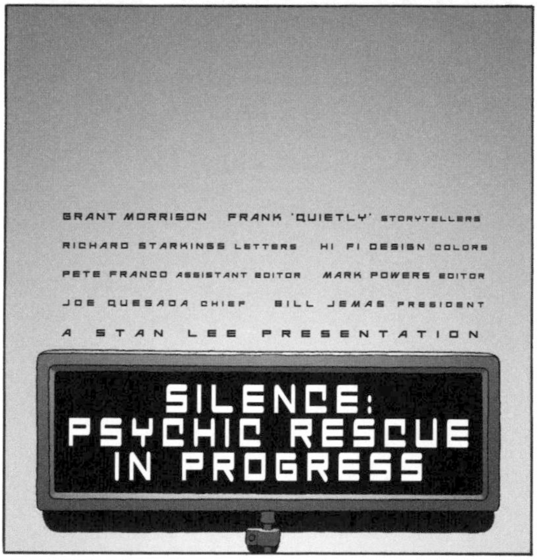
GRANT MORRISON FRANK 'QUIETLY' STORYTELLERS
RICHARD STARKINGS LETTERS HI FI DESIGN COLORS
PETE FRANCO ASSISTANT EDITOR MARK POWERS EDITOR
JOE QUESADA CHIEF BILL JEMAS PRESIDENT
A STAN LEE PRESENTATION
SILENCE: PSYCHIC RESCUE IN PROGRESS

PAGE 1

Frame 1 Establishing shot of the Xavier school gates. The sign is seen at a weird oblique angle, so that the perspective of the letters seems forced, diminishing into background. Huge oblique X near to us.

Frame 2 HUGE title credits page with the close up image of red glowing letters which read SILENCE:

TITLE/CREDITS:

PAGE 2 & 3

Frame 1   Spread page with two tiers. The top tier has eight vertical panels. The bottom tier is one cinemascope panel. First three panels show the X-Men - Scott, Logan, Emma , Jean standing outside the door where the SILENCE sign glows. Hushed moment of silent preparation. In this first is Logan..

Frame 2   Emma now opening the door to go in, looking back briefly.

Frame 3   Jean turns to Scott.

Frame 4   Kiss on cheek. Logan glances at Jean.

Frame 6   Scott about to say something. Jean puts a finger to his lips.

Frame 7   Jean makes a hush gesture as she turns away.

Frame 8   The door closes behind her.

Frame 9   Emma and Jean stand looking at Cassandra Nova...she's in a bad way on drips and life support...we're now in the sickbay area. Light is different.

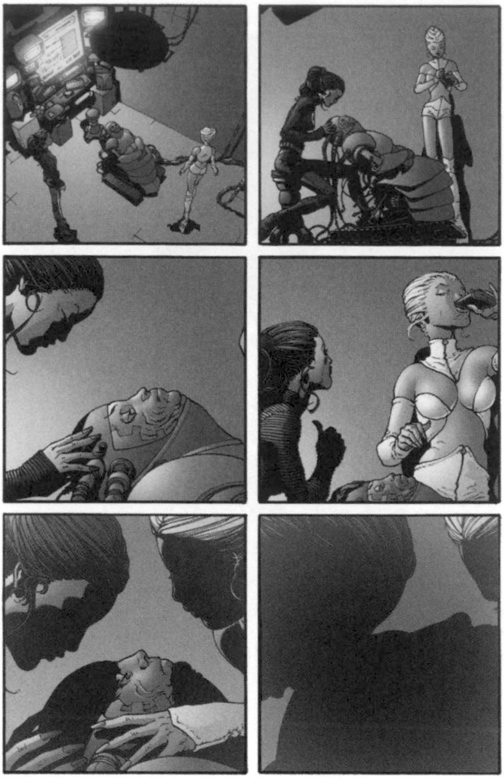

PAGE 4

Frame 1 Overhead shot. Emma takes her position in a chair behind the bed. Jean looks down.

Frame 2 Jean sits in her own chair beside the bed She touches Cassandra's head.

Frame 3 Closer. Jean leans down and lightly closes her eyes.

Frame 4 Jean looks up and gives a thumbs up to Emma. Emma knocks back a stiff drink.

Frame 5 Emma composes herself, closes her eyes. Fingers lightly on Xavier's temples.

Frame 6 Jean goes in. Whatever expression or pose you think would work best to suggest someone boring their way into someone else's consciousness.

PAGE 5

Frame 1 Six panels arranged in concentric circles, like ripples or a target. In the outermost ripple is filled with an abstract neuronal fuzz of twisted dendrites and brain fibres, with Jean superimposed as if diving away from us, down towards the centre of the page in a clockwise spiral.

Frame 2 The second tier is filled with Xavier faces, screaming laughing, howling, crying guardians - extreme emotional defence systems to ward off telepathic invaders. Pointing, accusing, hiding their eyes, pontificating. A smaller figure of Jean spins away from us, down into the center. Splashing into the one face which is calm, Christ-like in its quiet suffering expression.

Frame 3 Then in the third tier, looking down a fisheye perspective past the pillars and stairs and beams of a strange cellar filled with iconic dreamlike objects - a huge unnerving paper and wood fish sculpture is rotting there, papers and photographs of people from Xavier's past, all swirling in a wind which whips through the cellar, rearranging things.

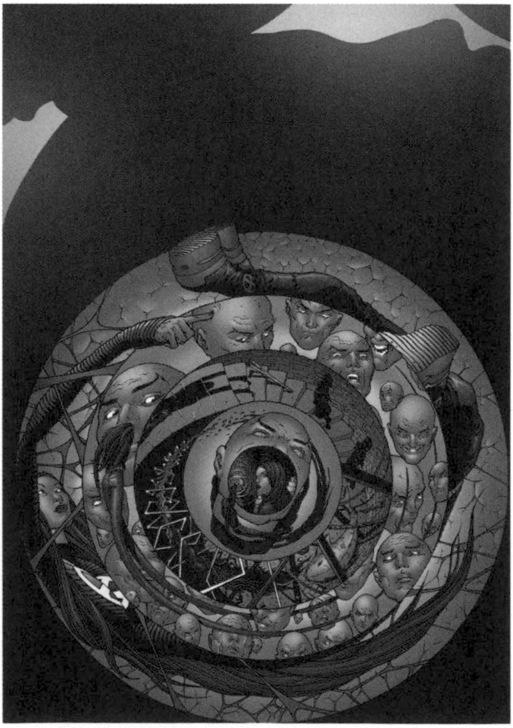

A bow. A crutch (all these things are associated with the letter X according to my trusty "abecedarium." Add other Peter Greenaway-esque details. This is the library of Xavier's mind. The memories and symbols of his ego. A smaller Jean spirals down like water into a plughole down the weird DNA stairs and bone bookcases.

Frame 4   A screaming Xavier face fills the fourth tier. Man at the end of his tether, holding onto his own identity and sanity with a sheer act of raging will. The tiny Jean hits this face as if there's a surface there which splashes up like liquid. She's in.

Frame 5   In the bullseye at the center of the page, is Jean's face in close up, turning to look back over her shoulder at us. Seeing something awesome off panel.

PAGE 6

Frame 1   Full page pic as we get to see it too. Jean is in Cassandra's brain. Longshot from behind her as she stands on a small, miserable looking beach hemmed in on three sides by tall black brick buildings. Out in the sea dominating the image there is a huge tower. Black and foreboding it rises up like a lighthouse of the damned. The tower has a strange superstructure - the central pillar is surrounded by a skeleton cage or helix of broken words, shattered symbols. Searchlights probe the isolated structure. At the edge of the beach are X shaped posts embedded in the sand, twisted through with barbed wire. It's like the beach at the Normandy landings. A feeling of oppression, police state tyrannical brutalism. The tarry rotted skeletons of boats in the shallows. Everything from here on in has the symbolic superreality of a dream.

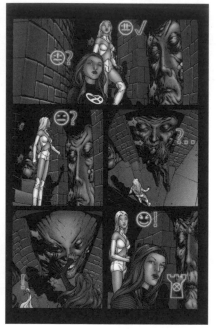

Frame 1   Jean head and shoulders in foreground looks off panel with a determined frown. In background on a narrow set of stone stairs which descend between tenements to the beach, we see Emma. She can't come any further than where she is.

We can see Jean's thoughts in the form of purple neon pictograms in the air near her head. They should translate as:

HE'S BEEN IMPRISONED. A MENTAL CONSTRUCTION A TRAP FOR HIS SELF...

Emma's telepathic symbols float in the air in front of her, glowing like purple neon and reading :

(*We'll talk about these symbols as you get to them Vin*)

Frame 2   Emma facing away from us in foreground on the steps extends her arm to indicate the faces of Cassandra in the doors lining the narrow stairwell. Each door is made of what looks like black Bible leather with huge clasp hinges. The Cassandra faces are like bas reliefs.

Frame 3   Jean looks at the sleeping face on the door.

Frame 4   It snaps at her and she flinches her hand back. Eyes surly, sleepy, partially opening for a moment.

Frame 5   Emma looks around, sensing danger. Jean is getting ready to move.

PAGE 8

Frame 1   The faces on the doors come to life. Eyes widen, mouths open into 'O's. Emma points across the beach to the sea and Jean takes off in that direction.

Frame 2   Jeans runs across the beach

Frame 3   The heads fire beams from their eyes. Emma consumed in the ferocious energy of the crossfire.

Frame 4   Mist fades. The heads grin, thinking they've destroyed Emma's thought-form. In the swirl of smoke we may glimpse a dim figure

Frame 5   Emma stands naked and diamond, beautiful. Her clothes are burnt away, her arms are folded across her chest and a wisp of smoke hides her naked loins. All she has on now is a wide belt. She looks pleased with herself and wickedly sexy.

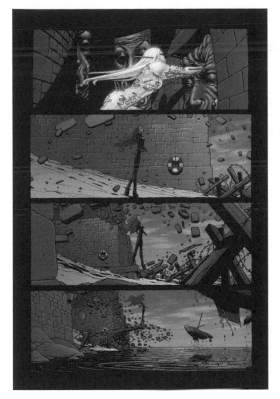

Frame 1   Emma plunges her fingers through the forehead of one of the Cassandra heads. Its eyes roll up and it squawks in death. Emma's costume forms around her, thought-controlled in this environment.

Frame 2   Jean slows as she walks towards the shoreline, gathering her thoughts. Her hair begins to rise up around her as though caught in a fan blast from below. Little flickers of fire run through the strands.

Frame 3   Jean walks forward dramatically, posing like an MTV star, lifting her arms at either side, palms upward, making things happen all around her as if by this simple gesture. Objects rise. Her telekinetic command is staggering in its scale and precision. Her flare flares up and whips around her.

Frame 4   Dream buildings coming apart, old boats rising from the dark foam. Huge orderly, towering processions of brick and mortar pass in avenues beside her.

PAGE 10

Frame 1   Tiny Jean in longshot, dwarfed by the great bridge she's building. A gorgeous span begins to form itself out of borrowed and mind-assembled debris, an incredible Kingdom Brunel bridge extending to the tower.

Frame 2   Jean walks as the bridge creates itself around her. She's very focused. The scale of her control is incredible

Frame 3   Overhead shot. We're looking at Jean as she walks across the bridge. Parts still fly into place.

Frame 4   Looking down from the tower itself. Cassandra gargoyles can be seen on the tower, rotating to fire upon Jean

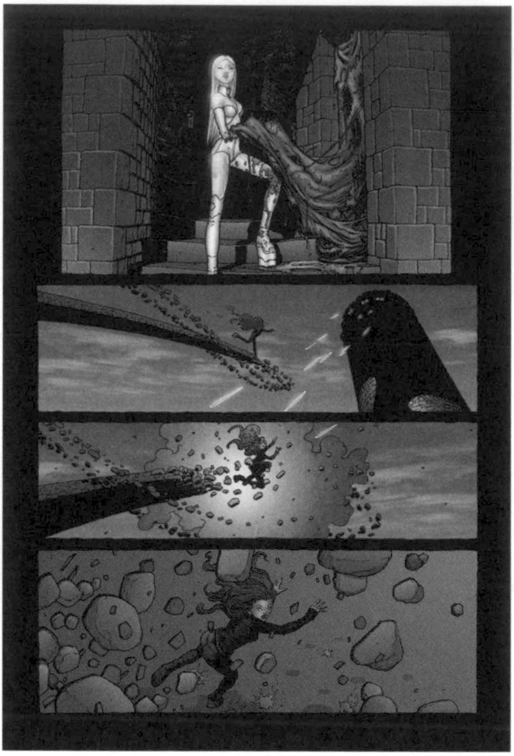

PAGE 11

Frame 1 Emma pause. She's got a huge Cassandra face in her hands, hanging limply from where she has it gripped between the eyes. She's ripped it off the leather facing of a door. In the stencil patch beneath, we see what looks like bleeding skin and knotted nerve cables of winking digital fibre optics and platinum circuit wire. She turns to see what's happening with Jean. The other heads shriek in fear, eyes twisting to look at Emma.

Frame 2 Jean runs across the bridge and we follow her as the gargoyles attack, launching destructive bolts from their mouths. The barred door at the base of the tower has an X motif with two crossed downward thrust swords.

Frame 3 We're looking up at Jean as she leaps across the collapsing gap of exploded smoking bridge.

Frame 4 Jean falls towards the ocean, looking off panel as if for some help from Emma.

PAGE 12

Frame 1 Emma sticks out her tongue wickedly. She has no intention of coming to Jean's aid.

Frame 2 Emma gets a shock as she looks down at the grinning face she's just discarded. It opens its mouth.

Frame 3 Jean hits the water amidst a fall of debris...

Frame 4 And the face bites Emma's foot, trapping it. The others purse their lips and spit on Emma. The flying saliva is red and filled with lots of little jumbled up letters like the rind in marmalade.

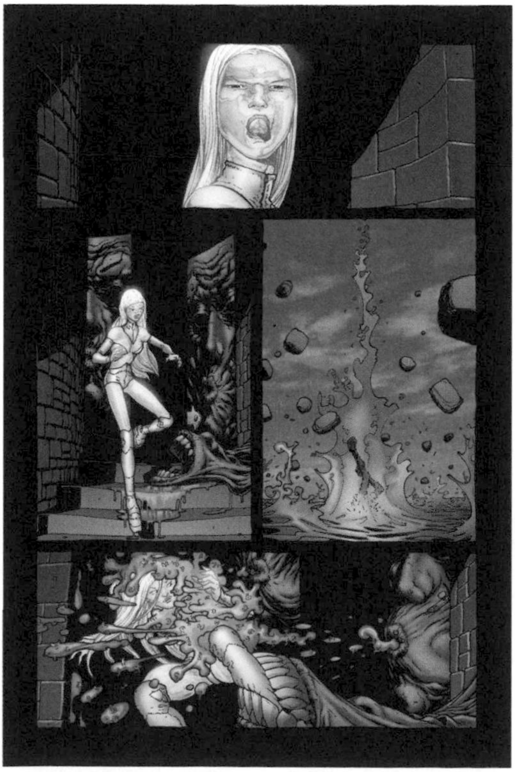

Frame 1   Jean hauls herself up out of the sea, really determined and pissed off now. The bridge is collapsed and sunken into the foaming sea behind, epic in its decay.

Frame 2   She walks towards the door, blows it open. Water flies off her telekinetically like a nimbus of rain. The great "X" seal on the door is shattered into fragments.

Frame 3   She walks into the hollow black tower. A weird room filled with symbolic stuff - bird skeleton in a cage, locked books, a rack of running shoes, gas masks, symbols of suffocation and fetuses in jars. Twin stuff hinted at everywhere. A snowglobe lifts towards her outstretched hand. She looks off panel, eyes riveted on the sight there ...

Frame 4   Charles Xavier in grotesque pose, holding his vast swollen dripping brain, like an Atlas. Xavier struggling with the gross weight of his own imprisoned thoughts, sunk to the thighs in bubbling slime and tar like some monstrous Blakean figure.

As a nod to Dali, there's an exploded wheelchair hovering in bits around Xavier . The components hang in strange splendor - Xavier's own version of the hyper-cubist cross. The terrible interior walls run with moisture and sport huge scrawled ghastly childlike drawings of the primal mummy and daddy. Any mad stuff you want to throw in to add to the density of visual information is fine.

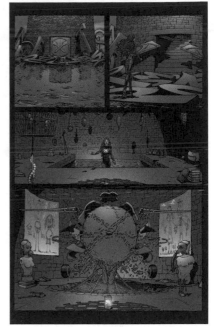

Frame 1   Close up. Jean holds up the snowglobe and we see that it contains a bride and groom - Xavier's mother and father. The snow inside, stirred into swirls by Jean's hand, is tiny tadpole swarms of sperm.

Frame 2   Zoom in on the snowglobe as she shakes it a little, into the driving rush of sperm and bubbles.

Frame 3   Xavier looks up from his torment, the huge head weighing him down.

Frame 4   Jean has been swept into the ultimate original memory - Xavier's DNA recall. Surprised, she's diving down towards us through a 3-d explosion of swimming seed as it heads for destiny. The sperm in foreground have intricate delicate glass heads filled with coils of information. Jean looks like she's diving with some exotic species of incredible luminous deep-sea jellyfish.

Frame 5   Jean slows to a stop and floats in the impossible symbol world. Her eyes are wide with cosmic awe. Lit from below by an unearthly primordial light. Fragments of fern-like XXX shaped villi float in the solution.

Frame 6   Outrageous cosmic moment as Jean hangs poised in the solution beside us, looking down at the dreamlike scene below. the primal moment of conception as the sperm surround the egg and merge into it. It's like a weird planet sunk in wet space, surrounded by thrashing tails and burrowing heads.

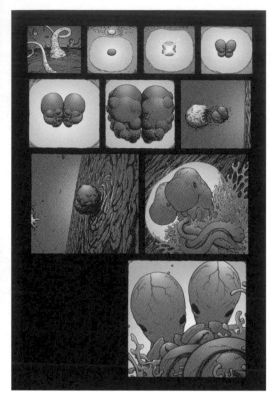

Frame 1   Microscopically accurate shots now as a single sperm forces its way through the coral-like structures of the zona.

Frame 2   The fusion. The X-gene activates in the pronucleus pair. A vivid signal flare, the clarion call of mutant conception.

Frame 3   Pull back to watch cell division in the egg. Something unusual is happening as twins begin to divide.

Frame 4   Two figures hooked up to the placenta - twin unformed fetuses identical at this stage. Charles and Cassandra emerging from undifferentiated cells into the red Eden of this primary world of total nourishment.

Frame 5   Close on the unformed alien newt face of Charles Xavier. Tiny organic Xs floating in solution. The eerie light of the deepest chambers of the human experience.

PAGE 16

Frame 1   Babies growing now to near term. All lit in eerie ultraviolet plutonian shades instead of the warmth of the womb scenes we're accustomed to seeing and experiencing.

Frame 2   Close up on the face of Cassandra - perfect light, pre-dawn divine light on the barely-formed face. She seems lit from within, godlike.

Frame 3   She and Charles float silently, calm, together. We circle around them in this timeless still place.

Frame 4   Then the supreme shocking moment as Cassandra's eyes tear open and stare at us.

Frame 5   Cassandra's POV. She reaches out her translucent hand and looks down at it with awe and understanding.

Frame 6   She makes a fist. A terrible smile crosses her face. It's worse because there should be no such expression on an unborn face. Her eyes shift to look at Charles dreaming in his prenatal trance.

CHARLES WAS BORN WITH HIS EYES OPEN, STARING...

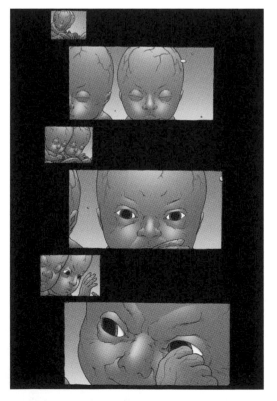

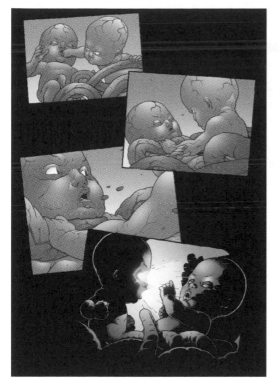

Frame 1   And suddenly it's War in the Womb as Cassandra hits her brother's face with her hand. A nasty backhanded blow. The tiny Charles yelps in first pain.

Frame 2   Thrashing internal tides, the tiny hands choke and battle.   Cassandra's face is gruesomely evil. Charles's eyes are closed, he's in distress as Cassandra attacks his face, blocking his nose and mouth.

Frame 3   Cassandra is killing Charles now, strangling him with his own umbilicus, pulling at his face. Seething toxic horror in the coloring now, amniotic fluid like urine and bile in the dark green light. Charles's eyes tear open, seeing the unseen universe for the first time.

Frame 4   The primal crime: Charles unleashes intense psychic power to destroy Cassandra. His mouth streams with energetic light and more pours from his eyes. Cass screams. Infernal scouring light fills the miniature womb world.

Frame 1   Outside it all. Mum in strobe-motion sequence across the panel, clutches her stomach, sways and then falls. Her belly glows in the first spasm and light shoots from her mouth and nose. Dad Xavier reaches to grab her.

Frame 2   Jean looking at the snowglobe as flowers of blood bloom inside it, snaking around the bride and groom. It floats up from her hand.

Frame 3   The snowglobe floats back into place as Joan walks towards Charles.

Frame 4   We're behind him as he hangs in his chains. Jean crouches down in front of him and the chains begin to come apart.

Frame 5   She takes his huge head in her hands, he looks up, eyes rolling tears. Monstrous, godlike in grotesque immensity Xavier seems like some suffering figure from a Renaissance fever dream.

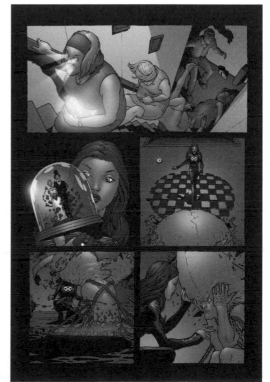

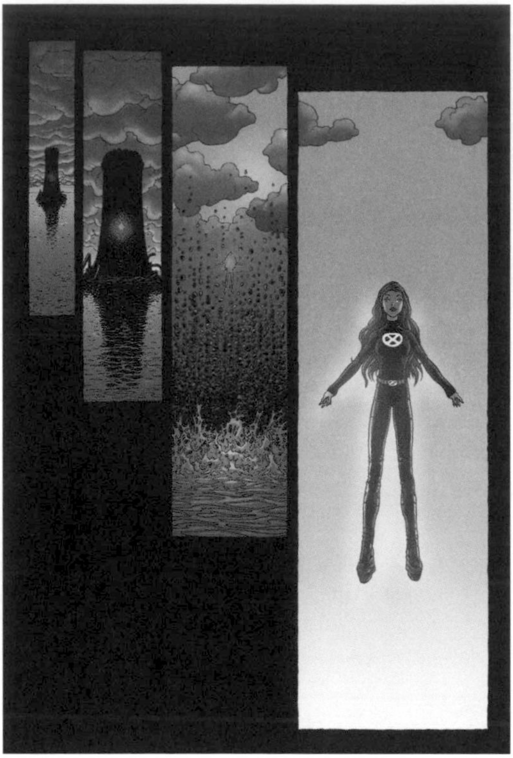

PAGE 19

Frame 1 A page of tall vertical frames, showing the anti-lighthouse prison of Charles Xavier. The bridge fallen.

Frame 2 A star appears in the center of the tower.

Frame 3 The tower crumbles. Sun bursts down out of the clouds.

Frame 4 Tower falls. The star is Jean.

PAGE 20

Frame 1 Emma is trapped under the sticky word goo of the heads. They aim their crackling eyes at her.

Frame 2 Emma struggles. Choking and pulling at the incoherent sticky gel filled with little letters. It's tacky like pizza cheese, covering her face, cutting off her breath.

Frame 3 Then it all splats into tiny gelatin globules and letters all around her. The door-faces go rigid with shock as though electrified.

Frame 4 Jean is there in the aftermath. All the faces are limp and dead now, like stroke victims. Smoke drifts from their slack mouths. Letters and jelly globules spin in the air, arranging themselves into HELLO EMMA THANKS FOR THE HELP

Frame 5 Emma gets up, dusting herself down look, shooting a venomous glance at Jean. Jean is talking no [redacted]. She point back towards the beach shels come from. A shape there maybe?

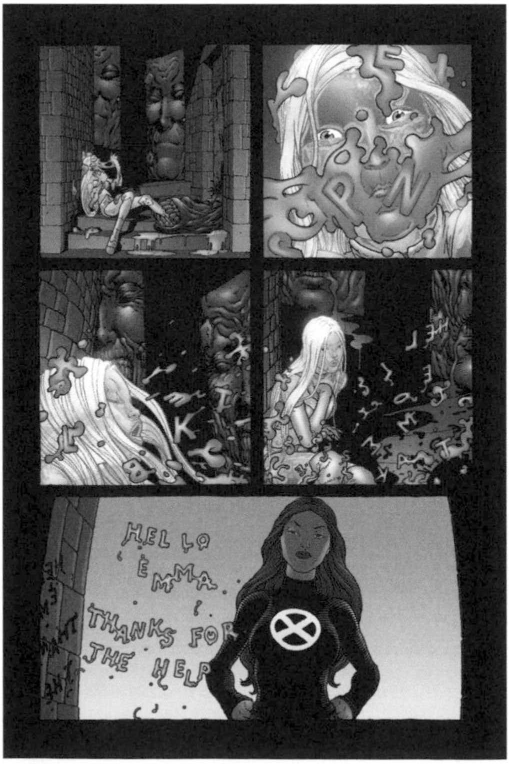
HEL LO
EMMA
THANKS FOR
THE HELP

Frame 1   Longshot. Emma kicks the fallen head angrily and one eye flies out to splat on the wall. Jean is grimly amused as she walks towards us.

Frame 2   Emma shoots us a placatory glance over her shoulder. I'm all right really...

Frame 3   Emma follows Jean as Jean issues a symbol command like this:

Frame 4   The crouched fetal autistic Professor on the beach with his huge swollen head.

Frame 5   Overhead, Jean crouches down, putting her arm around the monstrous Xavier self. They seem small and isolated on the beach. Emma stands by, looking down at the strange numinous scene.

Frame 1   Five horizontal insert panels in a double page end scene. First pic has the X-Men. Logan is reading ??? Scott is listening to his walkman, waiting. They sit apart and do not talk.

Frame 2   Logan looks up suddenly alert.

Frame 3   The red SILENCE warning light goes out.

Frame 4   Scott and Logan exchange glances as the door opens.

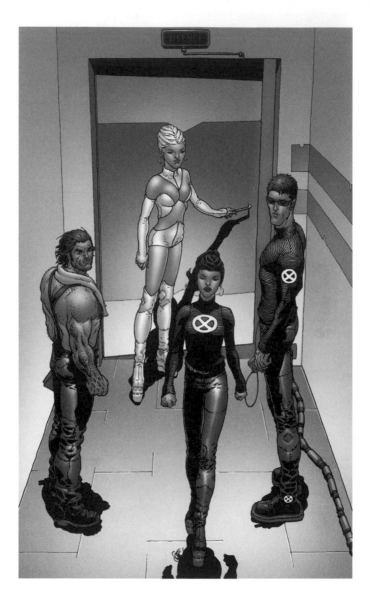

PAGE 23

Big pic taking up all of the final page. Emma and Jean emerge.

Jean looks grave. Emma is just behind and shoots the confident in control

Jean a sly, sullen glance. Emma doesn't like being beaten. And if she can't beat Jean with her super-powers then she might have to get ugly...

JEAN: PROFESSOR X TRIED TO KILL HIS TWIN SISTER WHILE THEY WERE BOTH STILL IN THE WOMB.

JEAN: WE OUGHT TO TALK...